GARDEN DESIGN

This is a Parragon Book
This edition published in 2004

Parragon
Queen Street House
4 Queen Street
Bath BA1 1HE, UK

ISBN: 1-40544-297-2

A CIP data record for this book is available from the British Library.

Acknowledgements
Illustrations: Kate Simunek
Special photography: Andrew Newton-Cox

Special thanks to Jennifer Bishop, Katie Cowan, Josephine Cutts, Dave Jones, Chairworks, Clifton Nurseries, Draper's Tools Ltd, Idencroft Herbs Jardinerie and Queenswood Garden Centre for the loan of plants, props and tools.

Printed in China

GARDEN DESIGN

Barty Phillips

Special photography
by Andrew Newton-Cox

p

CONTENTS

INTRODUCTION

The aim of this book is to help people with relatively little gardening knowledge make informed choices about how to plan and maintain their gardens. The upsurge of gardening as a leisure activity during recent years has been phenomenal and as a result the demand for information on practical gardening and plants to be grown in gardens has developed rapidly.

Everyone has a unique vision for their garden, but many people confronted with a garden for the first time feel intimidated by their lack of knowledge and the seemingly vast amount they think they will need to know if they are to succeed in managing their gardening. This book will show you that gardening need not be difficult – almost any garden, whatever shape or size, can be tailored to suit individual tastes, and as you gain confidence, you will quickly find your gardening horizons widening.

This book introduces you to garden planning and design, taking you chapter by chapter through the process of assessing your needs and the options open to you. Sections on different types of garden introduce you to the options available and chapters on planting design, the principles of planting, colour, and form and texture guide you easily through these areas.

Whether you're a first-time home owner with a small urban plot or tiny balcony, or have a large rambling garden in need of renovation, this book will inspire you to turn your garden into your own personal haven.

GARDEN PLANNING

**Your ideal garden might seem far out of reach
and unattainable. Don't worry; take your time.
A garden can wait and so can you.**

✿

The first step is deciding what you want and the second is
turning it into reality. A garden is a very personal thing and
everybody wants something different.

✿

Do not be afraid to play around with ideas; even the most
experienced professional designers will not come up with
the correct solution in an afternoon.

✿

Mistakes will be made – and indeed are often made
by professionals, too – but you can always change things.
Any garden is a living, growing entity;
it can always be adjusted.

YOU AND YOUR GARDEN

There are two aspects to the initial decision-making.
One is to think about your ideal garden – the garden you see in your
day-dreams, the equivalent to the Middle Eastern paradise garden.
What are your secret dreams for this small patch of land? The other is to
think about the practical aspects, such as providing storage for garden
tools and a place to dry the washing. It is useful to make a checklist of
what you require. Here are some possible ideas for your dream garden.
You will probably want to add others of your own.

CHECKLIST FOR YOUR 'IDEAL' GARDEN

ENTERTAINING can be one of the most enjoyable uses of a garden. A generous vine-covered patio, a barbecue area or a croquet lawn may be your dream. If you cannot incorporate all these features, some of them should certainly be possibilities. Other than entertaining, consider the following requirements, too.

Privacy and peace

❁ For some people the most important requirement of a garden is to create a private outdoor space. A tall hedge or trellis with climbers may not cut out all sounds but it will certainly help you to be less aware of them and will effectively separate you from your neighbours. A romantic arbour with a comfortable seat within the garden, surrounded by rambling roses, honeysuckle and clematis can provide a secluded, peaceful place in which to relax and enjoy the garden.

BELOW: *The romantic arbour, par excellence. This one would fit well in a small garden with its neat shape and simple wooden bench, and its surrounding of white roses and scented lavender.*

❁ Not everyone finds peace the ideal, however. You may prefer to sit in your small front garden and watch the world go by. Here, a hedge would get in the way, so you might prefer a paved area with pots of flowering plants and perhaps two larger shrubs to give the garden an entrance.

LEFT: *A herb border can be an attractive feature of a garden. This one has contrasting leaf sizes as well as scent and colour.*

LEFT: This small garden has been cleverly designed with ponds and interconnecting spaces to create the impression of spaciousness. The white sails are an attractive way of creating shade on hot days.

Water

❀ Water has a refreshing quality in any garden. Whether you want a quiet, still pool that will reflect the sky or take on an almost black mysteriousness, or whether you prefer the lively gurgle of a fountain or cascade, some form of water feature will give the garden an added dimension. Pools do not need to take up much space; a tiny pool with a miniature jet in a lined barrel on the patio, or a small basin with a narrow jet of water pouring into it from a lion's head on the wall can be effective. Place your water feature where you will enjoy it most, so that you can hear it without straining or gaze into it from a comfortable chair. You may even want a swimming pool and that may not be an impossibility in a moderately large garden.

Colour

❀ The green of foliage on its own can create a garden with a great sense of unity. At the same time, because there are so many different shades of green, and because leaves come in different shapes, rustle in different ways and catch the light differently, a foliage garden is endlessly interesting, without any extra colour.

❀ However, many people like bright colours and this is where a knowledge of plants, when they flower and where they will flower best, can be very helpful.

❀ To begin with, it is a good idea to add annuals or bedding plants where there are gaps, but as you become more knowledgeable you will find you like to experiment with all sorts of different colour and plant combinations.

Scent

❀ This is one of the most evocative aspects of a garden. It is worth trying to introduce as many scented plants as possible. In general, the scent from plants is most noticeable in the evening, so think of putting plants such as honeysuckles, scented roses and philadelphus where you are most likely to be sitting with an evening drink. Remember that some scents are more pleasing than others – privet, for example, has a rather overbearing scent, even during the day. Most of the scented flowers are also those that attract wildlife, and worth planting for that reason alone.

CHECKLIST OF GARDEN FEATURES

Before starting on your design, it is useful to make a list of all the requirements for your ideal garden. Some of these will be necessities, while you may have to compromise on others. Use this checklist at the planning stage.

BARBECUE ☐
BIRD-BATH ☐
COMPOST HEAP ☐
DUSTBIN AREA ☐
GARAGE ☐
GRAVELLED AREA ☐
GREENHOUSE ☐
HERB GARDEN ☐
HERBACEOUS BORDER ☐
LAWN ☐
PATIO ☐
PERGOLA ☐
PLAY AREA ☐
POND ☐
RAISED FLOWER BEDS ☐
SANDPIT ☐
SHRUB BORDER ☐
SUMMER-HOUSE ☐
SUNDIAL ☐
TERRACED AREA ☐
TOOL SHED ☐
VEGETABLE PLOT ☐

CHECKLIST FOR PRACTICALITIES IN YOUR GARDEN

HAVING pinned down your emotional feelings about the garden and what would make it your personal ideal, you then have to look at the practical aspects. Again, it is sensible to make a checklist, including all the things you need for the garden to make it function well for you. When finished, you will have to make compromises, but you will have the basis for dovetailing the practical with the ideal for a result that you can really savour and enjoy. Below are some possible ideas for your practical checklist.

Somewhere to sit

❀ It is useful to have a patio near the house, where food and drink can be carried in and out. However, if the sun shines best in another part of the garden at the time when you usually want to sit out, it would be better to make a patio there. It may even be a good idea to have two sitting areas, one for the sun in the morning and another that will catch the evening sun. Single seats can be dotted around in various places where they will be inviting at different times of day.

Sunbathing area

❀ This needs to be a hot spot, where the sun shines for most of the day. It also needs to be secluded. In a small garden the patio near the house is often the best place. Remember that if you grow tall plants or climbers to screen off neighbours, they may also screen the sun.

ABOVE: *Attractive in its own right, this miniature log cabin makes a playing area that will entertain young children for many hours.*

Somewhere to play

❀ Children may take up the whole garden for their play, in which case all you can hope to do is plant sturdy but decorative shrubs around the edges and wait until the children are older before planning a more subtle garden. If your garden is big enough and you can provide an interesting enough play area, you may get children to concentrate on that area, leaving at least a little space in the garden for your own pursuits.

❀ A climbing frame and swing can keep children happy for hours. Put plenty of bark underneath to cushion any falls. For younger children it may be more sensible to keep the play area near the house where you can keep an eye on them. A sandpit or a small pool can be located near the garden door and covered when not in use.

❀ By the time children go to school, they often become interested in gardening themselves. Giving them a little plot of their own with sturdy, quick-growing plants and workmanlike garden tools can encourage them to enjoy the garden in all sorts of ways.

Garden buildings

❀ Every garden needs a storage area of some kind. A large shed can be the answer but if you are short of space, there are many smaller sheds available. Using dual-purpose seating/storage units means you do not have to give up so much of the garden.

LEFT: *A secluded paved area offers peaceful shade for a quiet retreat. The planting is also subdued – mainly anemones and grasses.*

❀ A garden room can be something as slight as an open-sided summer-house or as sturdy as an insulated work-room, as decorative as a Swiss chalet or as basic as a garden shed with windows. If it will be very much part of the 'viewed' garden, a decorative shed may be best, but remember that modern paints can cheer up most buildings and careful planting can camouflage them.

Somewhere to grow and propagate

❀ A vegetable plot need not take up too much space and can be given a small, sunny corner of its own, perhaps behind a hedge or fence or through a flower-covered arch. Composting goes with food production. It is a way of using up waste material usefully and of getting rid of annual weeds and grass clippings. However, you should be aware that no small garden will be able to provide enough compost for its own requirements. You will have to supplement any you make with organic matter from elsewhere.

❀ A greenhouse is a good idea only if you are really going to have time to use, water, clean and generally care for it. Cold frames and cloches may be enough for beginners or somebody who has little time.

ABOVE: *This neat rubbish-bin cupboard takes up little space, has a waterproof roof and is stained an attractive dark green so that it melds in well with the garden.*

Accomodating wheelchair gardeners

❀ Remember that if you are making allowances for wheelchairs, you must provide not only paths wide enough for the wheelchair to negotiate but also turning spaces. Gravel is difficult for wheelchairs but bricks or paving are ideal. Raised beds can make gardening easier and more fun, while raised pools and water channels are more interesting, too.

BELOW: *This hexagonal summer-house adds a contemporary touch to the garden, with its cheerful blue painted woodwork.*

GETTING TO KNOW YOUR GARDEN

You have made checklists of your own needs and it is now time to assess the plot itself. There is a tremendous amount you need to know before you can confidently begin to design and, unlike a room within the house, the garden will repay you if you have patience and live with it for a year before making any drastic changes.

WHAT TO LOOK FOR

WHATEVER time of year you move into your new home, give yourself 12 months to observe the garden. It will almost certainly surprise you with unsuspected spring bulbs, dead-looking twigs that turn into splendid clematis or herbaceous plants appearing seemingly from nowhere.

❀ Use a notebook to jot down the interesting things that happen over the year, particularly those that are worth keeping.

❀ Look at the garden from the windows of the house and note where views are blocked or eyesores are open to view.

❀ Note where the sun shines for most of the day, which part of the garden gets sun in the morning only and which only in the afternoon. Note how the garden behaves in different weather; what suffers if there is a drought and what gets knocked flat in strong winds. Note whether noise comes from a particular quarter.

ABOVE: *Cheerful little hardy cyclamen can brighten up the garden in autumn or winter, depending on which species you choose, they cover the bare ground under trees.*

ABOVE: *Spring in a woodland garden with the heavenly blue of the Himalayan blue poppy (Meconopsis betonicifolia) and a speckling of varnished yellow buttercups.*

❀ Note if there is any wildlife. Lots of insects and worms mean the garden is fertile and plants should grow well. A complete lack of insect life – except, perhaps, whitefly and greenfly – means the soil badly needs air and compost or other organic matter. If you displace any frogs and toads while clearing out moist patches around drains, try to provide other sources of water because these are among the gardener's friends.

In spring

❀ Notice what bulbs come up that you didn't know about. Are they pretty and in the right place? Are there some missing that you would like to have? Snowdrops are an absolute blessing in the early spring garden and if they feel at home will multiply quickly. Are there any spring-flowering shrubs? Do not remove any dead-looking stalks at this stage. Many clematis and hardy hibiscus, for example, look like pieces of old sticks or string until they start to put out surprisingly sturdy leaves and buds early in the summer.

In summer

❀ Look for dull shrubs that are not pulling their weight; branches of trees that have grown too large and are cutting out necessary light. Few people realise how much light is excluded by overgrown trees and how this stunts the growth of other plants in the garden. Look for unexpected perennials poking through the soil – are they too leggy, or riddled with perennial weeds? Or are they a delightful surprise? Summer bulbs such as alliums and lilies may appear, too.

In autumn

❀ Watch for leaves that turn a wonderful colour or for brightly coloured berries that liven up the shorter days. Pyracanthas, so often used as hedging plants, are good 'security' shrubs because of their thorns but they also have pretty white flowers and spectacular berries in autumn. Bulbs often come up with surprises: look for autumn crocuses and, in later summer, tiny hardy cyclamen under trees. If you do not find these, put them on your wish list of plants. They are all exquisite.

In winter

❀ Look at the framework of the garden. Does it still look good when the flowers are all over? Are there any deciduous trees? If so, do they mean the garden looks rather bare, or do you like the feeling of light that this gives for a few months? Remember that spring bulbs and early flowers can grow under deciduous trees because of the light they receive early in the year, whereas many will not thrive under evergreens.

Front gardens

❀ In the front garden have a look at any rubbish bins. Are they well concealed behind a wall or a clipped hedge? Could they be better placed? Do people throw drink cans and crisp bags into the garden? A closely clipped, prickly evergreen hedge might stop this happening.

ABOVE: *The tall bearded iris is a late spring plant. This yellow and mauve one catches the spring sunlight and is seen here growing in a wild garden designed for low maintenance.*

ABOVE: *This garden backs on to a field, which allows the snow-covered trees at its perimeter to catch the late evening sun with a warm pink glow.*

INTERIM ACTION

ALTHOUGH it is best not to do too much planting or redesigning during the first year in a garden, there is plenty to be getting on with in the meantime.

Clear rubble and rubbish

❀ Many gardens have areas where the builders have tipped rubble rather than carry it to the dump. It is important that this is removed because bits of brick and cement are not conducive to growing things and often contain lime, which many plants do not like. If you have to carry rubble through the house, try to get old builders' bags, which are large, very tough and will shed less dust as you pass through. If the garden contains electrical items such as a microwave oven or refrigerator, it is usually possible to call the local authority and ask for them to be removed.

Clear bramble and weed patches

❀ If a patch of ground is infested with troublesome weeds like brambles, ground elder, nettles or the infamous Japanese knotweed, take the opportunity to clear it now. There is no point in cosseting any plant that may be growing among them. It is best to get rid of everything and start again.

❀ Nettles have shallow roots and it is usually possible to pull or dig them out. Brambles can be killed with brushwood killer but ground elder and Japanese knotweed are weeds of a tougher sort. It is best to use glyphosate in spring, when they are growing most vigorously, because the chemical runs through their sap and down into their roots. With both weeds you will

BELOW: *Do not be afraid to prune. The annual cutting back of these trees has encouraged new shoots and produced a wonderful display of contrasting colour without taking over the whole garden.*

probably have to give a second application when they come into vigorous growth again in late summer. To be on the safe side, you should apply the herbicide again the following spring. The chemical is no longer active when it reaches the soil, so if you are sure you have scotched the weed, you can plant when you want.

Prune trees

❀ Most people are reluctant at first to have trees pruned but, in fact, once pruned, they will spring into growth better than before, and letting light into the garden is absolutely essential if you want to grow healthy plants. However, trees may be protected and in some areas all trees are protected so you need to find out whether you need permission before you go ahead. You should check that the arborist is fully insured before you allow him or her to go up your tree and that the removal of all branches is part of the deal.

Mend fences and walls

❀ Unless you think you might alter the existing fences and walls, this is a good time to get them mended or replaced. Once you have done any planting, it will be difficult to get at fences without damaging the plants. Check that any fences are secure with good strong upright posts and that any trellis is solidly built and firmly fixed. Trellis often has quite a weight to bear if you grow an evergreen clematis or a vigorous climbing rose against it.

Provide temporary colour

❀ Even if the garden surprises you with unexpected treats, a neglected garden is unlikely to provide enough colour during the first summer. But there is plenty of temporary planting you can do to brighten up the garden for one season. Mallow plants are not expensive and one plant will grow to 2 m (7 ft) in a year and be covered with open pink flowers, giving a good display throughout summer and autumn.

❀ You can let yourself go with plants and containers. Pelargoniums will brighten up sunny places, busy Lizzies (*Impatiens*) are happy in light shade and abutilons will create an exotic atmosphere against warm walls. You can place pots with brightly coloured flowers throughout the garden. Of course, annuals and bedding plants will fill gaps. Petunias, verbenas, *Salvia splendens* and pelargoniums can provide plenty of colour.

Use the time

❀ It is good to use this year to inspect as many other gardens as you can. Look at their layouts, the details of their paths and steps and, of course, their planting. If something intrigues you, take a photograph and make a note of it. It may be useful when you are trying to solve a problem later on.

BELOW: *Containers can provide plenty of interest while you are waiting to tackle your garden. Here, various terracotta pots and a galvanised bin give a brave display of green and mauve that will be attractive all winter.*

GETTING STARTED

If you are feeling daunted by the amount of work required to get your garden into shape, follow these basic steps to see what is possible and what is not.

❈

First of all assess your site. Take into consideration which way the garden faces, where the sun reaches, privacy factors and soil type.

❈

Take the time to make a plan. Explore all the style, colour and planting possibilities, and refer to the checklist of features you want in the garden.

❈

Create a framework for your garden, taking into account your preferred style.

❈

Work out a seasonal workload plan so that you know what needs doing from month to month.

SURVEYING THE SITE

❦

Begin by making a site plan. It should be an accurate record of the boundary of your garden and the main items within it – the house, existing buildings, trees and ponds. It should show where the ground rises, where there are steps, which way the garden faces and where there are eyesores to be concealed or views to be enjoyed. Note on the plan those areas of the garden in the sun and those in shade. You should also note the type of soil and whether it is extremely dry, well drained or boggy, or whether it is dry in summer and soggy in winter, as are many gardens that have a heavy clay soil.

THE PLAN

I T IS best to do your survey on graph paper, which helps to get the measurements accurate. Measure the boundary of the garden first. You should use a 30 m (100 ft) measuring tape, and you will find measuring easier with two people to hold the tape.

House

❀ Mark where the house is in relation to the garden, and its size and distance from the boundaries. Show the position of the ground floor windows and doors and make sure you indicate which side faces north.

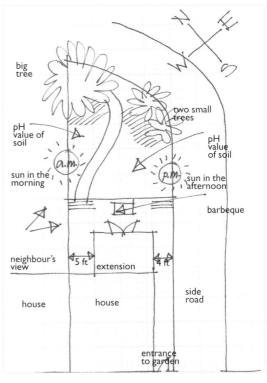

ABOVE: *A rough sketch of your garden need not be a beautiful drawing. Provided the measurements are correct and more or less in scale, you can sketch the garden several times, trying out different ideas. Here, the house is shown with its extension into the garden and its relationship to the road. The north/south aspect should be shown, as should all big trees, sheds and other structures; you can try different placings of paths, areas for barbecues and so on.*

ABOVE: *This pastel-painted seaside home needs plants that are able to withstand the salt-laden breezes. Ceanothus and wisteria do well, and there is a shelter belt of hawthorns further down the hill.*

LEFT: *Terracing a garden is a good way of dealing with steeply rising ground. The terraces can be very attractively planted, with each level offering a different type of garden. It is best to get such a site professionally surveyed.*

Alterations in level

❀ Show where the ground level alters and measure the width of any existing steps. It can be difficult to work out accurately the rise and fall of ground without special equipment. On a difficult site it is best to get a level survey done by a professional but if you do not need complete accuracy, you can use fences, walls and steps for guidance.

Aspect

❀ Mark which way the garden faces. This will enable you to decide on the best positions for seating and play areas, vegetable plots, flower and shrub borders and many other features that need to be either sheltered or sunny.

Trees

❀ Show all existing large trees and indicate where your neighbours' trees cast shade into your garden. If a tree is in the wrong place or has grown too large, consider getting rid of it and replacing it with something more suitable.

Shade

❀ Mark areas that are in shadow for most of the day. This may be a good area for a dog kennel or for a play area, although a little sun will be welcome, of course. Areas in deep shadow will require careful planting because only a limited number of plants will thrive in them.

Soil type and drainage

❀ Find out whether your soil type is basically clay, sand or loam. Clay is heavy, difficult to work and clogs into mud that comes indoors on your boots. It warms up slowly in spring but with lots of organic matter added it will become workable and more nutritious than other soils.

❀ Sandy soil is light, easy to work and drains easily, which means that nutrients are likely to drain away, too. Loam is probably the ideal. It is dark and sweet smelling, crumbles in the fingers and holds water well. Very dry soil can be given additives to help it retain water. Draining boggy soil can be expensive. Instead of draining you could create a specialist bog garden where suitable plants will thrive.

❀ An analysis of your soil will tell you whether it is acidic, alkaline or neutral (which is best for most gardens). The pH of a soil – its degree of acidity/alkalinity – is important as some plants require an acidic soil and others require an alkaline one. The pH can range from around 5 (acidic) to 8 (alkaline), 6.5 being neutral and suitable for a great many plants. Soil-testing kits are inexpensive and available from garden centres. Test the soil in several parts of the garden, since the pH may vary within quite a small area.

ABOVE: *The paved area in front of the house has been designed in a semicircular arrangement of bricks leading towards the house. The brick colour blends in well with the roof tiles.*

RECOMMENDATIONS AND PRACTICALITIES

Y OU have noted on your plan the salient points of the garden as it is, using the notes you made during the first year and the measurements taken during the survey.

You should now be thinking about how you want to alter the garden, what you want to remove and what you want to add. There are a number of practical considerations that will make creating the actual plan easier. For example, it is useful to know that the clearance needed for a swing is 7 m (23 ft).

Remember that everything should be in scale with the house. A very tall house will require a larger patio, taller trees and arches, and larger spaces. A bungalow will need everything on a slightly smaller scale if the garden is not to look pretentious.

Conservatory

❀ It is not good to have a conservatory on the south side of a house where it is too hot most of the time. A better position is the east or west side for sitting, or the north if the important thing is growing plants. As with other structures, a good conservatory will be in keeping with the house. A modern, simple building will suit a modern house, whereas a gothic creation will look fine added to a red brick mansion.

BELOW: *Similar bricks have been used here for both the paving and the wall to give a sense of unity to the design. The paved area is surrounded by a luxurious planting of pinks and purples.*

Steps and paths

❀ Steps should be comfortable to climb up and down. A leisurely scale is right for a garden. They are not like house stairs, which are designed to go up quickly. The slope should not be more than 40° from the horizontal, otherwise steps appear unwelcoming.

❀ The minimum safe riser (the vertical part) for steps in a garden is 100 mm (4 in). If they are shorter, someone might trip on them. The maximum is 200 mm (8 in). The tread should ideally be 300 mm (12 in) deep. A good proportion for garden steps is a 150 mm (6 in) riser with a 375 mm (15 in) tread, although in a small garden that may not always be possible. Steps do take up more room than is generally realised. Six steps, 1.8 m (6 ft) wide with treads 450 mm (18 in) deep, will take up 4.8 sq m (54 sq ft). This could take up a very significant proportion of a small garden.

❀ With stone or brick steps it is best if the tread projects slightly over the riser at the front to create a shadow line. This not only looks good but also helps to define the steps in poor light.

❀ If you are creating a long flight of steps, remember that you will need a 'landing' every 10 or 12 steps, which should be twice as deep as the steps.

❀ Paths can be wide or narrow, as scale or space permits. A wide path allows two people to walk along in conversation but may take up more space than the garden can easily allow. A narrow path will keep your feet dry in wet weather and may be all that is needed.

Pergolas

❀ A pergola is an important garden structure. The design and materials will affect the whole look of the garden. Supporting piers of brick or stone need large solid crossbars to be in scale. Wooden uprights with slender beams make a more elegant construction, suitable for smaller gardens and lighter climbers such as clematis and less vigorous roses.

❀ The height of your pergola is critical. The bar at the top will have something climbing on it, which will make it slightly higher, so 2.4 m (8 ft) is a good height. In a very small garden you could go down to 2 m (7 ft) and in a very large garden up to 2.7 m (9 ft).

❀ With any sort of opening, including arches, the wider and more generous it is, the more welcoming it will be.

Paving

❀ This also has an important structural role in the garden. It should always look good. Paving can be used for anything from patios and parking spaces to paths and steps; in small and urban gardens it can take the place of a lawn.

❀ Natural stone, concrete, brick, tiles, paviours and wood can all be used in different combinations. Do not try to use too many materials at once, however, or you will end up with an uncoordinated result. It is best never to use more than three different materials. This will help to create unity throughout the garden.

❀ Remember to make the patio large enough. You need room not only for a table with chairs tucked in neatly around it, but for people to pull the chairs out and sit in them. Any patio should therefore be at least 3 x 3.5 m (10 x 12 ft).

ABOVE: *A slightly curved flight of gravel and timber steps has wide treads and shallow risers, which give it an unhurried, relaxed quality.*

ABOVE: *Even the smallest space can be packed with interest by the clever use of different media, textures, colours and shapes.*

THE CONCEPT PLAN

This is where you get to fit all your requirements into your actual garden. You should have decided by now whether you want to bulldoze the whole garden and start again from scratch, or whether there is enough of a sensible outline to allow you to work round what you already have. Consider how you can make the transition from garden to house as smooth and pleasant as possible. French windows or patio doors are ideal and can be made secure with double-glazing, laminated glass and good locks. If you are not able to change the door, you can design the garden so that the view from the windows is enticing.

EXPERIMENTING WITH IDEAS

MAKE lots of copies of your initial survey sketch and try out ideas in pencil on these. Decide on the most important of your requirements and sacrifice the others, allowing a few generous spaces in your garden rather than too many slightly mean ones. This will make the garden less fussy and bitty and ultimately give more pleasure.

ABOVE: *Any ordinary garden shed can become an integral part of the garden by concealing it with ivy or creeper. Both are used here, with the creeper turning a bright red in autumn.*

Using photographs

❀ Your plan or 'map' is useful for getting a feeling of the balance of the different areas within the space, but will not give you a picture of the three-dimensional reality of the garden. For this it is useful to look at your photographs and try out some of your ideas on them. A good way of doing this is to lay pieces of tracing paper over them and sketch out different ideas – the more you do, the better. You will find you begin to revert to a particular idea. When your ideas begin to firm up, make a new plan with everything on it that you want to retain and everything you want to change.

❀ One of the most difficult things is imagining how the plants will look when they have matured and grown, particularly trees and shrubs. This is where your overlay and photographs can help. If you know a shrub is eventually going to become 2 m (7 ft) tall, you can see what effect this will have on the garden plan in a few years' time.

❀ On your initial sketches think of how you can make the garden more interesting and effective. There are several ways in which you can entirely change the appearance of a garden without too much outlay.

Alterations

❀ You might want to move a path nearer to a fence, or further from it, to provide a wider border, or take it diagonally across the garden to create two separate spaces. Diagonal lines across a narrow garden can make it look wider.

❀ You can move a small shed, instead of getting rid of it, to a place where it is less obtrusive and can be concealed behind climbers. Paint can give dull little buildings a more cheerful look.

Extending

❀ You can continue a straight border around in a curve to conceal a shed or surround the shed with shrubs. A greenhouse that is not particularly pretty can also be surrounded by low-growing shrubs. They cannot be too tall or they will cut out too much light and things inside the greenhouse will grow spindly in their attempts to reach the light.

Enlarging and dividing

❀ You can enlarge an existing patio or make it circular instead of rectangular; you might want to make a path wider, to emphasise its direction and lead people on. Using a tall, sturdy trellis fence to divide the patio and the garden can give privacy without completely cutting off the view. This gives an extra place for growing climbers.

BELOW: *In this garden, the patio has been extended into a pathway with planted borders to lead people through the garden.*

MORE IDEAS AND POSSIBILITIES

GARDENS are made up of spaces and shapes for various activities; the bits in between are your planting spaces. When you have sketched in the shapes for, say, sitting, paths, shed, pond, play and vegetable garden and you have eliminated the least essential, go through the whole process again until you have spaces that will fit well into your garden.

Thinking ahead

✿ If your basic framework works well, later on you will be able to change how you use it. For example, if you build a brick sandpit, butting on to a brick-edged lawn, as the children grow older, you will be able to exchange sand for water and have a garden pool. A playhouse can be a marvellous place for children to play in. If you have chosen a solid one you can have it insulated and eventually take it over as a retreat or even a serious workroom.

✿ One early decision, especially in a small garden, must be whether you want a lawn or would prefer to have paving. A small lawn can be a refreshing source of green in an urban winter. Some gardeners derive enormous pleasure from mowing a pocket handkerchief of greenery but a very small garden may not have room to store a lawnmower. Moreover, if the lawn is too overshadowed or impoverished, it will just look sparse and sad. In that case, it will be best to have it all up and lay paving slabs or a pattern of bricks or cobbles for a crisp and clean surface, which may better suit the urban environment or the busy working person.

Features beyond the garden

✿ Mark any good views on your plan and lead the eye to them by creating a gap in the hedge or a circular 'window' in a wall. A path leading in that direction and a seat facing the view will encourage people to enjoy it. Similarly, mark any bad views on your plan so that you can conceal your neighbour's rusty swing or ugly shed with trellis and climbers or a well-placed columnar tree.

✿ Make the best use of any attractive trees and tall flowering shrubs in neighbouring gardens. Doing this will not only provide extra colour in your own garden but also help extend the sense of space. Hedges can be cut a little lower to allow a view of a neighbouring blue ceanothus or pink camellia.

ABOVE: *A sense of spaciousness is achieved in a small area by narrow borders along the fencing and several unimposing features including a seat, trellis and central plant arrangements.*

ABOVE: *This miniature lawn will never need mowing, since it is made of camomile. Although only tiny, it provides a welcome touch of fresh green within this charming seating area.*

A feeling of space

❀ Small gardens can be made to seem much more spacious by designing in diagonals. A path running diagonally from one side of the garden to the other and then back again at an angle will divide the garden into three. The spaces made in this way can be separated by tall or low planting and will make the garden seem larger because the eye cannot see exactly where the garden ends and is intrigued by the planting between.

❀ Arches create a feeling of space by implying that there is more happening beyond them. Arches should always lead to something or the result is disappointment. A small gate under the arch will enhance the feeling of entering into a different domain.

A sense of unity

❀ When you have an idea of what you want, stick with it throughout the whole garden. This will give the garden cohesion and a sense of unity, which is one of the hallmarks of all successful gardens. Decide whether you want the garden to be formal or informal, or asymmetrical with overlapping squares and geometric shapes.

ABOVE: *A yew arch takes some years to grow to its full height and maturity, as here. Drawing in ink on a photograph of your garden will give you an idea of what an arch like this would look like when fully grown.*

CREATING A FRAMEWORK

For different parts of a garden to combine into a satisfying whole, a
cohesive structure is needed. Decide on your priority spaces and create
the framework around them. Keep everything simple. Boundaries and
divisions should have a unity that will provide a clear background for the
planting and join up the spaces harmoniously. For example, walls should
all use similar bricks, or all be rendered and painted the same colour.
Hedging plants should be compatible – either all native shrubs or trees or
one type of clipped evergreen. The lines of the framework, whether
straight, curved or squared, should be clear and firm. This is one of the
most important factors in garden design.

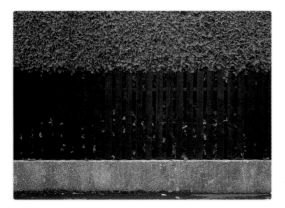

THE PLANTED FRAMEWORK

IF YOU use only deciduous plants all the framework shape
will be lost in winter when the leaves fall. Some
deciduous plants have interesting trunks and branch shapes
but you should include some kind of evergreen planting
that will stand out clearly in winter.

Dividing the space into separate areas is a good way of
preventing a long, narrow garden from looking like a
ribbon, but the technique is also invaluable in many larger
gardens to provide a variety of areas for different uses.

Boundary framework

❀ In small gardens, pyracantha and privet are often used as
hedging plants along boundary walls. They provide good
nesting sites for birds but they are greedy for space as
well as water and nutrients, and in urban areas it is
probably better to have trellis with climbers and
evergreens, interspersed with the occasional evergreen
shrub as a contrast and to break the straight line.

❀ In gardens by the sea or on a hill, where strong winds

LEFT: *Where garden meets roadside, this neat picket fence is backed by a
rigorously clipped conifer hedge, both of which are very much in keeping with the
feel of the garden as a whole.*

and salt spray can damage all but the toughest of
plants, the best sort of boundary is a hedge of mixed
shrubs such as hawthorn, *Olearia*, escallonia, hazel and
holly. This will act as a very effective shelter belt,
within which more tender and colourful plants can be
grown successfully.

ABOVE: *A clipped yew archway makes an attractive gateway to the front path
and frames the view of a solid red brick house with its small portico.*

❀ If the garden is bounded by a road, a clipped hedge often looks as neat as a wall and quite in keeping with the defined lines of the road. Beech makes a good and unusual hedge because, although it is not evergreen, it holds on to its leaves after they have turned colour and continues to provide protection and privacy throughout the winter.

Separating areas

❀ The framework for a formal garden is perhaps the easiest to design. You need a regular and level site. Once you have that, everything about the formal – its symmetry, regularity and mirror imagery – is in itself a framework. Low clipped hedges of box, taller clipped hedges of yew, clipped pairs of bay in tubs, a formal central fountain and paths crossing at right angles all reinforce the basic shape of the design. Everything adds up to a disciplined

ABOVE: *There are many different ways to give a garden form. A trellis is a practical and attractive method of creating an enclosed area.*

framework and, if it snows in winter, the whiteness emphasises the structure. An informal garden also needs its evergreens to create the framework, but the designer must be have an understanding of proportion and balance and trust his instincts.

❀ The most restful spaces are those with equal proportions, such as a circle or square. They make good seating areas or places in which to pause and relax. Long, narrow spaces, on the other hand, are an invitation to move on.

❀ Your framework should always define spaces that are there for a purpose. A circle should have entrances and exits. A path should lead somewhere; if it curves it should curve around something – a fountain, perhaps, or a feature shrub or sculpture. If it is straight, it should lead the eye to something intriguing.

ABOVE: *This narrow border of deep red roses and cotoneasters allows space for the pale old stone wall to be seen above the plants.*

THE BUILT FRAMEWORK

GARDEN structure consists of areas shaped by the vertical elements that surround and divide them. We have looked at ways in which planting can create divisions and surroundings. Now we can look at how built structures can reinforce and add to these areas.

❀ If you are dividing a playing area from a patio, you may want to be able to supervise what is going on in the sandpit or by the swing. You will therefore need to be able to see. Here you won't want a dense hedge, which would restrict your view, but you can create the effect of division by building a low wall or simply a pergola-type gateway. This will give the impression of entering a different area but you will still be able to supervise the children playing. Climbing roses or honeysuckle will soften the structure.

❀ An arch can be used to connect areas or to divide one area from another. It can be flanked on either side by a hedge or fence, but that is not always necessary. It will, all on its own, give the impression of a gateway into a different environment. There are many different types of arch. Tall, wide arches can be built at regular intervals, rather like a pergola but not so enclosed. If widely enough spaced, they will not cut out too much light and summer-flowering plants such as lavender can be grown beneath them so that you have a walkway to be enjoyed at leisure.

❀ The view through any arch should lead the eye to something interesting further down the garden – perhaps a sculpture, a gateway or a decorative shrub or urn.

❀ If you don't want to divide the garden with too many tall structures, low fences of trellis, provided the supporting uprights are sturdy and good looking, can provide elegant divisions while keeping an open vista at a higher level.

❀ Arbours and niches can divide up spaces, particularly if used on a corner where two paths intersect.

❀ Terraced gardens create good opportunities for structured framework. Long, shallow terraced gardens were popular in the 1920s and 30s. They had wide steps, balustrading and stone or brick cross paths and were often bounded by clipped box or yew on either side. The balustrading was often made of moulded concrete and it is very easy today to create a similar result with walls of concrete blocks, rendered and then painted. The walls should be no more than 45 cm (18 in) high so that people can sit on them.

Linking the compartments

❀ Having divided up the garden with a framework of planting or built structures, it is necessary to link the compartments or there will be no feeling of being one complete entity that a good garden needs. Use the same paving or brick for patios and paths throughout the garden. Walls should be topped with coping stones to match the paving, all of which will bring a sense of co-ordination and unity to the whole.

❀ When building pergolas, arbours and arches, again try to use similar materials throughout. If you start off with a simple metal arch use the same metal for any more arches and for arbours. With their clean lines and simple shapes, these are particularly suitable for urban gardens. Similarly, if you start off with a wooden pergola, follow through with wooden furniture, wooden gates and so on.

ABOVE: *This unusual cherry lined pergola has a double row of lavender at its feet, leading the eye to the gate and lake beyond.*

✿ A rustic pole screen can be used to divide a vegetable garden from the pleasure garden, but it should be in keeping with other divisions in the garden. Rough-cut wood would not be particularly suitable in conjunction with a sophisticated curved brick wall, for example, but would be perfectly acceptable if trellis or other wooden fences or evergreen hedges were used elsewhere.

The horizontal and the vertical

✿ When working out the structure, don't forget that you want a contrast between vertical and horizontal surfaces. Low hedges should be interrupted occasionally by a tall, conical tree or shrub. Expanses of open lawn should also have vertical interruptions here and there to keep the viewer interested.

RIGHT: *The multi-coloured brickwork on this terrace creates a pattern that is echoed by the careful planting.*

BELOW: *A rendered Italianate wall leads from a woodland garden through a rounded arch, giving an intriguing glimpse into the densely planted area beyond.*

GETTING TO WORK

Once you have thought carefully about how you want your garden to look, it's time to begin the hard work. Remember – every element of your house and garden must work together.

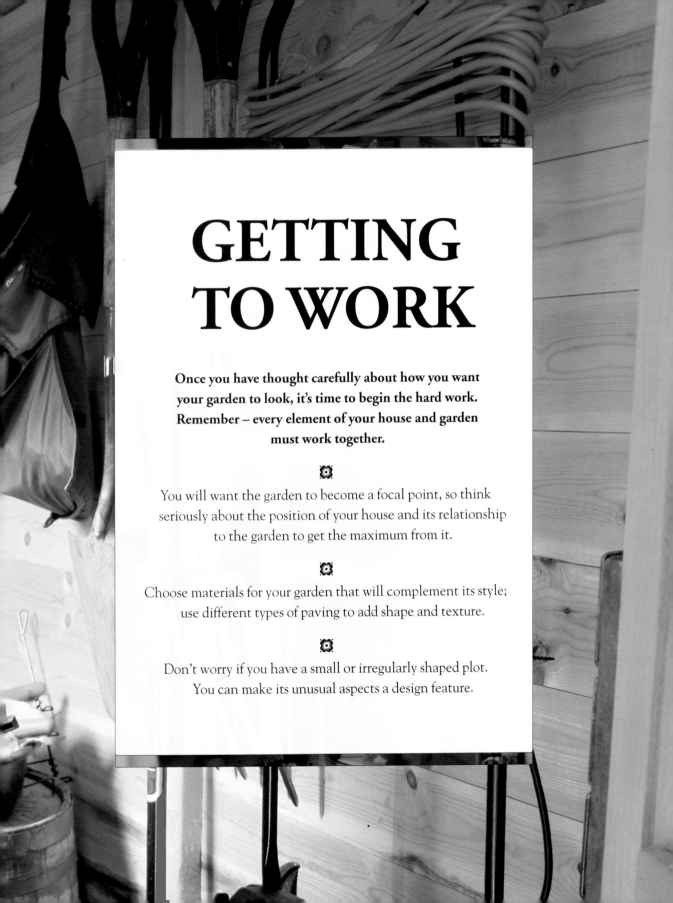

You will want the garden to become a focal point, so think seriously about the position of your house and its relationship to the garden to get the maximum from it.

Choose materials for your garden that will complement its style; use different types of paving to add shape and texture.

Don't worry if you have a small or irregularly shaped plot. You can make its unusual aspects a design feature.

INTEGRATING HOUSE AND GARDEN

❦

The entrance to your garden is important. An interesting and inviting environment should greet you when you step out of the door. Not every door will open directly on to the garden, of course, but a row of well-tended pots could point the way to the garden, or perhaps a trellis-trained flowering climber on the wall. Remember that a level garden seen from the ground appears foreshortened and shorter than it really is. Individual compartments will seem shorter too; so if you are planning a circular lawn, the circle will seem squashed unless you make it more of an oval, with the longest part facing the house.

DOORWAYS AND WINDOWS

THE ideal entrance to a garden is through French doors to a patio. This really makes the garden into another 'room', and even when the weather is cool or rainy the garden 'picture' can be appreciated through the protective glass.

Single doors

❀ If a large entrance is not possible, the garden door can still be given glass panels, which will make it seem less remote from the house. A scented shrub next to the door and pots or containers of summer-flowering plants will also be welcoming. Scented-leaved pelargoniums directly by the door will release their aroma as people brush against them. Lavender and rosemary will do the same.

Side entrance

❀ Some gardens can be reached only through a side entrance. Even if a side entrance is narrow and tunnel-like you can make it seem more spacious by painting the walls white.

ABOVE: An arched entrance leading from shadow into sunlight is one of the most romantic ways to approach an outdoor space. The wrought iron gates give the impression that you are entering a secret garden.

ABOVE: *These garden doors lead directly on to lush borders overflowing with flowers and fruit.*

❀ White reflects what light there is and always seems to enlarge a space. At the end of the alleyway you could install a wrought iron gate or arched entrance with climbers over it so that there is a hint of the promised garden before you get there. Always keep side entrances clear. There is nothing so off-putting as having to clamber over bags of compost or old prunings.

Windows

❀ Windows overlooking the garden should not be wasted but should look out on to a pleasant garden view. If the living-room window overlooks the garden, try to make sure the garden can be seen when people are sitting down.

❀ If this is not possible, you should at least ensure that some climbing plant or flowering tree is visible through the window. This is especially important for disabled or elderly people, who spend more of their time sitting down than others might.

Transitional entrances

❀ Porches, pergolas and conservatories all have very different functions but in one respect they are alike: they act as transitional areas between the house and the garden. Porches are usually erected as insulation from the weather. If they are very small they sometimes seem to act more as a barrier between house and garden than as a lobby joining one to the other. However, if they are glazed, they can be used to grow tender houseplants and become almost like miniature conservatories.

❀ A pergola by the garden door can complement the architecture of the house, while the planted elements can relate to the garden. A conservatory is also a meeting point between house and garden, relating both to the architecture and to the hardier plants outside.

ABOVE: *A narrow iron gate and enormous hydrangea entice you along the gravel path at the entrance to this garden.*

Proportion and scale

❀ Anything in the garden that is very large in relation to the house will seem excessive. Many a tree that is nicely in proportion when planted will grow far too large for its allotted space and not only prevent other things from growing but will diminish the house by its size. This is just as true of patios, terraces and paths.

❀ In a garden belonging to a small house, or a house with a narrow frontage, a grandiose patio will look out of place. A small patio with a carefully designed pattern of bricks or other paving and a concentration on the detailing and workmanship will look charming and could be surrounded by plants or a trellis, giving more of a courtyard effect.

❀ In a large house, on the other hand, elements that are too small will give a trivial, fussy effect. A broad terrace by the garden door will give the house a more suitable visual base. Use large paving slabs, and have the terrace or patio running the length of the house, particularly if the house has large windows and patio doors. It should be wide enough to take a dining table and generously proportioned chairs.

❀ Courtyards offer good opportunities for brickwork or paving. Again, the materials and patterns should be in keeping with the house, and any flowerpots and containers should be of similar shape and colour.

The view towards the house

❀ Remember that when you are at the far end of the garden, you will get a different view of its relationship to the house that is just as important as the view from the house into the garden. The house becomes a focal point and you will be much more aware of materials that do not match or co-ordinate with those of the house and be pleasurably aware of those that do.

ABOVE: *The tall plants of* Romneya coulteri *here break the hard line of the window frame, creating a softer look.*

ABOVE: *On the street side of this house, a burgeoning* Ceanothus *softens the brickwork and anchors the house to the ground.*

Anchoring the house

❀ Planting evergreen shrubs near to the house helps to anchor it to the ground. This is especially true of new or modern houses, which can seem rather bleak and unrelated to their surroundings. Climbers are another excellent way of anchoring the house. Those that cover the whole house are good for buildings that have no particular architectural interest. Virginia creeper, which turns the most astonishingly bright red colour in autumn, does the job well.

❀ A traditional house with some architectural interest will be better with climbing roses around the windows and nothing else to hide the materials and design. Interesting modern buildings, some of which are sculptures in their own right, may not need anything clambering over them but could benefit from groups of bold architectural plants nearby to act as anchors.

ABOVE: *In the garden of this modern single-storey building, a wide gravel walkway takes you at a leisurely pace back to the house.*

Paths

❀ Paths leading directly from the house should be as wide as you can make them; narrow paths are less inviting. Two people should preferably be able to walk together in conversation. This is not always possible in small gardens but it is something to aim for. Paths can get narrower as they lead into the remoter parts of the garden, but near the house the path is acting as a gateway to the whole garden and should reflect that fact.

Security

❀ The way in which the garden relates to the house can influence security quite seriously. The street door should not be concealed by tall, dense shrubs, which would prevent a burglar being seen while trying to force the lock. Low planting is advisable here, which would make anyone trying to break in much more visible.

❀ At the back, avoid growing trees and shrubs near the house that a burglar could use as a ladder. If you want to clothe the house in greenery, stick to thorny plants such as the unfriendly climbing roses 'Mermaid' and 'Albertine', or a *berberis* or *pyracantha*.

❀ Make sure you have a place where you can lock up ladders and heavy garden implements such as spades and forks. Padlocking a ladder to the wall is better than leaving it lying about, and certainly never leave one propped up against a wall as an invitation to intruders.

ABOVE: *This small garden is made to seem much larger by the divisions and cross-axes. Here, a brick path leads to a blue seat as the focal point, with the view interrupted only by a large copper planter.*

MAINTAINING LAWNS

A good lawn is an attractive feature but a poor one can
be a real eyesore. On clay soils in wet districts, for example, a really
green, healthy lawn is difficult to achieve. Many people tend to take up
unsatisfactory lawns and lay bricks or paving instead. However, if you
garden on clay and really would like to have an area of lawn, you can
lay new turfs on rafts of sand and rubble to ensure good drainage.
Lawns should be very slightly sloping to prevent waterlogging.
Aim for a minimum slope of 1 in 80 and a maximum slope of 1 in 4.
Steeper gradients are better terraced.

ABOVE: *A tiny tree in a lawn should not adversely affect the grass growth. This maple makes a stunning contrast against a green backcloth of foliage.*

Grass for lawns

❀ There are different mixtures of grass for different
situations. For example, some will stand up to bikes and
ball games, some will grow satisfactorily in light shade
and some will produce the sort of velvety green suitable
for bowling greens but are not so resilient as the others.

Lawn shape

❀ Although a rectangle is probably the most common
shape for lawns, it is often more pleasing to have an oval,
circular or irregularly shaped lawn. Avoid small and fussy
curves and awkward corners, which are very difficult to
maintain and mow.

❀ If you want to include island beds, make sure the verges
are wide enough to take a mower. When deciding where
the lawn should go, remember that all parts of a lawn
need to receive some direct sunlight during the day so
try not to choose too shady a part of the garden.

Access to the lawn

❀ You should be able to reach the lawn from several
angles. If you approach the lawn along only one path or
one small entrance or gateway, the soil will become
compacted and the grass worn and brown. Paths should
run alongside the lawn rather than across it, unless you
choose to lay concrete stepping stones.

ABOVE: *Lawns do best under lightly canopied trees. This lawn is flourishing under silver birches.*

ABOVE: *A well-situated lawn can be used as an outdoor room with judicious use of sunlight and shade and comfortable garden furniture.*

❀ A path between a lawn and a flowerbed can be useful in wet weather, and summer flowers tumbling over a path do look attractive. Lay paths and stepping stones below the level of the lawn and leave a narrow grass-free mowing edge between the lawn and path to make mowing and edging easier.

❀ Avoid using loose chippings as a material for paths next to a lawn. They inevitably get kicked on to the grass and will damage the mower blades.

Lawns under trees

❀ Lawns will not thrive beneath a dense canopy of leaves. Shortage of light and water and the dripping from the edges of the trees will make it difficult for the grass to grow. It will end up thin and wispy and moss will soon encroach.

❀ Cutting the lower branches and shortening the higher ones may help a little but you are still never likely to achieve a good lawn. The best thing is to remove the turf completely from around the tree trunks and create a large bed for bulbs such as hardy cyclamen and crocuses and shade-loving plants such as periwinkles (*Vinca*) and dead-nettles (*Lamium*).

❀ Specimen trees can look marvellous when planted in a large expanse of green lawn. If you want to plant a tree in a small lawn, choose a small tree such as the cut-leaf Japanese maple (*Acer palmatum* 'Dissectum'), which will take 20 years to grow to 1.5 m (5 ft). *Acer japonicum* 'Aureum' will grow to 3 m (10 ft) and has attractive leaves, which provide colour from early spring to early autumn.

The non-grass lawn

❀ Although grass is certainly the most reliable material for a lawn, you can create small areas of lawn with other plants such as camomile or thyme. They do not have the resilience of grass and should not be walked on too much.

❀ A good place might be at the base of a fountain or in the centre of a circular herb bed. A popular plant for this kind of use is *Anthemis nobilis*.

PAVED AREAS, STEPS AND PATHS

Probably the first step in designing a garden is to incorporate a paved area for relaxation, entertainment and family meals. Paved areas near the house form important transitional meeting places between house and garden. Hard materials carry the architectural feel of the house out of doors. Planted containers and shrubs nearby bring in the garden element. Paths and steps also provide an architectural element and should be carefully planned, as they will become part of the basic framework. Stick to one or two basic materials throughout or the end result will be fussy.

Patio shapes

The shapes you use in all garden spaces will be among the important things that set the style of your garden. A symmetrical arrangement will give the space a formal look, whereas a curving, asymmetrical one will suit a more relaxed style and a geometric asymmetrical one will suit an abstract modern garden.

ABOVE: A small area outside the house has been attractively bricked in a square shape and surrounded by interesting and varied plants. Even the smallest outdoor space can be made into a pleasant spot.

ABOVE: You do not need very much space to create a small oval or circular seating area. This one is gravelled and has mostly green planting with a little seat for contemplation.

❀ If your garden is surrounded by tall buildings, as is likely in an urban setting, straight, geometric lines are likely to work best, as they will complement the lines of the surrounding buildings.

❀ In a small area it is best to stick to one shape, just as it is best to stick to very few materials. It is also best not to try and mix diagonals and curves or squares and circles. Even in larger gardens, there will be better unity and cohesion if you limit the number of different shapes you use.

❀ Once you have decided on the shapes for the paved areas, you can design the patterns for the bricks or paving you are going to use. There is all the difference in the world between well-laid paving in interesting patterns and concrete slabs carelessly placed on the ground.

❀ Paving patterns can be divided into those that are static and those that are dynamic. Static patterns hold the eye within the area and have a peaceful quality. Dynamic patterns lead the eye along a path or paved area with a feeling of movement, an invitation to explore further.

Types of paving

❀ There are numerous forms of paving to choose from. Pre-cast concrete is available in many forms, including slabs that vary in size, shape and thickness. Clay bricks in many colours and dark engineering bricks are suitable for many areas. Granite setts (paving blocks) and cobbles are ideal for small awkward areas.

❀ Concrete slabs interspersed with small areas of cobbles can break up the blandness of concrete on its own. Some paving materials become slippery when wet; others, like brick, are highly non-slip.

Combining gravel and paving

❀ If you have decided against lawns and soft surfaces in your garden, one paved area can lead to another through a series of enclosures and paths. The whole garden can be given an extended courtyard effect, which will provide plenty of space for sitting and entertaining.

❀ Some of the paving can be given over to gravel, with 'stepping stones' of paving slabs to give a firm foothold and plants growing in the gravel. Many plants like growing through gravel because it drains well but also helps to prevent moisture from evaporating too quickly.

❀ Many alpines and Mediterranean silver-leaved plants flourish and will seed themselves. There are various types of gravel to choose from, including white limestone, white gravel chippings and washed pea shingle, which has rounded edges. It is best not to use white gravel in sunny areas where the light shining on it can make it quite blinding.

ABOVE: *This circular paved area is surrounded by a shady pergola and furnished with folding chairs, which can easily be carried indoors in wet weather.*

DECKING AND OTHER USES FOR TIMBER

TIMBER decking is a natural material with simple lines, which can be practical and attractive in a number of different situations. It is often used as an alternative to paving. The combination of doors, flooring, fencing, furniture and steps all made of wood can help provide a unified look, which is simple and yet stylish. Decking should ideally be made of hardwood, which needs no preservative treatment. Softwood must be planed or it will splinter, and it should be given preservative treatment, which should be repeated at regular intervals. Large areas of decking are not always successful in a cold, damp climate, where the timber may never have the chance to dry out fully and will eventually rot.

Construction

❀ An area of timber decking is not hard to construct. The decking timbers rest on beams and joists supported by posts held in the ground with concrete. This type of construction allows air to circulate, keeping the wood dry unless there are prolonged periods of snow or rain and the atmosphere remains moist.

Raised decking

❀ In the USA older houses were traditionally built with the living area above ground level, leaving space beneath for a cellar and to allow air to circulate. A wooden deck was often built as a way of extending the upper level to create an extra patio area.

❀ Decking is particularly suited to this form of extension because the air circulating around it helps to keep it dry and prevents the wood from rotting. However, it can also be used as a surfacing material at ground level. It is particularly suited to houses with timber clapboarding or shingled roofs and it can give a small space a pleasing look when used in conjunction with wooden fencing.

Decking on roof gardens

❀ Timber is a good material for roof gardens because it is much lighter in weight than other forms of paving. Many flat roofs have not been designed to carry heavy weights and decking will help to balance the weight of people walking on the roof.

❀ Square timber panels, similar in size to paving slabs, can be clamped together to provide flooring. They should be laid on a timber base above the roof finish so that water can drain to a downpipe. Before making any plans for a roof-garden you should find out whether you need permission to use it for this purpose and how much weight the roof can bear.

ABOVE: *Decking tiles in interesting patterns have been used here in geometric arrangements on two levels. Small blue glazed pots hold clipped evergreens that will be attractive all year.*

Decking and water

❀ Timber decking and water always look very natural together and landing stages for river boats have traditionally been made of decking. It can be useful for disguising the edges of artificial pools made with plastic liners and is also ideal for bridges.

❀ A real bridge can be constructed over a small pond or a mock bridge can be built to separate the pond from the water plants, thus making the pool seem bigger than it actually is. A 'landing stage' jutting out over a pond can be finished off with a timber balustrade, giving an attractive bird's eye view of the water. A small hump-backed timber bridge painted rich red is an excellent addition to a Japanese-style garden.

Timber decking in modern designs

❀ The regularly spaced lines created by boards of decking can be used to create exciting and attractive angles and changes of level. Timber decks look good in modern settings and make an excellent foil to plants and containers. Boards can also combine well with gravel, which on its own is not an ideal surface for wheelchairs or delicate shoes.

ABOVE: *This compact and well-stocked roof garden uses decking with rounded sea cobbles to soften it and add interest. A variety of evergreen, variegated and flowering shrubs provide interest all year.*

Wooden paths

❀ Wood is not often used for paths but might be a good choice as a continuation from a bridge or patio made of decking. Discs cut from tree trunks can be set into the ground but these usually look best in a fairly rural setting and are not suitable as a complement to decking used in sophisticated geometrical shapes. Discs are also likely to become slippery in wet weather so could be dangerous underfoot. Coarsely shredded bark can look attractive, although it looks better in a woodland or wild garden setting and is not right for a formal garden.

LEFT: *Decking and water combine well together. Here, decking is used along with brick to surround a pond with its lavish growth of evergreens and windmill-like sails, purposely designed to give shade.*

DEALING WITH AWKWARDLY SHAPED GARDENS

Many gardens are awkwardly shaped. They may be very narrow or have been awkwardly fitted between buildings on a new estate. They may narrow at one end to create a triangular plot. Basement gardens often have tiny patio spaces with very steep steps leading to dry gardens overshadowed by neglected trees. All these problems may be seen as challenges rather than disadvantages. There are many ways of approaching the solutions.

LONG NARROW GARDENS

GARDENS belonging to terraced houses are often long and narrow, sometimes almost ribbon-like in shape. The danger with this sort of garden is that it can feel more like a passageway than a garden. The part nearest the house may get used as a sitting-out area, but the rest of the garden is a repository for old furniture, and stinging or prickly weeds. One of the following solutions may suit this sort of garden.

A series of rooms

❀ The most obvious and usually most successful answer is to divide the plot into a series of separate compartments linked by a path. Each compartment can then be filled with a symmetrical design based on a square, a circle or an oval. By dividing the plot in this way you may be able to use the dividing barriers to hide an ugly barbecue or an intrusive large shrub or tree or to disguise a shed or screen a distant telegraph pole seen over the garden fence.

❀ The different areas will allow you to do much more with the garden. You might combine a small shrubbery or woodland area in which you could conceal a small shed, with a special play area with a swing and sandpit or a formal water garden with a fountain. If your main interest is in plants and growing things, one of these areas could be a small vegetable plot or could be devoted to growing show flowers.

Geometric divisions

❀ Rather than separating the areas with hedges or shrubs, you could use low walls and paving shapes to create interest and variety. Use diagonal lines, which will help to make the garden seem wider. A diagonal brick-lined pool could face a diagonal brick patio outside the garden door.

❀ A path could lead to the next area, perhaps a small lawn with flowerbeds around it. The path could then lead on to a small barbecue area. To prevent this sort of layout

ABOVE: *A raised wooden walkway built about a pond and bog garden allow the visitor to gaze down on to the water and the spectacular collection of irises.*

from seeming too flat, you could add vertical elements at strategic points. These might be small trees or carefully placed shrubs, arches or small pergolas.

❀ Each compartment should invite the visitor in with a visual surprise such as a sculpture, a water feature or an architectural plant and should have some form of seat so that people can stay and enjoy it.

A garden walk

❀ For extra narrow gardens, an alternative to the idea of separate garden spaces is to devote the whole garden to a deliberate garden walk. This will make an advantage of its narrowness. A path leading in gentle curves down the centre of the plot will create undulating borders on either side.

❀ Recesses or arbours can be created at intervals, where people can sit and read or relax and savour the flowers and their scents. At the end there should be a reward for those who have made the journey – a pool perhaps, or a fountain or statue. This kind of garden offers opportunities for urns and statuary at intervals along the walk and plenty of opportunities for formal or romantic planting.

ABOVE: *Long, narrow gardens can be made to look more spacious by the addition of features such as walkways or recesses and arbours. Perhaps you could place a fountain or a statue at the end.*

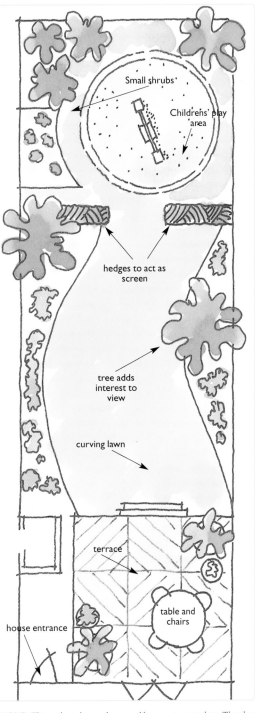

Small shrubs

Childrens' play area

hedges to act as screen

tree adds interest to view

curving lawn

terrace

table and chairs

house entrance

ABOVE: *This garden is long and narrow, like many town gardens. The edges contain plants of varying heights to conceal the edges, and the whole garden has been divided into 'rooms', each with its own character. The patio is near the house, separated from the compost heap by a hedge. The lawn is slightly curved to give a feeling of movement, and the children's play area occupies the end of the garden.*

TRIANGULAR-SHAPED GARDENS

TRIANGULAR plots are not as unusual as you might think. They are often found where the original building site met a road or a river. This shape can seem limiting and the apex seems to draw the eye uncomfortably, especially if the garden is new and bleak, surrounded by bare fences that exaggerate the awkward shape.

❀ You can use tallish trees and shrubs to conceal the awkward-looking pointed section. A small grove of trees or a group of shrubs at the apex will create a feeling of height and space and conceal the narrowness at the end of the garden. Or you could place a small summer house or arbour there as a deliberate focal point and full stop to the garden.

❀ You can also use false perspective, for example by gradually narrowing a flowerbed as it approaches the narrow end, giving the impression of a larger distance and making the garden seem altogether bigger. You can also suggest that the garden is larger than it really is by placing a smaller-than-usual sculpture or garden building at the end of the garden.

❀ Make sure you have some interesting feature in the centre of the plot, which will attract the eye and lessen the emphasis on the awkward point. A hexagonal or paved space or a circular lawn right in the centre will do this, especially if there is a central water feature or interesting container or sculpture in the centre. If this is reached by a path screened by shrubs, the whole area will be disguised and the triangular point becomes less obvious.

L-SHAPED GARDENS

AN 'L' shape, that is, a plot with two short 'arms', is in many ways not awkward at all but provides two gardens for the price of one. The position of the house is crucial to this sort of garden. It may form the inside corner with the garden on two sides. Or it may sit at one end of one of the arms. Almost certainly, one arm will be generally shady and the other mainly sunny. Careful choice of plants to suit these two aspects will be important and will create its own design to some extent.

ABOVE: The rather awkward narrowing shape at the end of this triangular garden has been planted with a small grove of trees to conceal its odd shape. A narrow patio at the back of the house leads to an asymmetrical lawn with a pretty seat as a focal point. The kitchen garden is behind the garage but conveniently near the kitchen.

ABOVE: A circular paved area acts as the link between the two arms of this L-shaped garden. A paved path leads from one part of the garden into the next under a tall pergola and through a gate.

❀ You can carry the same theme on from one to the other or create two completely different gardens. Whichever you decide to do, the important (and the trickiest) thing to do is to design the meeting point of the two sections so that the transition is comfortable. This meeting point

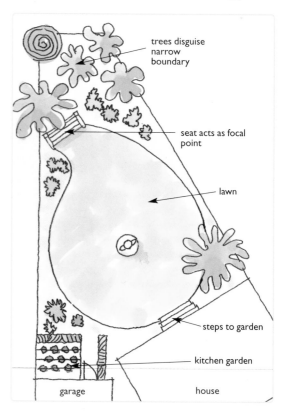

trees disguise narrow boundary

seat acts as focal point

lawn

steps to garden

kitchen garden

garage

house

could be literally that, a place with seats or a summer house where you can pause before moving on to the next area. It could be a third garden, entered from either of the others through arches or along a path bordered by shrubs.

❀ One traditionally successful device is to create a deliberately formal garden near the house, which becomes less formal further away from the house and eventually leads into a shrubbery, woodland area or wildlife garden around the corner.

WIDE AND SHALLOW GARDENS

A WIDE, shallow plot can be surprisingly awkward to plan for. It is generous in one way but its lack of depth from the house can make it difficult. For example, when sitting by the garden door, you may feel as though your nose is pressed against the boundary hedge opposite. However, there are a number of features that lend themselves to this shape of garden and with some careful planning, you can still create a feeling of depth.

❀ One way of tackling the problem is to create a plan of long narrow spaces divided by box hedging or low walls. Carefully detailed brick or stone divisions will emphasise the breadth of the garden and give an impression of space.

❀ Low arches and the occasional topiary feature or urn will encourage the eye to concentrate on the detail rather than the lack of depth. Opposite the house, an interesting detail such as a niche with a sculpture or a fountain will also distract attention from the lack of depth.

❀ Choose colours that will counteract the foreshortening effect. Avoid reds and yellow that will make space seem even narrower. Concentrate on mixing pale colours, for example lavender, santolina, pale blue hardy geraniums, catmint and herbs of all kinds.

BELOW: *This L-shaped garden has been designed with a formal area next to the house leading through a clipped hedge into something completely different – a much more informal lawn with a flower border and a path leading from the house through a small gate to the road.*

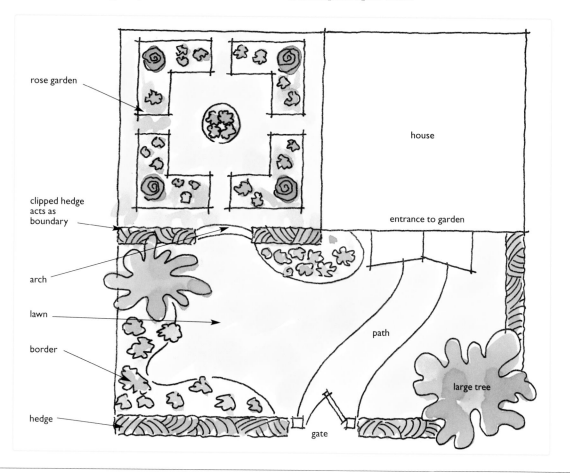

rose garden

house

clipped hedge acts as boundary

entrance to garden

arch

lawn

border

path

large tree

hedge

gate

SMALL FRONT GARDENS

GENERALLY, urban front gardens are difficult to cope with because they are often quite heavily shaded and also have to hold the rubbish bins. It is easy to give up on them completely but thoughtful planning can transform a front garden into a really attractive welcoming feature to the house.

❀ The first thing is to create some structure for the rubbish bin, where it will be easily accessible but concealed from people going in and out of the front door. Something simple, such as a three-sided 1-m (3-ft) tall brick enclosure is a good answer. One open side means the bin can be easily removed for emptying. A carefully constructed shed is less useful, being difficult both to keep clean and to maintain.

❀ Front gardens are seldom used for sitting in, being too public, but they do mark the approach to your home and should be well designed and welcoming. It is best to create a garden that will not require too much maintenance. Front gardens are often the forgotten areas of the gardener's domain and receive little watering, feeding or weeding.

❀ An important rule for the tiny garden is not to try to squeeze too many plants into it and it is often best to go for formality. Eliminate all grass, lay paving and install pairs of large pots planted with clipped bay or box. A

ABOVE: *This house sits directly on the pavement but its owners have managed to 'green' the area with planted boxes of ivy and colourful hanging baskets.*

small weeping tree in the centre of the plot can create an attractive feature. The weeping pear (*Pyrus salicifolia* 'Pendula') makes an excellent specimen tree in a small space and has a charming arching habit and pretty silvery leaves.

❀ Alternatively, go for a more informal look. This is not always easy in a small space and it is tempting to put in too many plants, which will soon grow out of control.

❀ One answer is to cover the whole area with gravel or pebbles and create a Japanese garden with a rock or two placed at judicious intervals and a silver-leaved plant to balance them. Otherwise, colourful groupings of pelargoniums or busy Lizzies (*Impatiens*) can brighten up a front garden magically. All these ideas will draw the eye away from the walled-off area of the rubbish bin and create a positive impression on those walking by.

ABOVE: *Front gardens should be simple and welcoming. This one has matching blue paint on the front door and planting boxes, which looks spectacular against the white walls. The two miniature willows with their attractive variegated foliage create a light, optimistic mood.*

ABOVE: *This restrained but effective planting scheme with one ivy covered wall and a ribbon of pink in front of a cotoneaster hedge suits this modern house.*

SLOPING SITES

IF YOUR garden is on a slope, you can create a wild meadow or sloping lawn, but other choices are limited because water will drain away quickly and many plants will suffer. In general it is better to terrace the site, using low walls to contain the different levels.

❀ For retaining walls use materials that complement the house itself. Brick houses look better with their garden walls and paths made of similar coloured bricks.

❀ For stone houses, try to use stone for retaining walls and paths. Rendered or pebble dash houses look best with concrete walls, rendered and then painted. Modern outdoor paints are available in a wide range of excellent colours. All walls should be topped with coping stones, which overlap the wall by about 4 cm (1½ in). Steps should be as wide and as shallow as the space will allow, using similar materials to the walls and paths.

❀ Each level of terracing can be treated differently. One level could be planted with yellow and orange plants, for example, while further down oranges, reds and purples could take their place; further down again, misty blues and mauves would seem to disappear into the distance.

❀ If the site is shady, this colour transition will not work so well, because you will not be able to grow the variety of plants necessary. Here a formal terrace could lead down to a less formal collection of mixed shrubs and herbaceous plants or a quiet seating area with a pool or fountain.

BASEMENT GARDENS

BASEMENT gardens often consist of a very narrow patio with steep, narrow steps leading up to the garden, which is normally too high to be viewed from below. The patio itself can feel cramped and dark and is not an inviting place to sit. In such cases, it may be best to sacrifice some of the growing space by making the patio a little larger and the steps a little more generous, giving you the opportunity to make both patio and garden more attractive.

ABOVE: *Steps should be as wide and shallow as space allows when leading from one area of terracing to another.*

WATER AND LIGHTING

Water has a magical quality in a garden. Quite literally, of course,
it brings the garden life, since nothing will grow without it.
Added to that, the sight and sound of water bring liveliness,
light and movement unmatched by anything else. Combined
with effective lighting, you can transform your garden into a brilliant
and enchanted place. Both water and lighting offer the opportunity for
beautiful and unexpected features.

ABOVE: A long, narrow garden deceives the eye with the creation of a
pond and a wooden bridge with a bright red hand rail, followed by a paved
seating area beyond. The edges are concealed by evergreen planting.

STILL WATER

PONDS and pools offer tranquillity. In the open they can
reflect the sky with a delightful magical mirror effect of
light. Such smooth planes of water can act as a foil to
planting either in the water or next to it. A pool should be
treated as an integral part of the garden's plan and should be
built of materials sympathetic to the shape, size and
materials of the garden and house. You can choose to have a
natural-looking pool or you can give it a much more formal
aspect with hard stone or tiles and a symmetrical shape.

Formal pools

❀ Formal pools look at home in symmetrical gardens, set
  in paving or some other hard surface and reached by
  straight paths or set in a terrace or courtyard. They can
  be sunken or raised and will reflect the stone or brick as
  well as any water lilies grown in them. They make
  excellent homes for ornamental fish, which can be
  observed at close quarters.
❀ Geometric shapes work best for formal pools – it is
  hard to beat a rectangular pond. A short wide one will
  look good on a terrace, whereas a long narrow one,

PLANTS FOR POOLS

WATER lilies (Nymphaea) are the ideal plants to
grow in a formal pool. They like the stillness of
the water and their flowers seem to float upon it.
Hardy water lilies include Nymphaea 'Escarboucle',
which is vigorous with large red blooms. N. 'Helvola'
has dainty, star-shaped canary yellow flowers throughout summer and is good for a tub or small pool; N.
'Hermine' has pure white flowers over a long period.

more like a canal, will look good beside a straight path or as the centrepiece in a narrow garden. Small circular, sunken ponds can look very pretty in tiny gardens. Ideally, this sort of pond should form an important feature in the garden and not be tucked away out of sight.

Wildlife pond

❀ You do not need a very large pond to attract wildlife and grow moisture-loving plants. A pond 1 m (3 ft) across is quite big enough to have its own population of water insects, damsel flies, frogs and toads. If you place your pond near a flower border, the plants will provide cover for shy creatures to hide in. A lawn nearby will provide an open space for birds. If the pond is completely surrounded by lawn or paving, remove some of the turf or slabs so that you can create a bog or rock garden or a wild flower patch, which will give shelter to small creatures. If young children are going to be playing in the garden you may want to avoid open water but you can still create a small boggy area for wildlife by digging a hole, lining it as for a pond, but filling it with soil. As this cannot then drain it is easy to keep it topped up with water.

ABOVE: *Ponds respond wonderfully well to planting, reflecting tall, elegant plants particularly well in the water. It is always best to keep the planting simple. Here, yellow water irises and water lilies make a spectacular show.*

BOG PLANTS

MARGINAL plants for the shallow edges include the yellow flag iris (*Iris pseudacorus*), marsh marigolds (*Caltha palustris*) and *Veronica beccabunga*. Leaves that float on the surface provide shade for underwater creatures and help prevent algae. They include water soldiers (*Stratiotes aloides*) and fringed water lilies (*Nymphoides peltata*). Plants for permanently wet soil near the pond include bugle (*Ajuga reptans*), creeping Jenny (*Lysimachia nummularia*) and lady's smock (*Cardamine pratensis*).

ABOVE: *Still water gives interesting and beautiful reflections as well as visions of the bottom of a pool. In shallow water, small water-loving plants will grow well around cobbles and over stones.*

MOVING WATER

ADDING movement to water creates a truly magical effect. Reflections are enhanced, the sound of moving water is soothing and musical, and fish benefit from the enhanced oxygenation of the water. Water lilies, however, prefer still water, so are better suited to ponds without fountains, or where a fountain is offset so that part of the pond remains still. Movement can be created by fountains, waterspouts, rills or cascades and is guaranteed to bring sparkle and dash to the garden. As always, it should be planned in scale with the area. A gentle trickle can be refreshing in a small garden, where a large fountain would be pretentious.

ABOVE: *An elegant formal fountain with a tall jet surrounded by smaller ones. The pale adjacent pink brick paving includes beds of lavender.*

Cascades

❀ Cascades have frequently been used in great and grand gardens, especially in Italy, to create spectacular stairs of water. The splendid cascade at Chatsworth in Derbyshire was built in 1694 and still amazes visitors with its tumbling staircase of water. It is quite possible to make more modest cascades in keeping with smaller gardens.

❀ On a sloping site, a narrow channel, interrupted at intervals by a short cascade and an occasional octagonal or round pool, can create an enchanted atmosphere not unlike that of a Persian or Moorish garden.

❀ On a flat site, an informal cascade can be built quite easily, the water being circulated by a small electric pump.

❀ An unusual cascade suitable for a small informal garden can comprise a series of watering cans or urns lying on their sides, each emptying into the one below to create a kind of cascade. This idea could be developed in different ways using a variety of receptacles.

ABOVE: *This sculpted glass fountain alters subtly as you walk around it, catching the sun and glittering as the water runs down it.*

Fountains

❀ Fountains have become popular recently, partly because of the availability of comparatively inexpensive reproductions of traditional designs, and partly because of the mass production of small submersible pumps, supplied with a fountain rose jet and sold in kit form. Installed in a part of the garden that becomes very hot during the day, a fountain has a distinctly cooling effect.

❀ Reproductions and copies of traditional fountain designs such as dolphins and cherubs are widely available. There are also some modern metal fountains in the form of leaves, twigs or birds, in which the water cascades down from one section to another.

OTHER TYPES OF WATER FEATURE

THERE are any number of ways of getting a small amount of water to bubble, trickle, flow or glint in a decorative and refreshing way. You can introduce the sound of running water by running it through a pipe in the wall, using one of the cheapest electric pumps and a small cistern.

Cobbles

❀ Rounded pebbles collected together are popular as a base for water to trickle over. (These are widely available from garden centres so please do not collect them from beaches.) A cobble fountain is simple and pleasant and does not need a pool. The effect relies on the sound and movement of water splashing over the stones into a reservoir, which is constantly recycled.

❀ You will need a tank large enough for a submersible pump and holding enough water to cope with evaporation from the surface of the cobbles on a sunny day. The size of the reservoir will depend on how often the system is topped up – it need be no bigger than a plastic bucket.

Millstones

❀ A large millstone has a strong architectural impact so should be carefully placed where it will balance some other strong feature. The water falls over the side of the stone and is collected in a reservoir below; again, no pool is required. A geyser jet can be used to introduce air if you want a more turbulent effect.

Bamboo spout

❀ In Japanese gardens, bamboo canes are used as spouts. Balanced on an upright, the cane fills up with water, tips it out on to pebbles below, then starts all over again. Some people find the regular filling and emptying peaceful, others find it monotonous.

BELOW: *A traditional Japanese bamboo spout deposits water into a large stone bowl that stands on a craggy rock with cobblestones below.*

LIGHTING SYSTEMS

ELECTRICITY in the garden has made it possible to create effective lighting schemes from the smallest to the largest gardens, and has equally made it possible to water the garden effectively and economically over a long period, even when you are not there. For garden lighting always use lights specifically designed for outdoor use. Any other lighting is dangerous if used outside.

Advantages of garden lighting

❀ Lighting adds another dimension to the garden and should be planned into your scheme from the beginning. A well-designed scheme can turn your garden into a completely different world at night. You can create subtle pools of light with a general illuminating effect or dramatically highlight particular trees, shrubs and garden features.

❀ The eye is intrigued and delighted by small lights nestling among the foliage and flowers of large containers and plants in surrounding beds. It is usually more flattering to light the garden rather than the house, unless your house has unusual architectural features that merit special highlighting.

How much light?

❀ For typical suburban gardens, one or two small floodlight fittings mounted on the back wall of the house will provide enough light for moving about safely and enable a patio area to be used for barbecues. However, much more can be done to highlight aspects of the garden plan or planting and make the garden more fascinating at night.

❀ Focal points such as sculptures and fountains can look particularly effective when well lit. Remember, though, even when aiming for dramatic effects, subtlety is important. It is very easy to be over-enthusiastic and overdo the lighting, ending up with something glaring and uncomfortable.

BELOW: *A handmade ceramic Japanese lamp gives the garden a pleasant glow in the dark and will guide you along a path.*

Lighting the outdoor room

❀ Lighting is particularly important where the garden is small and designed to be used for entertaining in the evening, as well as for displaying the plants. Here you want not only to highlight plants seen from the sitting area, which may be at the far end of the garden, but also to light the path leading to it. This lighting does not need to be as bright as daylight but bright enough to see where you are going, yet leaving the rest of the garden mysterious.

❀ A collection of small candle-lit lamps can light up a table perfectly adequately, casting a becoming light on both objects and people. There are many different and attractive glass and perforated metal holders for candles and nightlights and the flickering of a live flame creates interesting moving shadows.

Lighting seen from the house

❀ If you don't go into the garden at night, but want to be able to admire it from indoors or from the patio, you do not need to light the paths and can concentrate mainly on the 'picture' from the windows.

❀ Highlight decorative foliage, sculptures and other features. You will probably find that individual branches you have not really noticed before will respond like magic to being lit at night and will become positively sculptural when individually highlighted.

ABOVE: *Unobtrusive light sources are by far the most effective for night lighting. Here, the light source is hidden by the trees, giving a dramatic effect.*

Positioning garden lights

❀ A little lighting, if well positioned, can have a tremendous impact. Avoid dazzle and glare by keeping fittings and bulbs hidden. There are all sorts of places where you can do this, such as behind tree trunks or walls or behind plant containers or large-leaved shrubs. Try out their positions by placing lights temporarily and then walk around the garden to check that the source is concealed from all angles.

❀ Spike lamps are useful because they can be moved around but they should be regarded as temporary only and not for permanent installation. The plug should be removed from its socket and the lamp taken into the house when not being used. As with all lamps, it is important to use the bulb recommended by the manufacturer or there may not be a watertight seal and the lamp might shatter.

Lighting trees

❁ The texture and shape of tree trunks, branches, leaves and blossom provide endless opportunities for decorative lighting. Use tungsten halogen flood spotlights, positioned to shine upwards into the branches from a garden wall or a lower part of the trunk.

❁ You can fix a light fitting at the centre of the tree to create a soft glow. Strings of fairy lights strung through the branches give a magical effect, particularly if the bulbs are all white. Make sure you use lights designed for outdoor use.

❁ Bulb holders on this sort of lighting should be moulded on to the cable; the type with sharp contacts that bite through the insulation of the cable to make connection with the cores are extremely dangerous if used outside.

The magic of light and water

❁ Water and light are a magical combination and at night can provide extra glitter and sparkle. Use wide and narrow beam spotlights on fountains and moving water. When lighting a pond make sure that the source of the light is not reflected in it, which would diminish the mystery.

Lighting for safety

❁ You should always have some lights to show steps and other changes of level and check that these do not cast confusing shadows. There should also be enough lighting near the house so that when you come out of the bright light of the house interior or the patio, you are not blinded by the sudden darkness.

Light fittings

❁ As with all other elements of the garden's design, the light fittings themselves should be in keeping with the garden's style. There are many good-looking functional fittings available, made of high-grade materials to resist corrosion and sealed against the weather. They are therefore not cheap.

❁ Several designs will hold energy-efficient, compact fluorescent bulbs and any fitting designed to use standard light bulbs could take one of these. Several low-level light sources are more pleasing than a few very bright ones but it does mean that the cost can quickly mount up.

BELOW: *Lighting on water can produce a magical effect; here the different colours of the the lights give added interest.*

Light fittings powered by the sun are available. They can make good guiding lights, but the range of fittings available is not very large and some of them look as though they were designed for hotels rather than domestic gardens.

ABOVE: *Fairy lights twisted around the arches of this walkway enhance the flowers.*

Installation

All outdoor lighting should be installed by an approved specialist electrical contractor. Connections must be properly sealed and wiring must be of a special type, set in a conduit. Outdoor lighting is not cheap so test your chosen lights and make sure they are in the right places before you call in the contractor. Remember that plants will grow and the garden will change. Permanent lights that are complicated to install should therefore be positioned beneath mature trees and shrubs or sculptural items that are unlikely to change.

CONSTRUCTING
OUTBUILDINGS

Small buildings in the garden contribute greatly to
efficiency and often to the garden's charm as well. On the practical
side, they provide shelter and essential storage space for garden
equipment and furniture. They make pleasant places for conversation,
shelter and refreshment and can be excellent play spaces for children.
Visually they can contribute in an important way to the look of the
garden, providing architectural balance to the house or to some
other structure in the garden. Buildings of all kinds are potential
focal points, used to draw the attention and provide interest and
entertainment. They can also be eyesores, of course.

THE BASIC SHED

REASONABLY priced sheds are available in kit form to put
together at home. The smallest are large enough to
hold garden tools, folding furniture and games equipment.
The most basic garden sheds are not particularly pretty, but
there are ways in which they can be hidden. It is surprising
how often sheds are placed against a wall in the middle of a
small garden, where you cannot avoid looking at them.

BELOW: *Garden sheds are available to buy in kit form; they can be as basic or
sophisticated as your budget dictates.*

- If the garden is not quite rectangular and has the odd
  awkward corner, this might be the very place to put a small
  shed. Tuck it away out of sight behind some sort of screen,
  perhaps a shrubbery or trellis with climbers trained on it.
- Try to focus attention on some other interesting feature
  and away from the shed itself. It should be reached by a
  path so that it is easy to get to, even in wet weather.
- There are many different sizes of shed available and the
  more robust ones can be converted into workrooms
  with extra windows put in. They do not make
  particularly attractive buildings from the outside but
  should not be difficult to camouflage with paint or
  conceal with shrubs and climbing plants.

Alternatives for small gardens

- If your garden is very small and there is no room for a
  full-height shed, you can get seats-cum-storage units,
  large enough to hold implements such as spades, forks
  and trowels, small enough to place on the patio and
  attractive enough to hold their own with the regular
  patio furniture.

Brightening up a shed

- There have been great steps forward in exterior paints in
  the last few years. You can paint almost anything now in
  paint that will withstand the weather and comes in an
  exciting range of colours, from wonderful sea greens and
  blues to old rose and sunflower yellow.

✿ With these paints you can customise your shed by painting it in pale blue and white stripes, like a beach hut, for example, or in a really deep blue or green, perhaps outlining door and window frames in a different colour.

Garden rooms

✿ As homes become smaller and more people work from home, creating an extra room in the garden to use as a studio or office makes a lot of sense. There are many companies who specialise in building such rooms, so you can get an attractive chalet-type building or a cottage-like 'second home'.

✿ Shop around for different designs and qualities – prices vary enormously. One thing you must be sure of is that it will be weathertight and warm. You can quite easily carry electricity via special cables buried underground so that you can run lighting, heating and computer equipment in the room. You need to make sure that doors and windows can be safely secured and that the room is properly insulated.

ABOVE: *This very basic garden shed has acquired a personality all of its own by being painted a bright sea-blue. This colour seems to show up foliage colours particularly well.*

BELOW: *A well-ordered garden shed is a tremendous asset in any garden, however small. It is the perfect place to keep packets and tins, seeds and seed trays and other garden paraphernalia.*

CONSERVATORIES

THE purpose of buildings that use glass is to make full use of the sun and the daylight. The conservatory makes a useful, weatherproof link between inside and outside, but it can also create a magic of its own. In this extension of the home you can enjoy the jungle atmosphere of tender plants with their bright colours and exotic scents. You can use it as a light and airy dining room or a quiet space in which to read or snooze. Cane or perforated metal chairs and tables will emphasise the tropical aspect, and plenty of tropical plants and climbers in containers will add to the 'holiday' feeling.

Conservatory style

❀ Most conservatories are attached to the house and great care should be taken to choose one whose style, proportions and materials are in keeping with the materials and the architecture of the house. This does not necessarily mean that all buildings should be of the same period. In fact, a simple modern construction added to a traditional house can look very much in keeping. Getting the scale and proportion right in relation to the house are by far the most important things.

❀ Many conservatories are made of treated softwood and will require frequent painting, which is tricky and time consuming. Cedar can be used unpainted and will weather to an attractive silver-grey. Aluminium is expensive but almost maintenance free, as is UPVC.

❀ Georgian houses suit simple conservatories with arched windows and square panes, rather like the original orangeries popular in the 18th century for growing citrus fruits brought back from the Mediterranean. Victorian buildings, which are usually more eccentric and decorative, look good with a more flamboyant conservatory, perhaps with an ornamental metal frame, pointed windows and other Gothic detailing.

❀ Small cottages and houses suit small conservatories, which bridge the transition between house and garden

ABOVE: *This Gothic-style greenhouse/conservatory is firmly based on brick foundations. It blends in well with the garden, while the planting around it also helps to make it 'fit in'.*

RIGHT: *A wrought iron pavilion is a good focal point with its white painted curlicues and decorative seat. The whole effect is enhanced by an evergreen backdrop and a froth of Alchemilla mollis.*

without being too dominating. Simple designs with aluminium or UPVC frames and no frills will often look better than anything more sophisticated.

❀ It is easy to be tempted by the advertisements for 'period' conservatories. Many are over-ornamented, however, with decorative details that are completely wrong for the house. With conservatories, as with so much in the garden, simplicity is usually more effective than too much detailing.

A focal point

❀ A good-looking greenhouse can be a focal point in a small garden. The hexagon is an attractive shape, and hexagonal greenhouses with wood or aluminium frames can look charming. It can be used as a display area for colourful plants such as pelargoniums, busy Lizzies (*Impatiens*) and tender fuchsias, for example, as well as for growing seeds and cuttings.

Pavilions and gazebos

❀ Pavilions are largely built for romantic atmosphere in larger gardens and to give a sheltered resting place with a view on to the garden. The idea comes from ancient Rome, from ancient Chinese pagodas and Indian Mogul temples or pavilions. A gazebo is a smaller version of a pavilion.

❀ Pavilions are often circular or hexagonal, giving a view on to the garden from all sides. The roof should have a high pitch to give it a more commanding presence and elegance. Wreathed in foliage, it will offer an agreeable contrast between the geometry of the materials and the free form of the planting.

❀ A Chinese pavilion looks marvellous with light bulbs picking out the exaggerated shape of the roof at night. Pavilions and gazebos should be positioned in a sunny part of the garden but with some planting to ensure a certain amount of shade and seclusion.

BELOW: *This Victorian conservatory is very tall and is able to hold quite large trees.*

MAKING SMALL STRUCTURES

Pergolas, arbours, gazebos and other small garden structures
open to the air provide pleasant places for shelter or simply to sit in
and enjoy the view of your garden. They can also provide interesting
and attractive focal points in the garden. Features such as bridges
can transform the style of your garden, whether it is an Oriental or
traditional look you are seeking. It is important to make sure all
these structures are generously proportioned but not too large
or grandiose for the size and style of garden you are creating,
otherwise they will be overbearing and detract from the beauty
of the garden itself.

ABOVE: *A small white gazebo acts as a stunning focal point in this garden of lawns and foliage. It is carefully balanced by lead planters.*

ABOVE: *Small structures such as this little summer house provide welcome spots for shelter and relaxation in the garden.*

Pergolas

❦ Pergolas were used as long ago as 2000 BC, by the ancient Egyptians as supports for vines. They have continued to be a popular design feature of gardens throughout the ages and have many uses in modern gardens as paths, walkways and shelters. They have become particularly popular for their ornamental value. Festooned with climbers, they can be situated anywhere in the garden.

❦ They may run around the perimeter of a garden or straight down the middle of the plot. They can also be used to cover a patio, architecturally unifying the transition between house and garden. They are also particularly effective in joining two separate garden areas.

❦ Pergolas may be made of brick pillars with wooden cross beams or constructed entirely of wood. Once the main pieces of the structure are in position, lighter struts can be added to assist climbers to reach over the gaps.

ABOVE: *This is the epitome of English garden style with a mass of pink, red and white roses rambling over an arched pergola.*

❧ Metal or plastic arches can be linked together to make elegant pergolas that are very suitable for small gardens.

❧ If the supporting pillars seem too light, they can be made to look more substantial by planting evergreen shrubs at the base.

❧ In many gardens a central pergola running right through the garden may be too dominant. It is better to run it along one side, near the wall or fence.

❧ When it is used as a long shady walk, you can place a few seats underneath for people to sit and enjoy the planting. However, it is not necessary for a pergola to be this long; it can also be quite a short structure, simply covering a seat or arbour or the place where paths intersect.

Arbours

❧ An arbour is an open structure, strong enough to support climbing plants.

❧ Traditionally old-fashioned plants such as climbing scented roses and honeysuckle are used in arbours, although there is no need to berestricted by these and there are many other attractive climbing plants that will work just as well.

❧ The arbour usually encloses a seat. Once again, this may be made of wood or metal, or you can be even more creative and make the seat by simply by clipping a niche in an evergreen hedge such as yew.

✿ Arbours make romantic focal points and they, too, mark transitional areas where one part of the garden ends and another begins, or the meeting point of two paths.

✿ An arbour can be a large pergola-like construction, perhaps taking the place of a summer house, or it may be quite small. However, as with other small structures, it is important to ensure the arbour is in scale with the garden and does not take up too much space or detract from the planting.

Bridges

✿ A bridge offers exciting opportunities for design – from a simple timber plank or decking to a hump-backed Chinese or Japanese-style bridge painted a rich red.

✿ Bridges usually look best when seen from a boat on the water or from a path approaching from the side.

✿ As always, the style should match that of the garden. A modest, perhaps rustic style of bridge is best over a small stream; an oriental zigzag bridge constructed from posts and boards makes a suitable walkway over a wildlife pond. If the water is still, the bridge and any planting next to it will be reflected in it with magical effect.

✿ A false bridge next to a small pond can give the impression that the pond is bigger than it looks, perhaps suggesting that it continues beyond the garden.

BELOW: *This simple, but very effective, Japanese-style wooden bridge is complemented by colourful planting and a velvety green lawn.*

USING GARDEN ORNAMENTS

Sculpture, at its simplest, is placed in gardens to
provide pleasing forms or a way of marking and emphasising
spaces and contrasts, as a focal point or surprise, and to give a sense
of movement or stillness. Traditionally, sculpture had a certain
symbolism but, in general, this is not so meaningful today.
Sculptures and other ornamental objects stand in complete contrast
to the forms and colours of plants. Even 'found' sculptures,
such as granite boulders, and 'collected' sculptures of piles of
pebbles can act as a contrast to the flexible and soft forms
of things growing in the garden.

What sculpture?

❀ Many people associate sculpture with traditional
western forms such as large stone or lead figures from
classical literature. These are too large, too grand and
too steeped in the past to look at home in many of
today's small gardens.

❀ However, sculpture incorporates many other objects
that can add interest, focal points, humour or romance
to a garden. During the 20th century sculptors have
explored abstract forms and different ways of depicting
figures, and many of these are eminently suited to the
modern garden.

ABOVE: *Bright ornamental glass balls provide a dash of colour in
a snowy landscape.*

ABOVE: *These eyecatching stone frogs appear to be sheltering underneath a
hanging stone.*

LEFT: *Sculptures do not need to take pride of place. Some are most effective if 'chanced upon', such as this modern head of a young boy peeping out from behind a curtain of ivy.*

❀ A figurative sculpture can look spectacular in an alcove or bower. In general, one piece or a pair should dominate. Too many sculptures will compete with each other for attention and lose their individual impact.

Choosing sculptures

❀ Always use sculptures with discretion. If they are too fussy they will compete with the plants for attention. If they are too big, they will compete with the view. They may be in stark contrast with their surroundings or cunningly hidden among greenery.

❀ Traditional figures of shepherds and shepherdesses, and cherubs and nymphs should be smaller than their classical counterparts for most gardens today. There are many concrete-based copies available, which can look enchanting placed under a tree or hidden in a rose arbour. Modern sculpture is often abstract, lending itself to modern gardens and acting as a marvellous foil to foliage.

Uses of sculpture

❀ A sculpture may be large or small, temporary or permanent, prominent or half-hidden. Whatever its qualities, it should reflect the tastes of its owner and the style and size of the garden. A sculpture can attract attention to the end of an alley or become an integral part of a group of shrubs or trees.

❀ A figure or urn can be used to emphasise a particular aspect of the garden, such as an inviting green path or a pool or enclosed courtyard, or to draw the eye so that visitors are led around the garden to discover what will be around the next corner.

Placing sculptures

❀ Sculptures should be deliberately placed to create an impact. You can commission a piece specially for a particular place in the garden, or choose a piece you like and then find a place for it. You could search for objects such as fishing floats, which look sculptural, and hang them from trees or place them on stones or pedestals.

❀ Sculptures should always be positioned in strategic places – at the end of a vista, grouped in an open grove or balanced by a group of shrubs or other strong planting. A strong piece can be used as a distant eye-catcher to be seen from a rise in the ground. Pairs of urns are effective at the top of steps or as a gateway to a different area of the garden.

ABOVE: *The globe is an appealing shape. This glass globe has the added fascination of water that flows over its surface, altering the flowers seen through it.*

URNS AND VASES

THESE are important as garden ornaments. Like figurative sculpture, a large urn may be used as a focal point at the end of an avenue or vista, or as a terminal feature on a gatepost. Identical urns or vases on pedestals may be used in rows to line a path, with a backdrop of clipped yew to draw attention to their shape. Sometimes they may be planted with some eye-catching plant such as a single palm or a collection of silver and pink bedding plants. Sometimes they look best standing on their own.

❀ Antique urns and vases are very expensive but there are good reproductions in various materials that can give the right impression. Simple terracotta pots are available in many sizes, are comparatively cheap and can look very impressive. Reproduction troughs are also available in cement-based artificial stone and can look imposing on a terrace.

ORNAMENTAL FURNITURE

SEATS and tables take up a fairly large space in the garden. Too often they spoil the effect by being of unsympathetic materials or simply too large for their environment. Putting a group of furniture on a special area of paving helps give it a purposeful look and acts as a framework. Scale is important. It may be a good idea to enclose the area partially so that the furniture's bulk does not intrude visually into the garden.

❀ Plastic furniture, although cheap, lightweight and easy to move about, cannot be said to add aesthetically to a garden. It may be the most convenient sort of furniture to have on a patio, but for permanent seats and benches, which become part of the garden design, there are more sympathetic materials to choose from.

❀ One seat placed in a niche, or angled against a group of shrubs or tall perennials can look very sculptural. Stone seats are undeniably sculptural, although they are best positioned where they will warm up in the sun before you sit on them. Wrought iron can look graceful; treated, painted or stained timber looks particularly good in the context of a country-style garden. A bench can be 'settled' into its place with plants at the sides. This makes furniture look as though it has rooted and gives it a permanent look.

❀ A tree seat can run fully or half-way around a tree, providing a shady place in which to relax and an eye-catching decoration. Cast-iron reproduction Victorian furniture looks particularly good in rather overgrown, informal gardens. Cast-aluminium copies have the advantage of being light, but they lose the detailing of the decoration.

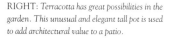

RIGHT: *Terracotta has great possibilities in the garden. This unusual and elegant tall pot is used to add architectural value to a patio.*

BELOW: *A traditional decorated terracotta urn can look good in a formal or informal setting. In a formal setting urns are best used in pairs or rows. Here, the background is somewhat overgrown and informal.*

PLANT CONTAINERS

WELL-grouped plant containers add a touch of luxury to a small courtyard, a porch or front door or the edge of a pool. The plants themselves contribute to the sculptural look so must be chosen carefully to enhance and complement the container. A large container with a short pelargonium poking out of the top will not look sculptural, no matter how colourful the plant.

❀ A timber half-barrel will hold a fairly large shrub and would look good with a standard clipped bay tree, particularly in country settings. A sophisticated alternative is the Versailles tub, which looks splendid planted with a lemon tree. Stone or tufa troughs can be planted with alpines or annuals.

❀ Metal buckets are unusual but attractive containers and look surprisingly good positioned on decking. Tall terracotta 'Ali Baba' urns with narrow necks are graceful and imposing on their own and best left unplanted.

BELOW: *This stone pedestal carries an elaborate container of helichrysum; a little stone pig sits to one side.*

Placing pots

❀ When using pots in groups try to keep similar materials and shapes together, otherwise there will be a lack of unity and the group will look fussy. Unglazed terracotta pots look good with each other but not so good with colour-glazed pots from China, for example. Stone pots look best sitting on stone paving and terracotta is best on brick, while stainless steel or galvanised metal buckets are popular for modern gardens and give a bright, fresh look to roof-gardens. A pair of pots placed on either side of a front door may be planted with well-cared for topiary yew, bay or box and will imply a welcome to visitors. Square pots are a good choice for the entrance to a rectangular area of garden, confirming its shape.

BELOW: *A tall, elegant, squared pot in the brightest indigo makes a striking focal point and co-ordinates with the rather paler grey-blue trellis behind it.*

GARDEN STYLE

There are two ways of approaching the design of a garden – the planned and the informal. Most garden styles fit into one of these.

Planned gardens are based on a central axis with cross-axes running at right angles dividing the garden into compartments. Informal gardens are curvaceous and natural looking.

❁

Within these two styles there are many different possibilities. Romantic, wildlife and exotic gardens tend to be informal, while roof gardens or tiny front gardens lend themselves to careful planning.

❁

Decide which effect you want to achieve before you start work on your garden and remember that it is not usually a good idea to combine planned and informal styles.

INFORMAL GARDENS

Informal gardens are characterised by flowing curves, non-symmetrical arrangements of features and spaces, and plants that are allowed to grow into their natural shapes. Traditionally, gardens have always had their most formal areas near the house, gradually becoming more informal as they get further away. This still makes sense today. Whereas in the formal garden you can see the backbone of the garden as part of the pattern, in informal gardens the underlying framework is almost entirely disguised by planting and the garden should look as though it has grown up naturally. Nevertheless, some structure needs to exist or everything will relapse into uncontrolled wilderness.

PLANNING FOR INFORMALITY

INFORMAL gardens are more difficult to design than formal ones. Since straight lines and symmetry rule the formal garden, balance is inherent. But the informal garden is ruled by irregularity and natural-looking planting, so the designer must create a balance through a mixture of instinct, experiment and experience. This is rather like painting a picture or like thinking of the garden as a sculpture.

❀ If you are trying to create informality in a plain rectangular plot, consider planning your design on the diagonal. A path might run from the right-hand side near the house, past an oval lawn and end up on the left-hand side at the bottom of the garden. On the way, trees and other planting will create informal screens.

ABOVE: *A medley of shrubs, grasses, fuchsias and low perennial plants make a charmingly informal border next to a large lawn.*

❀ On a sloping site you can create winding or zigzag paths and steps down a grassy bank, rather like the 'flowery mead' of medieval times, planted with bulbs in spring and wild flowers in summer. An irregularly shaped site is made for informal garden planning. You can use awkward spaces for creating secret gardens or for more mundane purposes such as hiding a greenhouse or making a play area.

LEFT: *Bright purples and pinks are easily found in the plant world and always combine well together. The gravel path gives form to what otherwise might be a rather straggling bed.*

Informal shapes

❀ An informal garden has carefully planned spaces but conceals its boundaries. You can create boundaries by using native mixed hedging such as hawthorn, holly and briar roses or, in larger gardens, by planting clumps of trees such as birch or rowan.

❀ Irregularity is achieved by organic-looking spaces and winding curves. A grassy lawn may lead circuitously to a wild garden or a rose garden. Make sure the shapes are generous. Paths should wind gently in large curves, not wiggle up the garden in a worm-like way.

❀ One large curve always looks better than two or three meanly angled ones. Informality implies relaxation, so the whole garden should seem relaxed. There should be plenty of space for slow movement around the garden and plenty of places in which to sit.

❀ At each bend a series of tall plants should conceal what is around the corner, so that there is always a new surprise – a flowering cherry tree, a sculpture half-hidden by ivy or a rural arbour – because this should not be a garden with strict patterns, but a garden of random walks and mysteries.

❀ In very narrow plots you can treat the whole garden as a walk, with undulating borders on each side of a gently curving path leading you down to a seat or other eye-catcher at the end. The path can be made of bricks, stone or even grass, although grass is liable to become worn in summer and soggy in winter, making it difficult to work in the garden.

ABOVE: A narrow border has been filled with plants with strap-like leaves at the back and low-growing perennials at the front. The mosaic pot gives the bed a focal point.

❀ At intervals on either side of the path, set back into the planting, you can create seating areas, allowing the visitor to pause and enjoy the plants. The plants themselves should be chosen for their colour and scent and they should have interest most of the year. The occasional small tree or large shrub will provide shade and height.

RIGHT: Even a very small garden can be made to seem larger and be filled with surprises by introducing winding curves, diagonal lines and tall plants to conceal what might be waiting round the corner. Here, a lawn is located fairly near the house and a herb garden at the bottom of the garden; comfortable seats invite the visitor to sit and enjoy the plants.

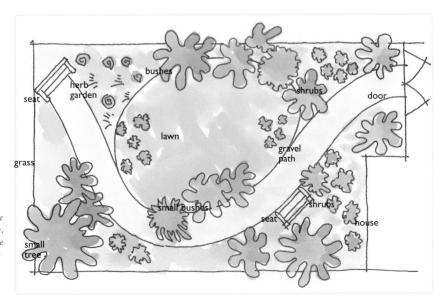

ABOVE: If your garden lacks tall trees or bushes, add something to bring height and interest into it, such as a planted obelisk.

Vertical elements

❀ Vertical elements in the garden create a necessary extra dimension. They provide interest, 'punctuation points', contrast with spreading plants and mark the ends of avenues. Used in pairs they can become frames to a wider view or gateways to other parts of the garden.

❀ In general, planting in informal gardens will include tall shrubs to create compartments and secret walkways. You will also need the input of taller trees to add to the vertical dimension and to provide shade. They will also hide the edges of the plot, and nearby buildings, and help give a secluded country feeling.

❀ Sculptures, obelisks and other ornamental features can all add a vertical element in low planting, either prominently positioned or lurking secretively behind foliage.

RIGHT: Willow supports sit attractively in the flowerbed, whether on their own or with flowers growing up them. Here, one is being used as a support for clematis, and the others allow various plants to bloom at their bases.

Flowers for the informal garden

❀ The informal garden revels in colour. Where the formal garden often looks best restricted to a variety of shades of green or green and white, the informal garden may revel in the riotous reds and pinks of pelargoniums and busy Lizzies (*Impatiens*), in nasturtiums, red salvias and sunflowers.

❀ Alternatively, you may choose silvers, pinks and soft blues. These are all colours that respond so well to a paler sun and a misty atmosphere. An informal rose garden should be filled with old-fashioned roses, sharing the space with complementary plants such as foxgloves, lavender and herbaceous clematis. The important thing is that the garden should have a natural look, as though all the planting had happened of its own accord.

Focal points

❀ Informal gardens do not have the straight walks and avenues that create obvious places for focal points. Their curves and hidden spaces should reveal eye-catching surprises at the last minute. As you round a corner, you should be confronted by something to please, astonish or amuse.

❀ Sculptures should have a sense of movement; this is why animal sculptures often work well. How you place these eye-catchers is all-important because, as they will probably be approached from many different directions, they must look good from all angles. Sculptures will enhance wherever they are situated: they can be hidden behind foliage, hung from the branch of a tree or placed beside a pool or pond.

A feeling of movement

❀ You can control the way people move around your garden by the way you plan the spaces. Long, narrow paths will encourage people to walk fairly quickly. If you want people to linger and look, you must provide wide paths of firm, dry material and seats for them along the way.

❀ A path next to a summer border should be wide enough for two people to linger and admire together, whereas a path going to a compost heap can be narrow and hedged. Paths that are too long, narrow and enclosed will make people feel uncomfortable – the higher the sides, the narrower and longer a path will seem.

A feeling of balance

❀ Balance in the formal garden is provided by symmetry. In an informal garden you have to create your own balance. A large, open space such as a lawn can be balanced by a strong upright tree or sculpture.

❀ A white seat, always a very prominent feature, can be balanced by a dark green background or by setting it in an arbour. A group of trees or shrubs can be balanced by an answering bulk of some kind, such as a table and chairs of a strong defined sculptural shape or a small building.

Water

❀ Natural-looking ponds and pools are ideal water features in informal gardens. You will probably get a better shape by digging the hole and lining it with butyl rather than by buying a preformed liner. Planting should include water plants, as well as marginal and bog plants.

ABOVE: *An intriguing and attractive scheme of mound-shaped flowering plants backed by tall spiky plants and, behind that again, a wall of climbing roses. The colours are predominantly red with shades of yellow, and the neutralising white burns in the middle.*

❀ Other water features could include a small stream or a rocky cascade, which can quite easily be created with a collection of rocks, a small reservoir and a submersible pump. Cobble, millstone and wall fountains can all be useful when you want to provide the sight and sound of water without giving up space to a pond.

ABOVE: *A bright, colourful flowerbed containing – among others – Calendula, Ligularia, lilies, delphiniums and roses.*

MATERIALS

Gravel is a good material for informal gardens. Concrete slabs set in grass or gravel provide a firm basis for wheelchairs or smart shoes. Bark is good for winding through woodland and will provide a soft landing for children if laid thickly under their play equipment.

ROMANTIC GARDENS

❦

The romantic garden is basically a dream – a garden of bowers and gazebos, of scent and pastel colour, where plants grow with soft, arching habits and sweet-smelling flowers that never outgrow their allotted spaces. Birds flit from branch to branch, ferny foliage is reflected in still pools and nearby are the sounds of waterfalls. The sun shines down on flowers of many colours growing in profusion, never clashing, never dominating, and nobody ever seems to do any actual gardening. Pictures of the flowery enclosures of the Middle Ages depict lovers meeting under apple trees and sitting on turf or camomile seats, while gazing tenderly into each other's eyes.

ABOVE: *A bench or other seat tucked into a small corner of the garden, or in a shady arbour surrounded with sweet-scented flowers, will create a perfect romantic hideaway.*

COLOUR AND SCENT

THERE is no reason why we cannot have a romantic garden in a modern setting. The most important things are colour and scent. The colours should be soft and gentle; pale pink, buff and white are romantic colours, and the flowers should be prolific. There are many new and old roses with pretty colours and delightful scents, which will flower for long periods and will not outgrow their spaces.

❦ Gazebos, garden buildings, arbours and seats with rounded arches or Gothic, pointed 'ogee' shapes are all easy to come by. Scented flowers can be grown next to seats and walkways and scented climbers can surround shady arbours.

❦ Shrub roses with good colour and scent include 'Gertrude Jekyll' with rich pink blooms, 'Constance Spry' whose clear pink flowers continue over a long period, 'Buff Beauty' and 'Felicia'. Climbers and ramblers include 'New Dawn', a light satiny pink rose that will grow over a north wall, and 'Albertine', a popular rose with very pretty dark red buds, warm pink flowers and fierce thorns.

THE VICTORIAN
ROMANTIC GARDEN

THE modern idea of a romantic garden follows a Victorian tradition. The Victorians were not only interested in the new plants being imported from all over the world, but they found the idea of the strange countries the plants came from wonderfully romantic, too.

BELOW: *This little garden is full of surprises, including the statuette peeping out underneath the rose-covered pergola.*

❀ The larger Victorian garden might include a garden devoted to roses of all kinds, including old scented roses; there were also rockeries, streams and ferneries. Then there was the so-called 'cottage garden', portrayed in idealised water colours by nineteenth-century artists, showing cheerfully chaotic beds of rampant perennial and annual flowers, growing cheek by jowl in front of thatched cottages.

TODAY'S ROMANTIC GARDEN

MODERN gardeners are highly imaginative and creative when thinking up romantic gardens that can look natural and still be manageable. Traditionally, the orchard is an important part of the idea of a romantic garden, but the idea is symbolic, of course, and there is no need to have rows of fruit trees. One apple tree, two fruit bushes espaliered against a wall or a 'hedge' of cordoned fruit trees will serve the same purpose and be a marvellous addition to your garden.

ABOVE: *Roses are the most exquisite of flowers, whether they are in bud or full bloom. If adequately fed and watered, many will continue to flower until well into autumn or later.*

❀ There are plenty of plants whose common names can give an indication of how romantic a garden was in the old days. Hearts-ease was the name for the purple and yellow viola. Black-eyed Susan, bachelor's button, love-in-a-mist, forget-me-not, sweet Alison, sweet Cicely and blue-eyed Mary are all names used for cottage garden flowers, many of which are still enchanting planted in natural or romantic gardens today.

❀ Today's romantic gardens are liable to be more deliberately designed, with fewer varieties of plants and an easy maintenance bias, but scent and colour, and a sense of timeless-ness are the essence of this style and these things are as attainable today as they ever have been.

LEFT: *The romantic garden is based on curves. Here, a camomile lawn has stepping stones for a path. Its pond is designed to attract wildlife. The pergola is covered with attractive vines, and from the seat you can see the only slightly formal element: a hexagonal summer house as a focal point at the far end.*

small tree

summerhouse

island

pond

camomile lawn

pergola with vine

informal border

paving pathway

seat

door to house

COLOUR IN THE ROMANTIC GARDEN

COLOUR depends so much on where, when and how it is seen. In the romantic garden colour is one of the most important aspects of the planting so choose plants carefully to look their best in a particular part of the garden. Make sure you design the garden not just to be seen from the house, but to be enjoyed as you walk through or sit in a shady bower. Many plants are best seen close up so provide plenty of seating areas and plant for the pleasure of sitting in these spots.

✿ Dark, rich colours such as purples and reds, and especially deep reds, are exciting when viewed close up with the light behind you. These colours, which include deep red roses and the crimsons, scarlets and loud pinks of pelargoniums, are best kept near the house. Pale colours look best from a distance and these

are the ones most suitable to the romantic style of garden. The pale blue clematis such as 'Lasurstern' and 'Perle d'Azur' are the most effective of all clematis colours in the romantic garden. The deep, rich 'Royal Velours', 'Ville de Lyon' and 'Niobe' clematises are best kept near the house, although the smaller-flowered *viticella* types with their pagoda-shaped flowers can be grown among paler-coloured roses in the main garden very effectively.

✿ Note whether the plants are best seen with the light behind you or behind the plants. The yellow forms of privet (*Ligustrum*), *Philadelphus coronarius* 'Aureus' and *Choisya ternata* 'Sundance' all look best against a dark background and against a north-facing wall. The high sunlight coming over on to the foliage will highlight the yellow beautifully against a dark wall or hedge.

TRADITIONAL PLANTS FOR THE ROMANTIC GARDEN

THERE are many plants that can add to the romantic quality of your garden. During the nineteenth century at least two dozen varieties of vines or wall grapes were grown as ornamental as well as productive plants. Walls were thickly covered with roses. Large colourful flowers were popular, such as peonies and oriental poppies. Scented flowers are an absolute essential in a romantic garden today, for example honeysuckles, lilies and old-fashioned pinks like the clove-scented white 'Mrs Sinkins'.

Climbing roses

✿ Repeat-flowering climbers are the most suitable roses for training up garden arches and bowers, whereas the vigorous but once-flowering ramblers may need the more substantial support of pergolas. 'Aloha' is one of the best repeat-flowering climbing roses, which will eventually grow to 3 m (10 ft). It is very healthy with lovely rich pink fragrant flowers and can be grown quite satisfactorily as a shrub. 'Golden Showers' is a good one if you like yellow. It is almost thornless but does not have much scent. 'New Dawn' is a beautiful pearly pink, highly fragrant and flowers almost continuously. 'Madame Alfred Carrière' is another almost thornless rose with white, scented flowers and satisfactory repeat-flowering. It will grow on a north-facing wall.

LEFT: *The top of this informal arch is almost completely hidden, as though it were wearing a bonnet of brightly coloured roses.*

ABOVE: *A hammock slung under a tree, surrounded by a summer border with sweet-smelling flowers such as stock, makes a truly romantic environment.*

❀ Rambler roses have only one flowering period, which begins about midsummer. They are easier to train than climbers and the flowers are smaller. They are very vigorous and may be difficult to accommodate in a small garden but worth a try if you have a pergola or

wall or even an old tree for them to climb. 'Goldfinch' is a strongly scented pale yellow rose, which grows to 3 m (10 ft).

Old roses

❀ Some of the old Bourbon and Portland roses are very desirable and exactly right for the romantic garden, offering billowing masses of soft colour and elegant habits of growth. Most of the old roses are exquisitely scented. 'Mme Isaac Perrière' is a Bourbon with exceedingly fragrant flowers with fully double globular cups and is said to be the most strongly scented of all roses. It can reach 2 m (7 ft) so make sure you allow it plenty of room.

❀ 'Mme Pierre Oger' also has deeply scented globular flowers of pale silvery pink and an arching habit, one of the most beautiful of all roses. 'La Reine Victoria' has a rather lax habit and may need some support. It has beautifully scented globular flowers, which open pale pink and deepen in colour on exposure to light.

LEFT: *With so many different roses to choose from you will be sure to find a variety to suit your garden, whatever the size, aspect or shape. Include roses in your romantic garden to add both colour and scent.*

WILDLIFE GARDENS

As with all gardens, in a wildlife garden you are not attempting to re-create nature itself, but designing a garden in which native species of plants, birds and animals will flourish. A wildlife garden can be used for human enjoyment as well. It can look well designed and modern without losing any of its attraction to small creatures, who mind not whether it looks rural and 'natural' and just want the plants and habitats they can feel at home with. If the soil near the house is filled with builders' rubble, you can cover it with decking. This will be useful as a 'patio' and also for observing the garden from a slight height.

WILDLIFE HABITATS

WILDLIFE can be enticed into the garden by providing a variety of habitats and sources of food. Ideally, the garden should contain a woodland area, a wild flower meadow and a pond, all features that can be adapted to fit into a small garden successfully. Make the most of the conditions that prevail in your garden. For example, a poor soil is ideal for growing a wild flower meadow, while a damp, shady area will suit many woodland plants.

❀ Other good habitats include a pond and a dry stone wall or a pile of logs. You need plants that will supply pollen, nectar, berries and seeds. Wild flowers will also encourage many small creatures. Give structure to the garden with a natural stone path set in grass or a forest bark path winding through a grove of trees. A slightly raised seating area will give a view over the garden. Surround it with a planting of tall shrubs so that it will offer opportunities for watching small creatures as they move around in your garden.

Planting

❀ You can apply the same ground rules for the design of this type of garden as with any other: creating well-proportioned garden spaces, focal points, areas of interest and varied planting.

❀ A sunny flowerbed is the perfect place for growing some of the old cornfield weeds such as corncockle, corn marigold, cornflowers and poppies. A mixture of poppies alone makes a really spectacular sight in summer.

❀ If you have a fairly large garden, you might like a central meadow with wild flowers and grass seed appropriate to

ABOVE: *A wild meadow in England with yellow daisies, cornflowers, oregano and many different grasses.*

BELOW: *The spectacular sight of a meadow planted with wild flowers in France. Seen here are cornflowers, poppies and daisies, making an astonishing splash of colour.*

the soil type. Choose a part of the garden that has rather poor soil if possible. Unlike most garden plants, wild flowers need soil with low fertility. This will help to restrict the more vigorous grasses so that the wild flowers have a chance to compete. Remove any turf and topsoil and replace it with subsoil.

❀ Buy an inexpensive kit for testing the soil so that you know its pH, and buy a mixture of seeds that will grow well on that. There are several seed companies selling appropriate mixtures. The plants should come into flower at roughly the same time, either all in spring or all in summer, so that you can cut the grass when appropriate. A spring-flowering meadow should be cut in midsummer and then mowed as usual until autumn or cut once again in late autumn. A summer-flowering meadow should be cut in late spring and again in late autumn.

❀ A true lawn will have its own wildlife community, too. Do not allow dandelions and plantain in, but you can add seed of white clover to the lawn seed or scatter it on to an existing lawn. You can mow a path through this meadow and around its edges so it is easy to walk round and admire the flowers.

BELOW: Treating the garden as a wildlife sanctuary means allowing flowers to retain their seed heads. Here, Agapanthus seed heads create interesting structural shapes.

ABOVE: *The cheerful little marigold* Calendula officinalis *will fill gaps in the summer garden and associates well with many different flowers.*

BELOW: *A wildlife garden implies a certain amount of laissez-faire. Do not try to keep it too neat. A small heap of sticks and prunings may encourage hedgehogs, for example. A pond with overgrown edges will encourage other small creatures to run back and forth. A woodland section will attract squirrels and birds and if you have a boggy area, you can grow a wider variety of plants.*

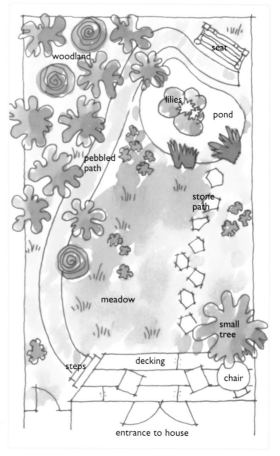

Woodland

❀ A woodland edge provides a rich natural habitat for
wildlife and may attract hedgehogs, bats and a range
of other creatures. You can re-create this sort of
environment even on a small scale to bring a great
diversity of creatures into the garden. A woodland area
should consist of several layers of vegetation, including
tall trees, smaller trees and a lower tier of shrubs.
Under these can be planted ground cover plants and
early bulbs.

❀ In a small garden, where large trees such as English oak
(*Quercus ruber*) and beech (*Fagus sylvatica*) would not
be appropriate, plant hazel (*Corylus avellana*), hawthorn
(*Crataegus*) or bird cherry (*Prunus padus*), all of which
will support wildlife. In a small town garden, use a
mixed hedge as the top layer or substitute climbing
plants including woodbine (*Lonicera periclymenum*)
grown up a trellis. Small shrubs for the intermediate
layer could include *berberis* and cotoneaster. Plants
such as wood spurge (*Euphorbia amygdaloides*) and wood
sorrel (*Oxalis acetosella*), which enjoy damp, shady
situations, are good plants to grow in woodland.

❀ Every wildlife garden needs a pond as a home for all
sorts of animal, bird and insect life and this should be
in the most open area of the garden. It will make an

ABOVE: *A variety of trees and dense ground cover using ivies, hostas and ferns make this a most attractive woodland walk.*

excellent focal point. Boggy and marginal plants will
make a natural-looking surround and offer cover for
little creatures.

Windbreaks

❀ Fences provide inexpensive instant windbreaks. They
can be of woven willow or hazel, or wattle in medieval
style. They are all good at gently filtering the wind.
Since this is an organic garden you will want to dedicate
an area to composting, hidden by shrubs or a hedge or
fencing to match that used in the rest of the garden.

❀ Hedges provide food, shelter, nesting sites and a safe,
sheltered corridor for travelling creatures. Choose a
flowering hedge such as *Rosa rugosa* 'Frau Dagmar
Hastrup', which is a pretty pale pink, or the pure
white 'Blanche Double de Coubert'. Alternatively,
plump for clipped holly or a mixed hedge. Conifers do
not mix well with other evergreen shrubs and do not
make the best wildlife hedges on their own.

LEFT: *A woodland area can be one of the most attractive parts of a garden, as shown here by the graceful shape and autumn colour of this small* Acer japonicum.

Shrubs for a mixed hedge

❀ Choose one species as the mainstay of the hedge. The common hawthorn (*Crataegus monogyna*) is an attractive choice, with its sprays of fragrant white flowers in spring, red leaves and purple haws in autumn. The blackthorn (*Prunus spinosa*) is another good mainstay hedging plant, with its white flowers in spring and blue-black sloes in autumn.

❀ Choose from the following to interplant with your main choice: buckthorn (*Rhamnus catharticus*), which provides food for the caterpillar of the brimstone butterfly; holly (*Ilex aquifolium*); dogwood (*Cornus sanguinea*); wild privet (*Ligustrum vulgare*), which has strongly scented white flowers in summer; hazel (*Corylus avellana*), with pretty dangling catkins; and spindle (*Euonymus europaeus*) which has extraordinary puce and orange berries, beloved by birds.

Variety is the spice of wildlife

❀ The best garden for wildlife is one with the most variety of plants. A bit of grass, some herbaceous plants, some roses, some vegetables, a tree or two, even a few weeds such as nettles and a privet that some caterpillars need to feed on, will make a good start. The garden borders should be wide enough to take several layers of vegetation.

ABOVE: *These cherry trees allow useful ground cover plants such as honesty and periwinkle to carpet the ground beneath them.*

ABOVE: *If you provide the right woodland conditions you may get hedgehogs visiting your garden. They should be welcomed, since they eat slugs and snails.*

❀ Make sure there are some evergreen shrubs for winter cover as well as winter interest, and some deciduous trees and shrubs to let some light through in the spring. Each layer of vegetation provides a habitat for different creatures. Thrushes are at home in the treetops, sparrows and tits congregate slightly lower down and blackbirds like to peck around and listen for worms on the ground. Spiders, beetles and mice will all make their homes in a pile of stones in a secluded corner.

Birdlife

❀ Birds can be encouraged to nest in the garden if you fix nesting boxes to the trees. Put these up in autumn or midwinter so the birds have time to go house hunting and explore them thoroughly before the next nest-building season begins.

❀ Nesting boxes with small holes (about 3 cm or $1^1/_4$ in) will allow smaller birds such as nuthatches and tits to use them. Larger entrance holes will attract a wider range of birds. A box should be fixed high enough so

ABOVE: *A thoughtful gardener has created a colourful spring-flowering garden at the edge of a wood where it meets the road.*

BELOW: *Soft greens and the palest of yellows provide colour and texture in a border between a meadow lawn and a hedge.*

that cats and squirrels cannot reach it. The positioning is crucial. It should be sheltered from wind, rain and strong sunlight and away from bird tables.

❀ Birds are attracted by such plants as asters, golden rod, cornflowers, teazel, cotoneasters, violas, fennel, lavender, forget-me-nots, scabious, sorbus, honeysuckle and pyracantha. Insects enjoy *Phacelia tanacetifolia*, a hardy annual with bell-shaped blue flowers with prominent stamens, which seeds itself around the garden even in poor soils. Insects also like thyme, mint, oregano, crocuses and ivy.

Butterfly borders

❀ Butterflies like to sunbathe in sunny, sheltered spots that are protected from the wind. In a perennial border grow *Aubrieta* to attract painted ladies, red admirals, brimstones and small tortoiseshell butterflies. The same butterflies use lavender as a nectar source, as do the small copper, common blue, meadow brown and small skipper. Later in the year they will be attracted by Michaelmas daisies (Aster), valerian (*Centranthus*), phlox and *Sedum spectabile*, which has fleshy green leaves and flattish heads of tiny pink flowers in late summer and autumn. It has thin narrow florets, into which the butterflies can reach for nectar with their long tongues.

❀ Honesty has heads of small purple flowers and is a good source of food for caterpillars of the orange-tip butterfly, and the lilac- or white-flowered buddlejas are well known for attracting peacock and tortoiseshell butterflies, which can absolutely cover the flowers on a sunny day.

Other insects

❀ Flowers are attractive to bees for both their nectar and pollen and they are also important as a continuous food larder from early spring to late autumn. Particular favourites are herbs such as thyme, marjoram, mint, lavender and lemon balm.

❀ Beneficial insects in the garden pollinate fruit and vegetables and prey on common garden pests. Between them, anthocorid bugs, ladybirds, hoverflies, lacewings, ground beetles and centipedes will eat caterpillars, midges, weevils, scale insects and red spider mites, slugs, snails, mealy bugs, thrips, scale insects, leafhoppers, aphids and cabbage fly and carrot root fly eggs and larvae. So choosing plants that will attract the beneficial insects is obviously sensible. Fennel (*Foeniculum vulgare*), with its flat heads of yellow flowers above feathery leaves, is a favourite plant of hoverflies. Pollen and nectar-feeding insects also love sunflowers (*Helianthus annuus*).

ABOVE: Gleditsia *trees and* Linaria *provide contrasting colours on the edge of a wooded area.*

❀ Other useful flowers are the annual pot marigolds (*Calendula officinalis*), the poached egg flower (*Limnanthes douglasii*), Californian poppy (*Eschscholtzia californica*), baby blue eyes (*Nemophila*), yarrow (*Achillea*), anaphalis, Shasta daisy (*Chrysanthemum maximum*), sea holly (*Eryngium*), wild strawberry (*Fragaria vesca*) and candytuft (*Iberis*).

Preference for species plants

❀ When choosing flowers remember that single flowers are best for wildlife. The extra petals in double forms are often formed at the expense of nectaries and anthers, which means they provide less food for insects. For example, the common bird's foot trefoil has a yellow pea flower, which produces plenty of nectar, but the double variety has none at all.

❀ In other plants, the extra petals on double flowers often make an insurmountable barrier for insects. This means that often they cannot get in to the flower to find the food at all.

❀ You need to check that nasturtium and columbine flowers have pointed sacs (or spurs) behind the flowers. These are reservoirs for nectar and are important for species like long-tongued bumble bees, an increasingly threatened form of wildlife.

❀ Delphiniums and larkspurs should also have spurs. When in doubt, choose old-fashioned varieties of plant and the nearest to the wild flower or species as possible. They are often more graceful and elegant in any case.

❀ Night-flowering nectar plants include flowering tobacco (*Nicotiana alata*) and night-scented stock (*Matthiola longipetala*). These will attract night-flying insects, which in turn may attract bats.

ABOVE: *A decorative* Rodgersia *stands out against a background of ferns in woodland.*

CONTAINER GARDENS

Pots and containers can be used to provide visual interest throughout the year; the most sculptural ones need have nothing planted in them at all. They can be moved around to fill gaps, rearrange the balance of some aspect of the garden, or add a particular colour. Used for tender plants, they can stand outside in summer and be brought inside during cold weather. Pots can also be used to hold climbers to enhance patios, terraces, balconies, courtyards and windowsills. They can be used to revitalise dull areas and introduce interest to the bleakest of tiny alleyways or basement areas.

CHOOSING CONTAINERS

THE range of possible containers is enormous. Almost anything can be used as a container, provided it has drainage holes and will hold enough compost to support the plant. Many are purpose made but there is plenty of scope for using containers not originally intended for plants, and these may be equally effective and cheaper. In Greece, for example, brightly painted old paint cans filled with red pelargoniums are often ranged along the street wall of whitewashed cottages.

❀ Old chimney pots can be simple in shape or very decorative and will add height where it may be needed.
❀ Wheelbarrows have become popular as containers, although definitely not for formal gardens, and old watering cans, buckets and pails, ceramic sinks and ancient water tanks are all possibilities.

ABOVE: *Chimney pots make interesting containers and you can experiment with plants to see which suit the style of pot best. Here, a fuchsia seems to be enjoying the shaft of sunlight coming in through the door.*

❀ Sinks are very heavy; once positioned you will not want to move one again. Shallow sinks are good for rock garden plants, miniature bulbs and dwarf conifers. White, glazed fire clay sinks can be covered in a substance known as 'tufa' to look just like stone. Alternatively, you can bury a sink in the ground, having first blocked up the plughole, and use it as a miniature bog garden for moisture-loving plants such as primulas.

LEFT: *A brightly painted container garden on different levels provides a colourful entrance to a seaside house.*

LEFT: *Wheelbarrows are often used to display an interesting selection of annual plants. Probably the most attractive barrows are those that have already done their stint in the garden, like this one, whose attractive grey-green paint is showing signs of wear.*

Other choices

❀ Cement-based artificial stone or plain cement planters can look handsome. Large concrete and timber planting cases and barrels can hold enough compost to support a small tree. In the eighteenth century, square or circular wooden tubs planted with orange and lemon trees were placed in rows in formal gardens and taken into an early form of conservatory, or 'orangery', over the winter.

❀ Plastic containers are very much lighter to lift than most other planters, which is a great advantage if you want to move them around. They do not look quite like terracotta but once full of plants and sitting on a patio, the containers themselves will not be very noticeable.

Clay pots

❀ Clay pots and containers come in a great variety of sizes and designs. Small and medium-sized pots are best grouped together because just one can look a little pathetic on its own in an open space. Very large, shapely ones can be used as ornaments in their own right at the end of an axis or some other prominent place.

❀ Clay pots can vary in colour from cream and pale pink to deep red and a rather brash orange. The colour will weather in time. Choose a relatively simple design so as not to distract attention away from the plants.

❀ Elaborate pots are really suitable only for special situations. Chinese-style pots with coloured glazes are available in useful, sturdy shapes. It is best to choose the same type and colour for pots that are going to be placed in the same area. Check that the pots you buy are frostproof.

BELOW: *This small courtyard garden has been laid with crazy paving and planted with large and small pots of plants to provide interest all year round. There are clipped evergreens for winter interest, pots of geraniums and busy Lizzies that will need to be taken in during the winter, and one or two tall shrubs to soften the edges.*

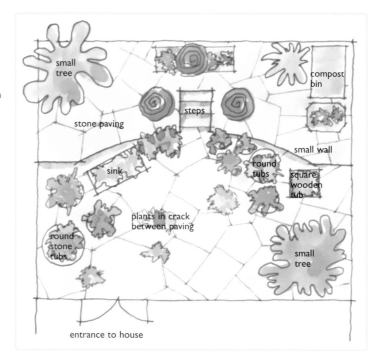

small tree

compost bin

stone paving

steps

small wall

round tubs

square wooden tub

sink

round stone tubs

plants in crack between paving

small tree

entrance to house

PLANTS FOR CONTAINERS

A S WITH all design, keep your planting schemes simple. Do not try to mix too many different varieties. Opt for just two or three that will bloom in succession to give a long season of colour. One variety to a pot often looks best of all. You can juxtapose the containers for their colour combinations after planting.

Planting for spring

❀ Fairly shallow containers with wide tops look great with low-growing spring bulbs such as crocuses and scillas. Taller containers can take taller stemmed plants such as daffodils and tulips. A long-lasting and attractive display can be made with crocuses and iris together with later-flowering tulips and daffodils in a container deep enough to take two levels of bulbs.

❀ Plant the tulips and daffodils at the lowest level. The satiny, almost black tulip, 'Queen of the Night', or a group of elegant lily-flowered tulips such as the snowy 'White Triumphator' are good container bulbs. For daffodils you could try 'Minnow', which has delicate creamy yellow flowers, two to four on a stem. 'Hawera', with pretty yellow heads, is one of the latest-flowering daffodils.

❀ Plant *Iris reticulata* and early crocuses higher up in the compost – when these die down, their leaves will not be noticed because the interest will have moved to the daffodils and tulips. These tiny irises have an upright habit and long slender leaves and look very good grown on their own in pots, although their season is not very long.

❀ Wallflowers (*Cheiranthus cheiri*) have the most wonderful scent in the late spring garden. Grow them with tulips and daffodils for a rich tapestry of colours. Tulips also look good underplanted with forget-me-nots (*Myosotis*), scillas and grape hyacinths.

❀ Polyanthus are excellent contenders for pots, too. Plant them with pansies or small trumpet daffodils and grape hyacinths. Their colours are wonderful. You can grow the whole palette of colours together, or try the blues and whites as a combination, or blues and pinks and so on. Double daisies (*Bellis perennis*) make good perimeter plants and associate well with forget-me-nots, wallflowers and pansies.

Planting for summer

❀ There are many interesting and colourful plants for summer containers. Variegated or silvery trailing plants such as small ivies, *Helichrysum petiolare* and *Senecio maritima* 'Silver Dust' can enhance any mixed planting. Useful summer bedding plants include busy Lizzies (for shady places), petunias, verbenas, *Felicia amelloides* and lobelias.

LEFT: A hot climate is just right for a cactus garden like this one. The garden walls have been painted white and accentuate the shadows of the pots. Even the dog seems to enjoy the sun.

Acid-loving plants

❀ Containers can be particularly useful for growing plants for which the soil in your garden is not suitable. Acid-loving plants such as dwarf rhododendrons, azaleas, camellias and heathers can be planted in ericaceous compost. Most of these are woodland plants and prefer not to be in full sun. All have shallow rooting systems, which makes them particularly suitable for container planting.

❀ Pots and pelargoniums might have been made for each other. Use them in window boxes and any other container on their own. Unlike busy Lizzies (*Impatiens*), pelargoniums like strong light. Their foliage has an amazing range of scents, from lemon and peppermint to apple, pine and rose so you can place pots where the aromatic foliage will send out its scent as soon as someone brushes against it.

BELOW: *The succulent plants in these terracotta pots introduce a variety of shapes that are set off against the sun's shadow on the painted fencing behind them.*

Planting for autumn and winter

❀ All clipped evergreen shrubs look good in winter, providing pattern and structure when everything else is over. The common snowdrop (*Galanthus nivalis*) is a hardy bulb not often grown in containers, but it will make a brave show of white and green from late winter to early spring. Flowering shrubs can provide interest, too, especially near the house, since during winter the garden will mostly be seen only from inside.

❀ The small deciduous shrub *Ceratostigma willmottianum* can be planted on its own in a medium-sized pot. It has bright blue flowers all through summer and well into autumn, when its leaves turn red. *Daphne odora* is an evergreen shrub with glossy dark green leaves and clusters of fragrant purplish-pink and white flowers from midwinter to spring. The heather families (*Calluna*, *Daboecia* and *Erica*) contain species and cultivars that will flower all year. Good winter ones include *Erica* x *darleyensis* 'White Perfection', *E.* x *veitchii* 'Pink Joy' and *E. carnea* 'Vivellii' (bright pink).

ROOF GARDENS

❦

A roof garden can be one of the biggest luxuries of city life. It is a true extension of the indoor living space, offering spectacular views over rooftops with a feeling of light and space that you cannot normally get in the urban environment.

HISTORY

THE roof garden has a long history. The Hanging Gardens of Babylon were really roof gardens, built over an arcaded palace in ascending terraces. On top of the arches, bundles of reeds and asphalt were laid and covered with brick tiles and thick sheets of lead to provide waterproofing for the decorated state rooms below. Water was raised up by pump. The whole thing was planted with flowering shrubs and trees such as larch, birch, cypress, cedar, acacia and mimosa.

❀ When Derry and Tom's department store was built in London in the 1930s, permission for a further storey was refused because the firemen's ladders were too short to reach it, so a roof garden was built instead. This was made up of a series of traditional gardens including a Hispano-Moorish garden, a Tudor garden and a woodland area complete with a small stream filled with fish and ducks. There was even a cascade and grotto. The garden is still open to the public, and although the introduction of flamingos has led to damage of some vegetation and loss of fish, it is still a magical place to visit and hard to imagine you are among the rooftops.

ABOVE: *This tiny roof space is a haven among the chimney pots in central London. The permanent planting is evergreen, while annuals are grown in tubs for summer interest.*

Practical difficulties

❀ Recent developments in waterproofing technology and materials and increased roof insulation have made the roof garden a possibility for anyone with a flat roof, and the luxury of extra living space in a small city flat cannot be overemphasised.

❀ Before you begin stocking your lofty garden with plants, there are a number of practical difficulties you should be aware of. Most roofs have a limited load-bearing capacity

LEFT: *This little London roof garden is not only attractive to sit in, but also pretty when seen from the street and the houses opposite. The planting is mostly shrubby and provides interest all year round.*

ABOVE: *On this extremely stylish roof garden, trellis has been used to form an outdoor 'room', creating a space with a Japanese flavour – open to the sky but concealed from the world.*

there may be regulations limiting or prohibiting screens or plants being visible from street level, so check with the local authority.

Room-like spaces

❀ High up spaces, open to the sky, can seem threatening, so the best idea is to try and create a room-like space with some sort of enclosure. If there is no low parapet or wall, you will certainly need to put something up anyway, simply from the point of view of safety. The other thing you will find on a roof garden is that the wind is much stronger than at street level and has a dehydrating effect, so plants will need more watering.

❀ You can surround the garden with trellis to act as a psychological barrier and also to help filter the wind to a certain extent. You can plant this quite lightly with ivy or clematis for privacy and leave parts of it unplanted so as not to block the wider view. Choose the most robust trellis you can find and fix it firmly to supports, otherwise the wind will blow it over in a very short time.

and may not be able to support the extra weight of surfacing materials, soil, containers and so on. You may have to have the structure strengthened or you may have to keep pots and plants around the perimeter, close to the structural walls, where the roof is supported.

❀ You must make sure the roof's waterproofing is sound and will not be interfered with. So before you begin, get a structural engineer to check the site for you. In historic or conservation areas,

RIGHT: *The first priority for a roof garden is to establish that the roof is strong enough and waterproof and has planning permission for use as a garden. Paving should be as lightweight as possible – thin tiles or decking are probably the best materials. Any pergola should be sturdily fixed to prevent it rocking in the wind and pots should be ranged around the edges of the roof where it is supported.*

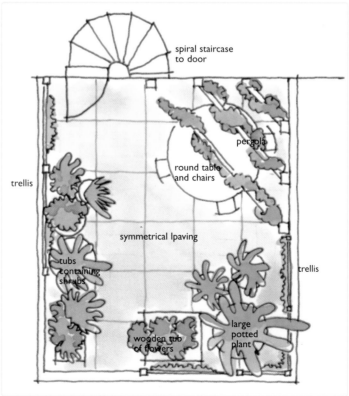

spiral staircase to door

pergola

round table and chairs

trellis

symmetrical lpaving

tubs containing shrubs

trellis

large potted plant

wooden tub of flowers

Adding a pergola to a roof

❀ You can add to the enclosed feeling by introducing a
small pergola for shade and to support climbers. This
will also reduce the effect of the possibly rather
oppressive area of sky and provide privacy from nearby
roof gardens. It should be attached to walls and sturdily
fixed seats and planters to ensure stability.

BELOW: *This attractive, sunny little roof garden is protected from the
elements and neighbours by ivy and a small bay tree. Evergreen herbs
such as rosemary are brightened up with the reds of geraniums and pinks
of sweet peas.*

ABOVE: *The plants in this small roof garden are mostly low growing so as
not to suffer from the wind. They include a Mexican orange blossom
(Choisya ternata 'Sundance'), some low bamboos, variegated hostas,
broom, ceratostigma, lavender and, for climbers, solanum and clematis.*

Flooring materials

❀ Lightweight gravel is a good foil to small containers.
Decking is comparatively lightweight and therefore
suitable for a flat roof. Timber tiles are available, which
are easy to lay and convenient to carry upstairs. If you
have enough space, you can add a raised area of
decking to use as a table or for sunbathing.

❀ Roberto Burle Marx, the celebrated Brazilian garden
designer, uses brightly coloured mosaic designs as a
prominent feature on the floors of his roof gardens and,
provided you have a suitable surface, this is an idea
that would look cheerful on small roof terraces, too.

Planters and containers

❀ Most flat roof spaces have some unfortunate built-in features such as a water tank or air-conditioning unit that you cannot get rid of. Portable timber planters of varying heights can be used to hide such eyesores. Fill them with lightweight, moisture retentive compost and plant them up with small trees to make an effective screen. You can paint containers to match any trellis or wall. White is always effective, but there are many excellent colours to choose from and you might prefer a pastel colour or something bolder like a deep blue.

Plants for the roof

❀ If your roof space is open to the sky, it will probably be best to choose a few carefully placed sculptural plants that will thrive in difficult high-rise urban circumstances, or put containers around the perimeter, planted with wind-resistant shrubs and small trees. Cacti and succulents are sun lovers, and require the minimum of watering. If the temperature is too cold for them, use grasses, which do not need much maintenance and will look very attractive blowing in the wind.

❀ If the space is small and partly enclosed, you could create a bower of flowering shrubs and climbers with a few small conifers for height, variety and shade. Plants that tolerate seaside conditions are often good for rooftop gardens; varieties of *Escallonia*, *Berberis* and *Lauristinus* should all be able to cope with high-rise conditions.

Balconies

❀ A balcony can become a useful visual and physical extension to the living area. A very effective way of integrating the two areas is to stand a few pots on the inside as well as the outside to act as links and make the balcony seem larger. Use identical pots and flowers to emphasise the sense of unity. If your scheme involves structural work, get advice from a structural engineer as to the weight capacity of your balcony, as you would for a flat roof.

Window gardens

❀ If window boxes and hanging baskets are the only garden you have, make the most of them. It is wonderful that English pubs have gone so wholeheartedly for

ABOVE: *This large, sunny roof garden has been treated rather formally, with rows of white-flowered geraniums in black pots along the bottom of the window and purple violas climbing up the steps.*

highly coloured hanging baskets and window boxes. Many are truly splendid in their rich and varied plantings, but all the best ones have very deliberate colour schemes. They are not simply a chaos of any old colours planted together.

❀ If you like these cheerful displays, note down what plants have been used to create them and do the same at home. However, not every window box gardener wants to be quite so flamboyant. There are plenty of other ways of making the most of window boxes. The mixed colours of red and white pelargoniums with some trailing ivy will look bright and cheerful all summer.

❀ Herb window boxes can be both charming and useful. Choose herbs that all like the same conditions and that will grow to much the same sort of height or the display won't work or will look unbalanced. Sage, golden marjoram, a dwarf lavender and chives could make an interesting and tasty display.

❀ If the window is on the shady side of the house, you can plant miniature bamboos in window boxes, which will provide a sort of lacy curtain of green. Choose containers that suit the style of the house and make sure the boxes are firmly secured.

PLANNED GARDENS

❧

Planned gardens are precise and often arranged symmetrically around a central axis, which divides the garden down the middle. The central path may have paths crossing it at right angles, dividing the garden into rectangles or squares. A very small and square garden might not have a straight path, just a central feature with paving around it. The positive symmetrical shapes of the garden must be kept very defined and clear. Paths should be carefully detailed, hedges precise and evergreen shrubs clipped into disciplined shapes. Several features have been associated with the great formal gardens of early times. Many can be introduced into small gardens with great success. The style is particularly suitable for square or rectangular level sites where the symmetry fits well into the basic shape of the plot.

Hedges

❀ Because a symmetrical pattern is the important thing, hedges are often used to mark out the pattern like piping on a cushion. Many of these are low so that they emphasise the basic geometry and do not hide one part from another. Box is one of the most popular shrubs for low hedges, as it grows slowly and is easy to clip.

❀ Tall, clipped hedges of yew, privet, hornbeam or beech can create divisions between different areas or mark out the perimeter. Straight avenues can be lined on either side by pleached hornbeam or lime. Pleaching means planting the trees equal distances apart, cutting off the lower branches and intertwining or grafting the side branches to meet at about eye level, making a

ABOVE: *A vegetable garden laid out in a carefully planned manner with contrasting stone steps and paths and clipped bushes introducing symmetry.*

clipped hedge on tall 'stalks'. In larger gardens two rows can be planted to create a dense double hedge with a tunnel in the middle.

Knots and parterres

❀ Knot gardens were popular in Tudor times and were based on ancient mazes. These developed into small, rectangular, intricate geometrical patterns planted in a continuous, unbroken line. A knot garden may be complete in itself or filled with colours to accentuate

LEFT: *Simple geometrical patterns in knots or parterres can enhance any garden – no matter how small.*

triangles, hexagons and octagons. This need not necessarily mean straight lines. An oval shape can be very satisfactory in a rectangular plot and circular shapes have often been used very successfully inside square plots.

❀ Adjacent shapes can touch, overlap or be separated by a gap. It is usually best to choose one shape, such as a square, and then arrange squares of different size in a formal pattern.

Axis paths

❀ When making your axis lines, you can reinforce them by planting clipped hedges along each side. Box is the most popular for this but lavender or rosemary will also make attractive low hedges. If you want something taller, plant standard roses on supports.

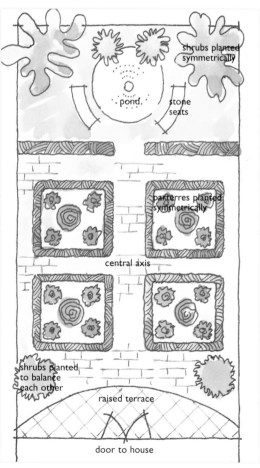

the shapes. Traditionally, different coloured gravels and coal or perhaps low-growing herbs such as thyme and lavender were used. Today recycled glass chippings and coloured glass pebbles have added to the possibilities.

❀ A parterre is simpler than a knot – often planted in individual squares, not joined up together. Parterres were developed from knots in 17th-century France where they were designed to be viewed from first-floor windows. They are usually larger and more open and the plants grown inside them can be taller, for example shrub roses such as 'Felicia', 'Ballerina' and 'Iceberg'. Parterres can also be used for growing vegetables.

Symmetrical shapes

❀ Symmetrical shapes are those that are regular in outline. Although squares, rectangles and circles are the most common shapes, it is also possible to use

RIGHT: *This garden leads, via two steps, from a curved patio of square slabs to four squares of clipped yew set in brick paving. Each square has a standard small rose or bay tree in the centre. A clipped hedge divides this area from a circular pond with seats for peaceful contemplation.*

ABOVE: *The wooden garden chair provides a focal point here, with the eye being drawn from the herring-bone patterned paving by the symmetry of the carefully clipped bushes on either side of the seat.*

BELOW: *Geometrically shaped beds of box make up this parterre. They are divided by narrow brick paths and filled with a variety of white flowers, mainly with silver leaves.*

Vertical elements

❀ Because so much of the pattern in planned gardens is derived from paths and low hedges, it is necessary to bring in some vertical elements to provide height and interest. These can be introduced in various ways. A sundial or bird-bath on a pedestal or a stone fountain can make a good central feature. Yew or box clipped into tall shapes or mop-headed box or bay trees in tubs can be positioned in rows on either side of a path.

Focal points

❀ A focal point is something that attracts attention. It might be a small building or tree on the horizon or a sculpture or urn. A focal point should be deliberate. You do not want the eye attracted towards a washing line or tool shed. The eye likes to go to a focal point in a straight line, so formal gardens are asking for focal points to be positioned at the ends of straight paths and avenues.

❀ A focal point may be a specimen tree, a well-designed bench in an arbour, a small summer house or a white painted seat (white is an instant focal point).

❀ A view could also be a focal point. To do this you will need to frame it with planting or create a 'window' in a clipped hedge through which to see it.

Materials

❀ Formal style is highly disciplined. Paving materials need to be very carefully chosen so that they are in sympathy with any nearby buildings. Even mixing different kinds and colours of bricks can produce a disruptive effect.

❀ All materials should be well defined. It is best to use as few materials as possible so that the overall effect gives a sense of unity. If using paving stones, they should be placed in a geometric manner, not as crazy paving, which is seldom suited to a formal plan.

❀ When laying bricks you will find that a herring-bone pattern has a softer effect than when the bricks are laid in straight lines. Paths can be edged with small cobbles to give them an 'outline' to reinforce the pattern. Both brick and stone make a warm, static ground cover that marries well with brick walls to give a unified design.

❀ Gravel is not usually a good choice for the symmetrical garden. It is too easily kicked around and does not provide a clear enough outline for the geometric garden. One exception is a very small garden that is more for viewing than for walking around, where gravel can make an effective background for a central clipped shrub or stone sculpture.

Water

❀ Water is very much part of the traditional formal garden. It harks back to the desert gardens of old with their irrigation channels and refreshing central pools.

❀ A central pool of circular or geometric shape, perhaps with a fountain in the centre, or indeed any central water feature with a symmetrical shape will look in place.

❀ Narrow channels can run alongside paths and long, rectangular ponds with matching seats on either side will enable visitors to sit and enjoy water lilies and the reflections of the sky. A long, narrow rectangular pond can have a fountain at each end to add interest.

❀ If water is the central element in the garden, it creates an atmosphere of great tranquillity. The reflecting quality of the water in a large pool, plus pale-coloured paving, will give the centre of the garden a very light, optimistic feeling.

RIGHT: Graded heights make these yew topiary shapes very intriguing. Combined with the red standard roses and the white shrub rose, they make an impressive sight.

❀ The pool should of course be symmetrical and balanced. In an enclosed area, more water can be added via wall fountains. Even water plants can be placed symmetrically.

❀ A wide paved path allows the visitor to get near the water, and steps can lead right down to the water's edge. A symmetrical row of small trees or a clipped hedge will act as a framework to the pool, giving a general feeling of privacy and accentuating the formality.

CHILDREN IN THE PLANNED GARDEN

THERE is no reason why young children should not be able to play in a formal garden. Clipped hedges are usually pretty sturdy, particularly in tubs, and the very fact of having paved paths and straight lines means that running and cycling, roller-skating and skate-boarding are made possible. Remember that paths should be wide enough to make all these activities easy and it is a good idea to provide turning circles at each end.

SMALL GARDENS

The key to the formal garden is repetition, unity and geometrical patterns and spaces. Small square or rectangular gardens belonging to urban houses are well suited to formality. The symmetrical shape is good for the geometric division of spaces and for straight lines of plants. Remember that although clipped hedges are a highly finished kind of formality, the mere lining out of identical plants in rows is in itself a formal arrangement. There are several ancient and traditional models of formal garden on which to base a design.

A Persian garden

❀ The first pleasure gardens in Egypt and Persia were based on water and their long narrow canals ran in grid patterns, stemming from the idea of the four-square paradise garden. Where these channels met, there would be a large central pond or tank with fish and water lilies. The royal paradise garden was large, with raised pavilions to catch the slightest breeze. Here you could sit under the shade of trees and enjoy the sound of running water and the scents and colours of flowers.

❀ Although in temperate areas water does not have quite the same significance as it does in desert areas, we still find water soothing and relaxing. Most gardens, large or small, are more interesting if they include a pool, fountain or stream. In city gardens an enclosed garden designed along Persian lines can keep ugly neighbouring buildings out of sight. Even in tiny gardens a narrow channel of water can be created, either running alongside a path or taking up the centre of the plot.

❀ Narrow flowerbeds can run around the perimeter with seats or spaces for sitting under shady trees. In a small garden you can use paths rather than water as your grid with some formal planting on either side of standard rose bushes and clipped shapes in box or yew. Fastigiate (having erect branches) and mop-headed trees will provide shade without taking up too much light.

A Moorish garden

❀ There are many similarities between Persian and Moorish gardens, for example the shady trees, scented flowers and the idea of water channels. But whereas Persian gardens were enclosed to keep out the desert, in Moorish gardens the rigid and confined lines were opened up to give views of orchards, olive groves and distant hills.

❀ Patios, porticos and arcades made an almost seamless transition between the house and the garden. Similarly, the wall or hedge of your four-square garden could open out to reveal a tree or an interesting piece of

LEFT: *A very small space can be given interest by the pots used. Here, a pair of chimney pots has been planted with clipped box, giving a striking and unusual appearance. The box leaves serve to echo the green of the door.*

Box-edged borders

❀ An elaborate parterre may be too large for the smaller garden but simpler box-edged borders are very suitable. Although the plants may take some time to get going, they will eventually form a solid block of foliage that is a good foil to other plants. The variegated varieties, although pretty, do not create such a good background and are best grown as features on their own.

LEFT: *Simple borders – such as this carefully laid out lavender border, with its attractive cloche at the centre – are often best for a small garden.*

BELOW: *Formality can be achieved with repetition, unity and geometric lines. A small fountain in the middle is surrounded by a low hedge and a perimeter of grass, the width of a lawn mower. Formal seats are set in niches created by clipped yew hedges and sheltered by topiary shapes.*

architecture outside the garden itself. Summer houses could be constructed with columns, giving a cloister-like impression to be reflected at one end of the water.

A parterre

❀ The parterre is basically a 'flat' pattern, often best seen from a height, such as a first-floor window or a raised terrace or mount. Even where there is no raised area, a parterre can still be enjoyed while walking through it. It may be part of a larger formal garden or can take up the whole of a small garden.

❀ The simplest parterre, perhaps a rectangle or square of clipped box or shrubby honeysuckle such as *Lonicera nitida*, makes an excellent design for a small front garden, which is usually viewed in passing, rather than actually entered.

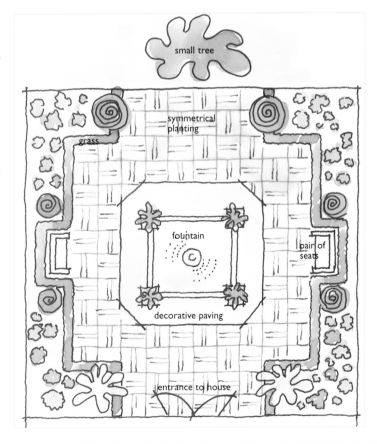

small tree

symmetrical planting

grass

fountain

pair of seats

decorative paving

entrance to house

FORMAL FRONT GARDENS

A VERY small garden may not offer much scope for an extended symmetrical arrangement but even one small standard tree in a square bed edged with box will make a charming formal front garden. You could place a clipped bay (*Laurus nobilis*) in a tub at each corner of the bed and use paving slabs or gravel as the surrounding material.

❀ If the site is sunny and you do not want the shade of even a small tree, the silvery leaves of the small shrub *Convolvulus cneorum* in a small sea of gravel will look pretty all year round. In a shady area, grow one bold plant of *Hosta sieboldiana*, whose bluey-green leaves are large and important looking.

Clipped hedging plants

❀ Although box is probably the longest-lasting hedging plant, there are several others that will make attractive edging hedges and you may prefer the silvery look that many of them offer.

ABOVE: *Careful planting, pruning and clipping of bushes such as bay can introiduce a sense of fomality into even the smallest of garden areas.*

LEFT: *This tiny, narrow garden incorporates careful planning in the decorative paving work, the small ponds mirroring each other and the planting along the pathway.*

❀ Lavender, rosemary and santolina were all traditionally used as clipped hedging plants and are still very attractive used in this way. They are not as long lasting as box and if you want them to live for many years, they must all be cut back really hard. They do not like to be crowded and hate any competition for light, moisture and nutrients so make sure there is a gap between the hedge and the planting inside it.

Formal but soft

❀ A very long, narrow plot can seem difficult to deal with formally because its ribbon-like shape already accentuates the straight lines and constricted space. You can soften the lines of straight paths by creating circular areas along the way, planting dome-shaped plants and clipping shrubs into rounded shapes.

❀ Similarly, the path can be lined with round-headed flowers, for example the soft rounded shapes of golden marjoram and alliums, which will produce big round flower heads in summer. Gravel rather than paving or brick will also soften the outline.

Axes and vistas

❀ One of the first decisions to make is the direction of the main axes. This will determine where the main vistas will lie and the garden's relationship to the house. The ornaments and features that close a vista can be added at a later stage. In most cases you will want the main axis to relate to the main door of the house so that garden and house can be seen as one entity in the plan.

❀ Cross-axes should be at right angles, but this is not always easy to achieve if the ground is not level or the plot not rectangular. At Sissinghurst in Kent the axes are not always at right angles but this has been cleverly concealed by the planting.

Materials

❀ The choice of material for hard surfaces and how it is laid can make or spoil a formal garden. Gravel is a versatile material, which combines well with other surfaces, including concrete and granite setts (paving blocks).

❀ Always get the best quality of any material that you can afford. York stone is unfortunately too expensive for most gardeners but there are acceptable forms of reconstituted stone, which can look perfectly good. Granite setts make good substitutes, too.

❀ Rounded cobblestones are attractive visually but uncomfortable to walk on, so should be used only for decorative details among other paving. They are useful as a contrast to other materials and as part of a decorative paving pattern. They can also be used to mark transitions between two separate areas or the change of direction of a path. Tiles laid on their edges can also mark changes of direction or provide interesting edging between other materials.

Plants for formal gardens

❀ Edging plants are useful for emphasising the line of a straight border. Choose those that will be of interest over a long season and use one plant along the whole length of the border to give a sense of unity. Possible plants include *Alchemilla mollis*, a pretty greeny-yellow plant that associates well with almost everything.

❀ The catmint *Nepeta cataria* is another good edging plant if your border is wide enough. *Bergenia cordifolia*, otherwise known as elephant's ears, will give a border a striking dark green edging, which turns red in autumn.

CONTEMPORARY GARDENS

Many modern buildings have simple, rectangular shapes, repetitive forms and the minimum of applied decoration. It is the shape of the whole structure that is important – the spacing and proportion of windows and doors and the relationship of the different planes. To complement such buildings, we need to design gardens of great simplicity, elegance and style, which will reflect the geometric lines of the house with their own geometric lines, softened by planting.

MODERNIST IDEAS

MODERNIST principles in gardening come from the Modernist style of architecture, which emerged at the beginning of the twentieth century. This made use of the newest technological developments to design buildings that did not have to rely on traditional building techniques. Reinforced concrete could be moulded into exciting new forms, creating lighter buildings with bigger, interconnected spaces and uncluttered interiors.

❧ Today there is a new wave of Modernist thinking, which regards the garden as an outside room whose link with the house is paramount. Key elements of the building's architecture such as doors and windows will be repeated as elements of the garden. Wooden floors inside the house can be repeated outside with wooden decking, and stone floors with stone paving. A lawn or rectangular paved area outside can be related to a rug indoors.

❧ Even if your house is not particularly interesting architecturally, you can feel free to interpret a traditional style in a modern way, bringing new ideas to an old theme. Whereas the classical formal garden is based on a central axis, Modernist gardens are always asymmetrical. Nevertheless, they are unmistakably formal. The lines are geometric, the ideas and plants are few but repeated. The angles and spaces are dynamic, implying energy and life, but the uncluttered terraces are also tranquil.

❧ The trimmings are the plants, which include spring and summer flowers, grown in pots and urns or galvanised metal buckets and dustbins. They can be

moved around as desired. Such gardens are designed for minimum maintenance, often for people with busy lives and exacting jobs who want to use the garden for leisure and entertaining, not for propagating and growing. There is no aping nature here; this is an artificial environment and proud of it.

Forms and shapes

❧ All shapes should be simple, functional and unpretentious. If you are designing an exotic garden or one that uses architectural plants, clarity of geometric form is desirable as a balance to the untidiness of plant growth. If you choose to design your garden in the geometric manner, use it confidently.

RIGHT: A tall, curved concrete wall has been painted deep ultramarine and decorated with sea creatures and flying ducks. The mosaic table adds extra colour and interest.

LEFT: *Square containers and a restricted planting scheme will complement many modern gardens. Here, a galvanised container has been filled with bold and colourful plants using only reds and yellows.*

Narrow gardens

❦ The paving in a typically narrow city garden can be done inexpensively with concrete slabs. Along one edge you could cut the concrete to form a generous curve which will leave room for a flowerbed with some depth. This means that at the widest part, you will be able to grow two or three tiers of plants, which will give opportunity for more plant height and variety.

Courtyard gardens

❦ You can modernise the Italianate courtyard style by using a formal pool of water with an elaborate but modern fountain in the centre, surrounded by terracotta tiles with brick edging. As for plants, keep to formal, clipped evergreens in very simple containers. Galvanised containers include buckets and dustbins. Just one or two of these planted with architectural palms, for example, will create an outdoor room of great style.

❦ In a small front courtyard, you can paint the walls in any deep colour. The introduction of new ranges of outdoor paints has enabled gardeners to paint fences, walls and whole courtyards in colours that will highlight plant forms and leaves to great effect.

❦ The style will suit any modern building, whether made of concrete, brick or timber, and can be used with modern mock Georgian or other brick houses, especially where the gardens are rather squeezed in between buildings. Often, these oddly shaped plots are asking for a geometric solution to the design.

RIGHT: *The modern garden takes the idea of the garden 'room' quite literally. The lines are geometric, the feeling architectural, the plants few but sculptural. Modern materials such as engineering bricks or decking can be used, and water is often present in the form of a sculptural fountain, again using modern materials such as stainless steel or glass.*

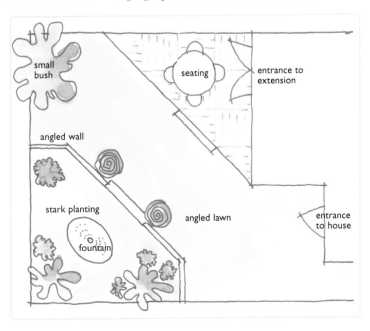

small bush

seating

entrance to extension

angled wall

stark planting

angled lawn

fountain

entrance to house

ABOVE: *In this garden, the owner has painted a curved line on the fence, which leads the eye into the curved line of the actual garden where it turns into woodland.*

Small rectangular gardens

❀ If the garden is very small, you can divide it up diagonally, the long line creating a feeling of more length. Mark the line with a change of level or a change of material, perhaps using gravel for one side and concrete slabs for the other.

Materials

❀ The first consideration in a modern garden is not necessarily the planting. Indeed, there may be very few plants or even none at all. The surfaces of the walls and floors of the garden offer opportunities for decoration. The traditional garden used mostly brick, stone, granite setts (paving blocks), sand or gravel.

❀ The modern garden designer can add to such materials glazed tiles, mosaic (especially on walls), glass bricks, mirrors, coloured glass beads and rubber and reconstituted materials. Glass bricks need some support but can be let into suitable frames. There are also bright stainless metal containers, poles and columns, which can be the supports for 'sails' for shade, rather than the traditional garden umbrella.

RIGHT: *Modern gardens should be functional and unpretentious. The tall and secure fence of this garden is made of simple wooden poles painted in graded shades of blue and purple.*

❀ Traditional materials are often perfectly suitable for the modern garden but used rather differently. Slate can be cut and laid with great precision. Precision cutting suits the spare 'hard-edged' designs of contemporary architecture. Alternatively, it can be sawn in random lengths and laid as a patio, path or surround for a geometrically shaped pool or L-shaped canal.

❀ Green slate is ideal for the modern garden but the surface should be roughened so that it is non-slip in all weathers.

❀ Any paved area should have a unified feeling, and this is especially important to counterbalance any exotic planting.

❀ Timber decking is a good material for many modern gardens, particularly roof-gardens. It can look magnificent with the dark, rough texture of railway sleepers used as retaining walls or with brick, and surprisingly perhaps, it also seems to go very well with modern galvanised containers.

❀ Concrete can be coloured with the addition of coloured cements. The various stone colours are usually the most popular because they are the 'kindest' and quietest foil to grass and plants.

Vertical elements

❀ Fine timber laths can create elegant vertical structures such as pergolas with a definitely modern look. They can symbolise tree trunks and create the feeling of a small copse or grove, but are very far removed from the deliberately rustic look of the traditional pergola. They will complement the straight lines of narrow decking. Timber obelisks can take the place of fastigiate trees with their erect branches, such as junipers or yews.

❀ Modern lighting can also add to the vertical effect. Globes on metal 'stems' give a modern effect. The stem can rise up from a group of dome-shaped shrubs, which themselves echo the shade's rounded shape.

Paint

❀ Walls, fences, furniture and containers can all be painted. White reflects more light than any other colour and will brighten a shady wall. It is also a good colour for highlighting foliage shapes.

❀ However, the enormous advances made in outdoor paints and the colour ranges now available give the modern gardener a really exciting choice. Blue-green and grey-green seem to be universally attractive colours in a garden and again, most foliage and flower colours and shapes look well against them. However, the brightest orange and the deepest blue can look right, too, when used with confidence and minimal planting, and many sculptural objects, particularly abstract ones, can look marvellous against them.

The plants

❀ Plants without flowers are ideally suited to the Modernist garden. Ferns such as *Athyrium filix-femina* can be massed together in front of a large-leaved ivy such as *Hedera helix* 'Montgomery'. Groups of three small trees planted together, such as *Betula pendula*, especially those with interesting bark, will remain small and look attractive. Their lacy foliage and narrow trunks will allow you to see the architecture through them.

❀ Large square or rectangular containers will also relate to the architecture and you can grow exotic plants such as palms, hostas or grasses in them.

Colour

❀ If you do want to introduce colour, it is best to choose restricted colour schemes so that the colour will not detract from the bold lines and geometric spaces of the garden plan. You can plant in blocks of geometric colour using pelargoniums or bedding plants and you can use foliage colour such as the red forms of *Phormium*.

BELOW: *Modern paints are available in a range of colours as bright as garden flowers themselves. Here, panels of a concrete fence have been painted in uninhibited shades of green, red and yellow.*

JAPANESE GARDENS

Japanese gardens have developed over many centuries and have been refined and shaped by religious and philosophical ideas, ranging from Shintoism, Hinduism and Taoism to Buddhism – very different from the classical roots of Christianity and Islam that have shaped European garden traditions. The basic principle behind Japanese gardens is a quest for harmony and an important element is the idea of retaining the spirit of the place and appreciating the beauty of the natural rock.

THE PRINCIPLES

IN early Japanese gardens design principles included the idea that rocks already *in situ* should be respected for their own inner stillness, and that rocks, islands and ponds represented nature and should always be placed asymmetrically. Symmetrical elements represented humans.

ABOVE: *This is an unusual but attractive and appropriate way to fence off a Japanese-style garden, using bamboo poles knotted together with rope.*

BELOW: *Bright red fish in a still pond are not difficult to keep, and they coordinate with the red paint used on many Japanese bridges.*

❀ The representation of a mountain is essential and refers to the Cosmic Mountain at the centre of the universe. The Island of Immortality can be represented by an island or a rock. Rocks are arranged in groups of three. In old Japanese gardening books this is explained as representing three forces – horizontal, diagonal and vertical – which correspond to the structure of the universe – heaven, earth and mankind.

❀ The aim is not to overpower nature but to enter into a partnership with it. The garden is a place for divine spirits and when harmony is achieved, the good spirits will be drawn into the garden while the hostile ones will leave it in peace.

ABOVE: *Japanese design is always very disciplined. The black decking and the single shapely plant in a pot very much reflect the Japanese sense of design.*

❀ Everywhere in the garden there should be devices to ward off evil spirits. Trees and stones should be grouped in odd numbers – threes, fives and sevens. Devils are thought to walk in straight lines so garden pathways are made to twist and turn.

❀ In the Japanese garden non-living features are paramount and plants are not the prime ingredients. One of the most important items is water – the Japanese word for gardener means 'He who makes the bed of streams'. Others are stone, sand, gravel, bamboo, aged trees and space.

❀ There is a 15th-century Japanese diagram that shows how a landscape should be deliberately designed to look natural. It has 16 pieces of land and water arranged around a central 'guardian stone'. The design is asymmetrical but carefully balanced, and each piece has a distinct function and importance. The pieces include mountains (near and far), rocks, beaches, islands, a lake and a cascade.

❀ Every item is balanced by something else. Tall plants grow next to bushy ones. Sharp angles are balanced by gentle bends. Any stream should be as natural as possible, moving from the east, going underground and flowing into the 'ocean' at the west. A stylised form of well head symbolises freshness.

❀ Some Japanese gardens have no water but are made up simply of rocks and gravel. This is because in the 15th century the Japanese Civil War put a stop to all gardening except in Buddhist monasteries. Here the monks kept up the tradition but in a very simple form. Sand represented the ocean and was raked daily to create wave forms. Uncut and weathered stones represented gods, mountains and animals.

The boundaries

❀ Japanese gardens are always separated from the surrounding land. Bamboo can be used for boundary fencing and for fencing to divide various parts of the garden. It should be tall and solid enough to conceal distracting views when contemplating the stones. Stepping stones laid on gravel are deliberately spaced to slow you down and leave behind your daily cares.

❀ A typical feature of Japanese gardens is a small bamboo pipe pivoted on a stand. When the pipe is filled it tips forward and then drops back on to a 'sounding stone' with a clack. This device was originally designed as a bird and animal scarer to protect crops.

BELOW: *Simplicity is the hallmark of a Japanese-style garden, as is retaining the spirit of the place. If there are old trees or rocks, try to retain them in your design. Gravel with stepping stones, a regularly shaped pond and characteristic plants such as bamboo and cherry trees are all within the spirit of the style.*

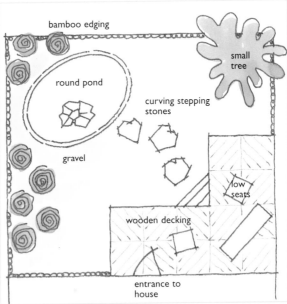

THE TEA HOUSE GARDEN

IT IS thought that the Zen monk Muratushuko (1422–1502) probably originated the tea ceremony. He built a little tea hut in the middle of Kyoto, furnished with simple utensils, and this idea of simplicity and austerity caught on. The main feature of a tea house garden is the path of rough stepping stones preventing the visitor from trampling on the beautiful moss. Stone lanterns light the way at night and a stone bowl stands outside the tea house for cleaning the visitor spiritually and physically before entering the house.

❀ The tea house itself should resemble a small rustic retreat and was based on the traditional Japanese farmhouse. Traditionally, there should be no windows in this little house because there should be no view of the garden from inside. There might be a veranda, from which the shape of the garden can be viewed.

❀ The whole garden is in muted colours with plenty of moss, kept damp and green by watering, sprinkled on paths and stepping stones. Everything should appear totally natural. If there is a pond, it should be sinuous with jutting peninsulas and deep inlets, often shored up with rocks so that you can get a dramatic overview from the tea house veranda. Shrubs and bushes are clipped into shapes suggestive of mountains.

ABOVE: Rocks are essential to a Japanese garden. They are chosen and placed with the greatest care and balanced by both the planting and other objects in the garden.

BELOW: Although appearing to be informal, this is in fact a very formal garden, planted with the utmost discipline so that everything balances and is reflected in the pool.

THE STROLLING GARDEN

THIS is basically a garden walk in which visitors are taken around a deliberately designed pathway so as to see the various changing vistas and set views designed for that purpose. Artificial hills, artificial ponds, broad winding streams and waterfalls with islands, rocks and topiary emphasise the rustic ideal. There are paths and bridges in great number and variety, with a tea garden tucked away in a small separate garden within the strolling garden.

✿ Bridges can take several forms. The Steep Bridge is arched and usually painted red and black, but bridges are often simple planks laid across a narrow stretch of water. There may be stepping stones across the water as well as in the gravel or moss. Typically, both plants and rocks are rounded bun shapes and vertical elements are provided by trees. The ponds are full of golden carp.

✿ The gateway to the strolling garden is a pergola-like structure with a roof. The whole garden is dotted with trained and shaped conifers and miniature conifers. Ponds have many rocks and grass right up to the edges. This sort of strolling garden can be bounded by bamboo screens or it can merge gradually into natural woodland. Clipped paths and interestingly shaped rocks can show up to advantage against a white-painted wall.

BELOW: *This gravel garden represents the ocean with green islands floating in it. Such disciplined raked patterns are meant to be seen, rather like the parterre, from a window above that looks down on the garden.*

THE DRY GARDEN

THE dry landscape garden can represent a pond or the ocean and is often raked into wave-like patterns. It can look very stylish simply with cherry blossom hanging over it in spring. This sort of garden can be the answer to a small front garden overhung by trees where little will grow and which is more of a viewing garden than a garden to go into. This means the gravel will remain undisturbed and continue to look good for an appreciable length of time. Rocks can be set into the gravel and perhaps a dwarf pine tree such as *Pinus mugo* 'Mops' or an ornamental cherry.

SUITABLE PLANTS FOR JAPANESE-STYLE GARDENS

THE range of trees and flowers is fairly limited. If plants were used the main idea is to make the most of the different seasons. Pine trees, cherries and plums have a special place. Bamboo is an obvious choice of plant, being both natural looking and architectural. *Prunus* x *yedoensis* 'Shidare Yoshino' is a weeping cherry with pink buds ageing to pure white in short racemes. It grows to 4 m (13 ft) in 10 years. *Acer palmatum* 'Dissectum' forms a mound with arching shoots and has finely cut leaves turning gold in autumn. It will grow to 1.8 x 3 m (6 x 10 ft).

EXOTIC GARDENS

The exotic can be achieved simply by creating the effect of something foreign. The Victorians were fascinated by foreign ideas and had gardens inspired by many different countries. The nineteenth-century garden at Biddulph Grange in Staffordshire – now owned by the National Trust and restored to its original splendour – was designed in separate compartments, reflecting styles of different parts of the world, including a Chinese garden, an Egyptian garden with sphinxes and a Japanese garden.

TROPICAL-LOOKING PLANTS AND CONSERVATORIES

THE Victorians also used tropical-looking plants which had to be taken into conservatories in the winter in their summer borders. No truly tropical plant will survive outside in temperate climates but recent technological advances in propagation have produced a number of tropical-looking plants, which can tolerate a temperate climate even in winter. This gives tremendous scope for creating exotic, jungly gardens, especially in milder areas or in cities where the temperature is always several degrees higher than in the areas surrounding them.

❀ Conservatories expand the possibilities, too, and even the smallest one offers opportunities for creating really flamboyant effects with climbing plants, hanging baskets and epiphytic plants (those that grow on other plants) hanging from branches, as well as orchids and bromeliads.

ABOVE: *The stately yucca always surprises with its tall spire of white bells in summer. It has a good architectural quality and will provide height in a border or stand on its own.*

LEFT: *Bananas and canna lilies are truly exotic and the robinia tree behind them has an exotic look as well. They will all grow in sheltered spots in temperate areas, although you cannot expect the bananas to fruit.*

Creating a hardy jungle

❀ A jungle is lush with foliage, with many large, differently shaped leaves growing at different heights in curtains of green, all overlapping and intertwining. You can create this effect in the garden by using vigorous climbers in association with large-leaved hardy plants. Many plants grow very tall in the jungle, climbing up

ABOVE: *A lush and exotic water garden with a small walkway across the stream is positively tropical in feel.*

into the trees towards the light. You can simulate the height of a forest canopy by installing tall scaffolding screens. Make sure the scaffolding is robust and firmly fixed because many plants become very heavy when in leaf and need strong supports.

❀ If the site is sunny, the golden hop (*Humulus lupulus* 'Aureus') is a good candidate and perfectly hardy. Any vigorous climber with large leaves will add to the effect. The crimson glory vine (*Vitis coignetiae*) will eventually grow to 24 m (80 ft) and Virginia creeper to 15 m (50 ft). The leaves of both plants turn bright red in autumn. The evergreen *Clematis armandii* is another vigorous climber with plenty of large shiny leaves and will make your screen look like a snowstorm in spring with its masses of white flowers. For a shady site, *Hydrangea petiolaris* is a vigorous, hardy climber with handsome, flat, white lace-cap flower heads, which will reach 3.5 m (12 ft) on a wall or 5 m (16 ft) growing up a tree.

❀ For lower plants use *Fatsia japonica*, with its enormous palm-shaped leaves, or phormiums and yuccas. *Yucca glauca* is a mass of straight, thin grey-blue leaves 1.5 m (5 ft) across. Plant it in drifts close together. *Yucca* 'Vittorio Emmanuel II' is one of the biggest and best. It will grow to 1.8 m (6 ft).

RIGHT: *This small, sheltered garden relies on a few architectural and semi-tropical plants to give an exotic quality, relying on sculptural shapes and gaudy colours. Tall scaffolding provides a screen for vigorous climbers such as Virginia creeper, providing a jungle-like enclosed feeling. Palms, yuccas and large-leaved shrubs add to the jungle quality and a fountain provides sparkle and life.*

❀ For a moist site choose *Gunnera magellanica*, *Zantedeschia aethiopica* and *Rodgersia aesculifolia*. Bamboos are easy to grow and can contribute to the exotic feel of a garden. Choose ones that will not spread, or grow them where you really want a jungle or keep them in pots. *Phyllostachys aurea* is well behaved and will grow to 4.5 m (15 ft).

Creating a tender jungle

❀ Many tropical-looking plants, often from Mediterranean areas, although difficult to propagate, are not difficult to grow. Some prefer an exposed site; others grow best in dappled shade. The hardier eucalypts and the holm oak (*Quercus ilex*) are dense enough to keep the heat in and sparse enough to let light through, especially if you cut off their lower branches. *Eucalyptus aggregata*, *E. perriniana* and *E. parvifolia* all make good canopy trees.

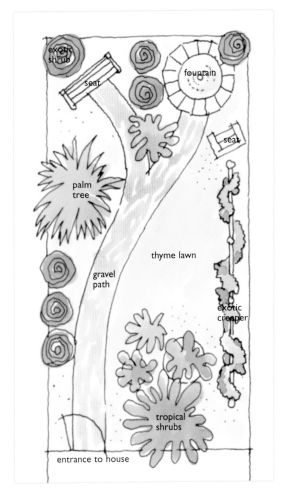

exotic shrub

seat

fountain

seat

palm tree

thyme lawn

gravel path

exotic creeper

tropical shrubs

entrance to house

LEFT: *This is a plant for a desert garden, a rock garden, a raised bed by a sunny wall or a container. Grow in poor, sharply drained soil in full sun. Where the temperature drops below 2°C (36°F), grow it in a cool greenhouse.*

Almost hardy exotic-looking plants

❀ There are some small evergreen trees that can look highly exotic grown on their own. These include mimosa (*Acacia dealbata*) with pretty, grey-green ferny leaves and masses of tiny ball-shaped yellow flowers in spring. *Acacia* 'pravissima' is a small weeping mimosa with triangular leaves, suitable for a small garden.

❀ The monkey puzzle (*Auracaria araucana*) comes from Chile and is strikingly exotic. It is the only one of its family hardy enough to be grown outside in temperate zones. In the nineteenth century it was a fashionable tree to grow in front gardens. Grow it as part of a grove or as a specimen tree near enough to the house so that its fascinating flowers and fruits may be seen from an upstairs window. The red-barked strawberry tree (*Arbutus* x *andrachnoides*) is evergreen, fast growing and winter flowering, as well as having attractive bark.

❀ Bananas are really herbaceous plants but they are tall enough to act as trees in the exotic garden. They look good at the edge of a pond where they are reflected in the water. The hardy banana (*Musa basjoo*) has enormous tattered leaves, which can be used for anything from wrapping paper to picnic plates or umbrellas! Other bananas, including edible ones, must be kept in a conservatory.

❀ The two hardy palm trees are the chusan palm (*Trachycarpus fortunei*), which will reach 7 m (23 ft). The dwarf palm (*Chamaerops humilis*) has broad green fans on prickly stems and grows to 4 m (13 ft). It is the only native European palm and will withstand wind better than *T. fortunei*. Tree ferns are both stately and feathery, a surprising and attractive combination. *Dicksonia antarctica* has 2-m (7-ft) fronds. You will have to water or spray its trunk in summer and wrap it up in winter, but it is certainly worth it if you have a sheltered spot in which to show it off.

❀ *Melianthus major*, from southern Africa, is a dramatic plant with serrated grey-green leaves. It is actually a shrub but best treated as a herbaceous perennial. It will survive in a warm position in many areas, if protected in winter.

RIGHT: *Hedychium densiflorum is a clump-forming perennial bearing tubular, fragrant orange flowers in late summer. It will grow to 5 m (16 ft). It needs moist soil with shelter from the wind. It may survive outdoors in winter if given a deep winter mulch.*

ABOVE: *The cardoon (Cynara cardunculus) is an imposing, statuesque plant that should be grown in fertile, well-drained soil in a sheltered spot in full sun.*

All these exotic plants will add an architectural dimension to the garden and can be grown in association with hardier large-leaved plants such as *Rodgersia*, *Ligularia* and *Astilbe*, or add height to a bed of ground cover plants such as *Sedum* and *Polygonum*.

Exotic plants for pots and conservatories

❀ These plants can be placed in the garden during summer, but really need the protection of a greenhouse or conservatory during the winter.

❀ The cannas are exotic in both form and flower. *Canna indica* has banana-like leaves, grows to about 1.5 m (5 ft) and has bright red and yellow flowers in summer. *C. indiflora* is bigger and good for summer bedding or for pots. It has shocking pink flowers and will grow 3 m (10 ft) in a year. *C.* 'Purpurea' is a purple-leaved form with orange flowers. Cannas are best dug up in autumn and stored under a bench for the winter, then planted out again in spring.

❀ Agaves are succulent perennials grown for their large, fleshy, sword-shaped leaves. *Agave americana* has curvy-toothed grey-green leaves armed with short spines. It needs to be kept in a pot so it can be moved indoors in winter.

Poolside exotica

❀ Surprisingly few swimming pools have had any attempt made to integrate them with their environment. But why put up with municipal surroundings if you have your own pool at home? Hedges, walls or trellises can all create an enclosed private space that you can make as exotic as you wish.

❀ The pool could be integrated into a spacious patio or terrace with room to stand large pots of citrus fruit or tropical-looking plants, which will be reflected in the water.

❀ The pool itself can be any shape you wish. It can be long and narrow, reminiscent of the Moorish gardens of Spain. Standard clipped mop-headed box trees can stand sentinel alongside the pool. A cloistered Moorish changing room with rounded arches could face one end of the pool. Or you could have a Baroque pool built with scrolls, statues and more clipped plants.

KITCHEN GARDENS

One of the pleasures of vegetable gardening is being able to pick the produce while it is fresh, and cooking or eating it straight away. Many people imagine that an allotment-sized plot is needed to grow vegetables, but this is not true. A pocket-sized patch in any small garden can be used to grow salad vegetables and a couple of growing bags on a sunny patio will give you a satisfactory crop of your own tomatoes or beans.

VEGETABLE APPEAL

CAREFULLY chosen and imaginatively grown, vegetables can provide a surprisingly aesthetic pleasure garden in their own right. Anyone who has seen the glorious decorative vegetable parterres at the Château of Villandry in France's Loire valley will know that vegetables can be as colourful and appealing as flowers, so there is no need to relegate your vegetables to an unseen part of the garden. The enormous expanse of the lower terrace of this great garden is planted with rows of brightly coloured vegetables in great variety inside clipped hedges.

❀ Happily, you do not have to be the owner of a large château to make wonderful use of the fascinating shapes and colours of vegetables in your own garden.

BELOW: An elegant home-made wigwam has been made for this box parterre potager, to support sweet peas and runner beans. The whole potager is intended to be as decorative as it is practical.

THE SITE

VEGETABLES should not be planted in heavy shade. An open site is best but they do need shelter, particularly from the wind, so a hedge or woven fence to filter the wind would be ideal. Provided the area is not too shaded, the ideal place for the vegetable plot is near the greenhouse and shed, with space enough to have a compost heap.

❀ This means that the utility parts of the garden are all in one place. It gives unity to what might otherwise be a scattered group of buildings and work areas. The vegetable plot itself does not need to be part of this area. It can be fenced or hedged off but it will be practical to have the working area nearby with a firm path leading from one to the other.

BELOW: These very attractive rows of vegetables have been chosen for their colour and shape, not just for their taste. They include Longbow leeks, and Rubine and Icarus Brussels sprouts.

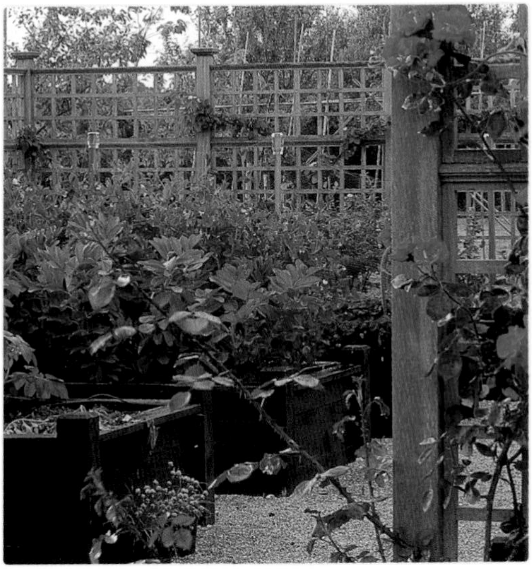

LEFT: *This well-organised space uses square wooden tubs and trellis to create a colourful and high-yielding potager, mixing vegetables such as broad beans with climbing red roses.*

- A plot can be arranged in a circular pattern divided by radial paths, and the pattern marked out by edging stones. Circles always look elegant. Their outlines can become valuable focal points and need not conflict in any way with an otherwise purely decorative garden.
- Vegetables grown in rows within the divisions will give an attractive coloured pattern to the design. Square or more complicated geometric shapes can be used if you have the space. Beds with straight lines can be edged with purpose-made edging tiles or you can use wooden boards.

POTAGERS

A POTAGER is a sort of cottage garden where the main ingredients are vegetables rather than flowers. It is a decorative vegetable patch and can be more or less disciplined according to your preference. At its most defined, it is not unlike a parterre, with vegetables growing in spaces delineated by low hedges or brick or gravel paths. Then it becomes a larger, more varied version of the formal herb garden.

The formal potager

- Strictly ordered rows of vegetables can be attractive if they are well maintained, but it is not necessary to grow them like this. Build raised beds and surround them with brick paths. They may be square or rectangular, each being planted with one or two varieties to give order to the whole design. Dwarf tomatoes can be grown alongside dwarf beans; leeks next to ornamental cabbages. Globe artichokes in the centre of a bed will give height and structure; strawberries provide a decorative edging for some of the beds.

BELOW: *A vegetable plot can be among the most decorative of gardens. This one has been designed rather like a formal herb garden. It has four square beds, each comparatively small so they can be easily reached for garden work, with a decorative bay tree in the centre. The greenhouse and the compost heap are both conveniently nearby.*

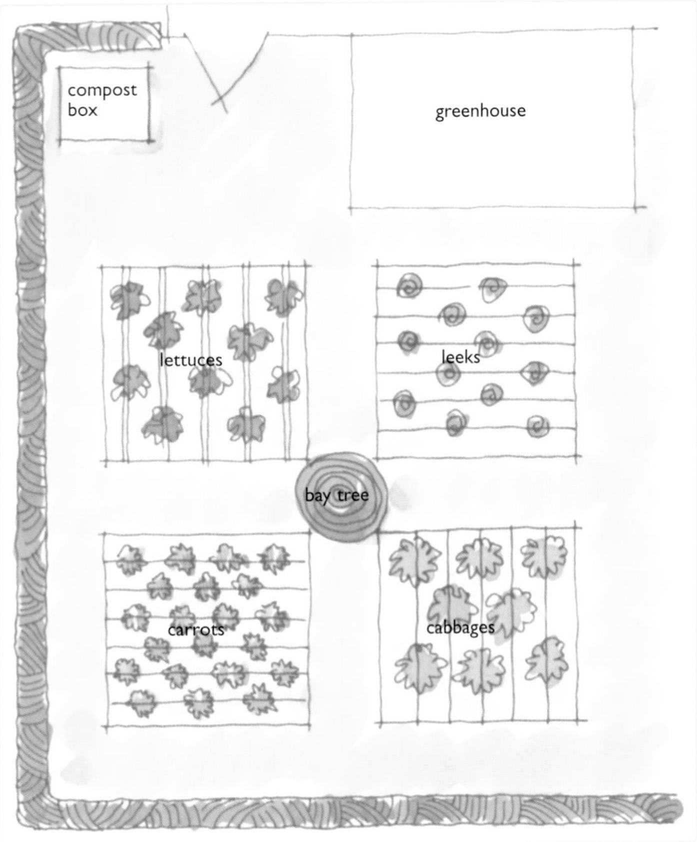

The informal potager

❀ In a small garden, or if you have chosen an awkwardly shaped part of the plot as your potager, an informal vegetable patch will probably be a more sensible option. Here you can allow the plants to grow in a somewhat haphazard, more natural manner than in the formal plot.

❀ You will therefore need a strong framework because, although the luxuriant growth in summer will tend to conceal the edges, in winter you will want the shape to reappear. You can mark out the area with wicker fencing, which will be quite appropriate to the design, or you could use espaliered apple or pear trees whose branches will look attractive when they are both in leaf and dormant.

❀ Give some height to the beds with standard soft fruit bushes such as gooseberries or black and redcurrants, which will be easier to maintain and to pick and will

ABOVE: Some of the most mundane vegetables can look enchanting if they are grown where the sun can shine on their young foliage. This Swiss chard is called Rainbow and ranges in colour from green to red and bronze.

help give form to the area. Other vegetables can be planted in more or less organised patterns, as you prefer.

❀ Ornamental cabbages, tall and round lettuces of as many different colours as you can find, Swiss chard, leeks and dwarf sugar snap peas can all be interplanted with herbs and standard or shrub roses for extra decorative value. Rhubarb is a dramatic plant in its own right. One plant will be enough to feed a family with rhubarb crumble for a season and its magnificent leaves and attractive pink stems make a good, strong impression and contrast well with other plants.

The basement potager

❀ Basement flats often have tiny patios with steps to gardens at eye level or higher. People generally sit in the patio area because the steep, narrow steps to the garden are uninviting. Such plots are good candidates for vegetable gardens. If you can push the garden out by enlarging the patio area, making the steps wider and shallower, you will lose some growing space but make the whole place feel much more open and spacious.

❀ You can decorate the patio with large flowering shrubs in containers and set up table and chairs there, and concentrate your growing skills in the upper part of the garden. Ornamental cabbages with their round,

LEFT: Ornamental cabbages are astonishingly decorative. They can be grown with other vegetables in a decorative mixture, but often look best on their own in rows, like this pink and turquoise variety called 'Benihato'.

LEFT: *Vegetables can work well in the flower border, a particularly useful characteristic if you want to grow vegetables in a small garden and cannot afford space for a separate kitchen garden area.*

❀ Ruby chard is a coarse, spinach-like vegetable with deep purple leaves and spectacular scarlet stems and veins. It associates dramatically with herbaceous plants at the front of a border. Ornamental cabbages have wonderful winter colours of bright purple and blue-green, sometimes with cream markings and firm, rounded, symmetrical shapes. They are at their best in winter and can brighten up a dormant border in the colder months.

Vegetables and fruit on the patio

❀ Apples on dwarfing rootstocks, tomatoes, runner beans – in fact a complete miniature kitchen garden – can be grown in containers on a patio. The colours, the different leaf forms and the fruit and vegetables themselves can prove an attractive combination. Strawberries look particularly attractive poking out of strawberry pots. A practical advantage is that you can slip out and pick a few fruits or vegetables as needed. You must make sure you feed and water them regularly or the results will be disappointing.

brightly coloured shapes, the feathery pale green leaves of carrots, chives with their bluey-green spikes, the tall strap shapes of leeks and soft, round spinach leaves will make contrasting patterns on the lower terrace.

❀ Tall, stately vegetables such as cardoons can grow right at the back. Carefully planned and with the addition of some summer-flowering perennials and shrubs, this can become a pleasant place to sit, especially when the sun is on the garden and not on the patio.

VEGETABLES IN MIXED PLANTING

Vegetables can also take their place in the mixed border, along with herbs, perennials and shrubs. This relaxed attitude to growing vegetables allows you to add plants for colour and to fill gaps. It also has practical value as the more varied the planting, the more it helps to prevent a build-up of the pests and diseases attracted to particular plants. French marigolds (*Tagetes*), for example, and pot marigolds (*Calendula*) attract beneficial insects and deter harmful ones, so planting vegetables in a mixed border next to them will be beneficial.

RIGHT: *This delightful corner of a flowerbed shows an intriguing piece of mixed vegetable and flower planting, using red and white busy Lizzies with a towering lettuce growing at the centre.*

HERB GARDENS

Every garden needs some herbs, whether they are grown for their charming flowers, aromatic foliage or culinary qualities. During the four centuries of their rule the Romans introduced many herbs to Britain which we still grow and use today. Many of those herbs would have been lost during the war-torn Middle Ages, had it not been for the monks who, safely inside their monastery walls, continued to grow herbs for healing and cooking. In the early years herbs were primarily grown for use as medicinal plants – indicated by the species name officinalis. The monks grew them in neat, rectangular beds and meticulously categorised and labelled them.

PLANTING HERBS

THE tradition of herbs grown in ordered beds has survived to the present day, partly because many are neat, low-growing plants, which look particularly good grown in this way. In the 17th century they were grown in formal patterns in parterres, purely for decoration.

❀ In a modern garden, growing herbs in patterned beds is not only visually attractive but also practical because small beds separated by low hedges, paths or stones make tending and harvesting the plants easier.

BELOW: This circular herb garden has been created in the centre of a lawn surrounded by hedges to keep out the wind. There is a wide variety of herbs, grown both for their colours and contrasting shapes.

❀ However, herbs will find a place in any style of garden; the range of possibilities is enormous. They can be grown among other plants in a mixed border or, if you lack space, a few pots can look good on a kitchen windowsill or you can create a little herb garden in a window box.

❀ Ground-hugging creepers such as pennyroyal, some thymes and mints can be planted among paving slabs or bricks; hummock-forming plants such as oregano, common sage, and chives make charming front-of-border plants, and tall stately plants such as fennel, lovage, angelica and sweet cicely can provide structure.

BELOW: This herb garden has a formal framework of stone, yet quite informal planting, in which the herbs have been allowed to grow into their own shapes. The small willows and the little fruit tree add height.

it should be as near to the kitchen as possible. Even if you enjoy a stroll through the garden to reach the herb bed, you may not always have the time (although you can always grow a separate collection of herbs in pots for cooking).

❀ Most herbs will benefit from being grown in an open, sunny part of the garden, since many of them come from Mediterranean areas where the climate is hot and dry. Many herbs smell delicious when walked on or brushed against, so large herbs can be grown by an outside door. Others may be planted along pathways – thyme, eau de Cologne mint, peppermint and coriander can be planted near paths and creeping varieties of thyme and camomile between flagstones.

❀ The whole herb garden can be enclosed by a clipped yew hedge, or simply divided from the rest of the garden by a clipped hedge. If your garden is on different levels, a circular herb garden at the lower level, sheltered from the elements by walls and shrubs, can make a good sun trap for both plants and people to enjoy.

❀ If your garden is on heavy clay, it may be worthwhile creating raised beds so that water can drain away quickly. Add gravel and sand to the compost, since most herbs prefer a poor soil.

LEFT: *An outsize mortar planted with thyme lends character to this small herb plot. Around it are a selection of artemisias and other feathery plants.*

❀ The well-behaved habit of most herbs (mint is an exception) makes them useful in formal gardens, while their soft foliage colours make them good companion plants in herbaceous borders or in the cheerful disorder of cottage gardens. Many will do well in containers, and a cluster of pots near the kitchen door is both attractive and convenient.

Where to grow herbs

❀ Where to put your herb plot is an important consideration. If you are going to use the herbs for cooking,

RIGHT: *The cartwheel shape can make an attractive and practical herb garden, the 'spokes' dividing different herbs from each other and providing narrow paths useful for planting, weeding and picking. Here, the wheel is the centre of a square, sunny garden with roses and shrubs around the edges and a bench from which to enjoy the scents and sights.*

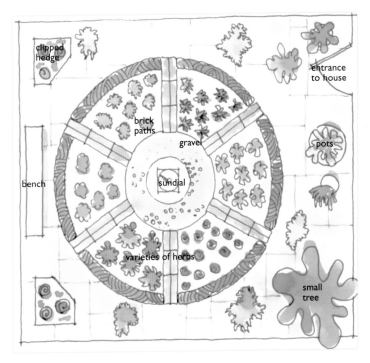

HERB GARDEN STYLES

Aformal herb garden is often designed in the form
of a parterre with closely clipped low hedges of box,
which give a defined frame to the herbs. There are other
suitable plants for hedging, however. *Santolina
chamaecyparis* gives a beautiful silver frame to the design,
wall germander (*Teucrium* x *lucidrys*) has neat triangular
dark green leaves, and the dark green foliage of rosemary
and the dwarf lavender 'Munstead Dwarf' can be effective.

❀ Hyssop and thyme will also grow dense enough to be
   regularly trimmed, and chives can make a very pretty
   edging during the summer, but will disappear in winter.

❀ Work out your design first on paper and then mark it
   out on the ground with string or hose pipe before you
   start planting. Rectangular, circular and square shapes
   can all look good. Triangular shapes are more difficult
   to manage but may suit a particular plot. The whole
   thing can be as large or small, as simple or complex as
   you like.

❀ In a small garden you can use a cartwheel shape, laid
   out in stones or bricks, and grow the plants between
   the 'spokes'. It is best to separate the plants with
   narrow paths or stepping stones of brick or paving or
   they will grow into one another and spoil the clarity of
   the pattern.

❀ Add height by planting standard roses at regular
   intervals and a vertical eye-catcher in the centre of the
   plot such as a sundial, a fountain or other water feature
   or a large urn on a pedestal.

Using herbs informally

❀ A formal herb garden does take up space and may
   not be the best answer in a basically informal garden.
   Formality is successful when linked to a grand or
   formal building but does require constant maintenance
   with frequent clipping to keep it under control.

LEFT: *The pale and interesting stalks and dark seed heads of these Egyptian
onions have been allowed to remain to add winter interest to the garden and to
feed the birds.*

BELOW: *Even when there is not much room, herbs can be grown very
satisfactorily in pots. Here, an interesting variety of herbs, including basil,
tarragon and sage, are growing in terracotta pots conveniently situated near
the house.*

❀ A more sensible way of herb gardening for those with a busy lifestyle is to incorporate herbs in a mixed border, as you would any other flowering plants.

❀ Rosemary makes a tall, stately shrub with sky-blue flowers all along its branches in spring and summer. It can be used as a structural plant in a border or as a specimen plant, on its own against a sunny wall or freestanding. Angelica, lovage, and sweet cicely, too, are all tall, stately plants, which can provide structural elements in a border. Bronze fennel, with dark feathery leaves, can provide good contrasts with other plants. Chives, sage, golden marjoram and other plants with similar habits can make good companion plants towards the front of a border. Garlic chives have narrow, strap-like leaves with flat heads of small white flowers in late summer and autumn.

Paved herb area

❀ You can create a dedicated herb garden in a paved area of the garden by creating square beds between brick paths. Plant masses of the same variety of herb in each square for a deliberate pattern of habit and colour. More informal would be a gravel garden with concrete stepping stones in which the herbs can be allowed to grow and spread naturally in a seemingly random manner.

❀ Tall plants like globe artichokes (*Cynara scolymus* 'Green Globe') and angelica can be grown at the back; in front you could grow pot marigolds with their cheerful round orange heads, the silvery-leaved curry plant (*Helichrysum augustifolium*) and varieties of artemisia. Orris root (*Iris florentina*) will provide strong strap-like vertical interest. Add some shrub roses and one or two *Alchemilla mollis* to create pretty associations and a discreetly colourful garden of great charm.

Herbs in window boxes and on balconies

❀ Some herbs such as basil, scented geranium and lemon verbena may do better indoors or in sheltered window boxes and balconies rather than outdoors. Success depends on where the window box or balcony is situated, which direction it faces and whether it gets enough sun and not too much wind. You can introduce a herb corner on a balcony with a few containers of herbs that are easy to grow. You can sow some herbs such as chervil, summer savory, borage and sweet marjoram directly into their containers. Certain perennials such as thyme and lavender can be kept for several years if you keep them dwarfed by clipping them.

BELOW: *A herb garden can be quite dramatic like this one, where the usual central square parterre is filled up with tall spiky seed heads.*

CHOOSING YOUR PLANTS

Choosing plants for the garden need not be confusing if you bear in mind the following simple principles.

A plant's requirements in a garden depend on where it comes from in the wild. For example, if a plant likes harsh Alpine soil, it will not thrive in a woodland environment.

Always test the soil in various parts of your garden before choosing plants and always buy healthy specimens – stunted plants will not reach their full potential. And finally, be aware that plants can soon outgrow their allotted spot in the border.

If you apply these simple principles consistently, you are unlikely to go wrong with your choice of plant.

LEARNING PLANT NAMES

The ancient Greeks and Romans began classifying plants over 2,000 years ago. In the monasteries and universities of Europe where the work was continued, the universal language was Latin. So for centuries Latin names were used to describe individual plants. Each plant needed a long sentence to describe it so that scholars could recognise it. The scientific descriptions were unwieldy and did not always correspond to each other in different parts of the world, so there were many misunderstandings. Common names for plants were not satisfactory either. One plant may have several different common names in different localities and, conversely, the same name can be given to different plants.

THE BINOMIAL SYSTEM

IN the 18th century the Swedish naturalist, Carl Linnaeus (1707–78), created a system for methodically naming and classifying the whole living world 'from buffaloes to buttercups'. His system, the binomial system, consisted of two names for each plant.

❀ Since then, the Linnaean system of classification has been developed by scientists so that the entire plant kingdom is divided and subdivided into what amounts to a 'family tree' according to each plant's botanical characteristics. There are now international rules as to the naming of plants.

❀ Linnaeus grouped plants together into families and then divided each family into smaller groups called *genera* (singular genus).

Plant families

❀ All flowering plants are grouped into particular families based purely on the structure of their flowers. The family name always has a capital letter and ends in –aceae or –ae. For example Rosaceae is the rose family; Ranunculaceae is the buttercup family; Liliaceae is the lily family; and the Umbelliferae family includes plants that have clusters of small flowers like cow parsley and angelica.

RIGHT: *Twelve pansies and violas painted by Joachim Camerarius the Younger in 1589. He called them 'Little day and night flowers' – Linnaeus did not introduce his binomial system for the naming of plants until the eighteenth century.*

Genus and species

❀ Each plant family is then divided into smaller groups called genera. The binomial (two-name) system gives each plant name two words. The first word is the genus name, for example *Ilex* (holly).

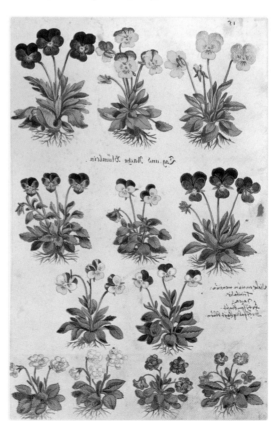

ABOVE: *A row of modern pansies (*Viola wittrockiana*) growing with lavender in front of a clipped hedge of privet.*

❀ The second name is the specific, or species name, (which is equivalent to a person's Christian or given name), for example *aquifolium*, which means 'pointed-leaved'. Thus *Ilex aquifolium* is the name for the common holly tree and means 'holly with pointed leaves', whereas *Ilex platyphylla* means 'broad-leaved holly'. In the binomial system the genus name is always given an initial capital letter, and the second, species name, which applies to that plant alone, starts with a small letter.

❀ A plant may be named after the plant 'hunter' who first discovered it in the wild and brought it back to civilisation. For example, *Dicksonia antarctica* is named after James Dickson, who discovered it in Antarctica.

❀ Subspecies (denoted by 'subsp.') indicates a distinct variant of the species, usually because it has adapted to a particular region.

Cultivars

❀ There are many plants that differ from the normal form of the species. These may have occurred spontaneously in the garden by mutation, or have been created by plant breeding or induced from radiation or chemicals.

❀ These used to be called varieties when naturally occurring in the wild, and cultivars when produced by humans.

More recently, all variants are now described as cultivars. Cultivar names follow the species name and have a capital letter and single quotation marks. For example, *Rosa rugosa* 'Blanche Double de Coubert' is a white-flowered *rugosa* rose and *Rosa rugosa* 'Frau Dagmar Hastrup' has pink flowers.

Hybrids

❀ Hybrids are plants produced by crossing two different parent plants. These are most common between two species of the same genus because they are closely related. For example, *Viburnum* x *bodnantense* is a cross between the two species *Viburnum farreri* and *Viburnum grandiflorum*. However, there are some crosses between species from different genera, for example the very vigorous x *Cupressocyparis leylandii*, which is a cross between the genera *Chamaecyparis* and *Cupressus*.

❀ Hybridisation and selection have produced many cultivars with similar characteristics. For convenience these are often classified into groups or series, for example Delphinium Pacific Hybrids or Elatum Group.

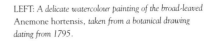

LEFT: *A delicate watercolour painting of the broad-leaved* Anemone hortensis, *taken from a botanical drawing dating from 1795.*

NAME CHANGES

Sometimes it is necessary to change a plant name, which can be very confusing for gardeners. There are several reasons for this. The plant may have been wrongly identified or an earlier name for it may have been found, in which case the International Code specifies the earliest name should be used. Another reason is that two different plants may have been given the same name.

❀ The reason it is important to know the correct name of a plant is that two different species from the same genus may be very different from one another.

❀ For example, take the spurge family (*Euphorbia*). These plants have unusual blooms and good foliage and make excellent plants for creating decorative effects or background foliage in the garden.

❀ But you do have to choose the right one. *Euphorbia wulfenii* is a large, shrubby very hardy plant, which forms a loose dome of large yellow flower heads and grows to 1.5 m (5 ft) tall. It is a splendid plant for creating an architectural effect, whereas *E. myrsinites* is only 15 cm (6 in) high and *E. obesa* is a tender ball-shaped succulent requiring greenhouse cultivation.

LATIN NAMES AND THEIR MEANINGS

Many genus names and even more species names have a particular meaning, which helps to identify them.

RIGHT: *This detailed watercolour is of a snowdrop anemone* (Anenome sylvestris)*, first printed in a botanical magazine that was published in 1796.*

Genera names

❀ Generic names sometimes commemorate classical gods and heroes or famous botanists. For example *Achillea* (yarrow) was named after the warrior Achilles, who was slain by an arrow in his heel; Daphne was a maiden pursued by the sun god Apollo; Iris was the goddess of the rainbow. All come from classical literature.

❀ Plants named after famous botanists include *Aubrieta*, after Claude Aubriet (1668–1743), a French botanical artist; *Clarkia* after William Clark (1770–1838), an American explorer; *Dahlia* after Anders Dahl (1751–89), a Swedish botanist; *Magnolia* after Pierre Magnol (1638–1715), a French physician and botanist; *Mahonia* after Bernard McMahon (1775–1816), an Irish-American nurseryman; *Nicotiana* after Jean Nicot (1530–1600), a French traveller; *Rudbeckia* after Olaf Rudbeck (1660–1740), a Swedish botanist; *Saintpaulia* after Baron Walter von Saint Paul-Illaire (1860–1910), a German traveller; and *Tradescantia* after John Tradescant (c. 1570–1638), English royal gardener to Charles I.

Species names

❀ Species names can be even more informative. They may honour people who had a direct connection with the plant. Often a plant used to be named after the plant 'hunter' who collected it or the nurserymen who propagated and sold it.

❀ *Darwinii* after the genus name of a plant, therefore, commemorates the English scientist Charles Darwin

LEFT: *Scarlet poppy* (Papaver rhoeas) *from a book entitled* Familiar Wild Flowers *by F. Edward Hulme, published in 1894.*

(1809–82); *douglassii* denotes David Douglas (1798–1834), a Scotsman who collected many conifers in North America; *farreri* denotes the English collector and author, Reginald J. Farrer (1880–1920); *fortunei* is for the Scottish collector, Robert Fortune (1812–80); *veitchii* is for the English family nursery firm of Veitch, which flourished in Exeter and London between 1808 and 1914 and which sponsored several successful plant hunters; *willmottiae* is for Ellen Mary Willmott (1860–1934), an English gardener; and *wilsonii* for Ernest Henry ('Chinese') Wilson (1878–1931), English collector and botanist.

❦ Some names refer to the geographical area where a plant originated, although these are not always reliable. Botanists sometimes made mistakes.

For example, several plants introduced as from Japan (*japonica*) were later found to be natives of China.

❦ Linnaeus himself regarded Indian (*indica*) and Chinese (*sinensis*) as virtually interchangeable. Geographical names often used include *cambricus* (Cambria or Wales), *capensis* (Cape of Good Hope), *damascenus* (Damascus), *gallicus* (Gaul or France), *hispanicus* (Hispania, Spain), *lusitanicus* (Portugal) and *neopolitanus* (Naples).

❦ There are hundreds of names that simply describe aspects of the plant. Just a few common examples are given in the table above. They are almost all of Latin origin.

LEFT: *These colourful Iceland poppies have the Latin name* Papaver nudicaule, *which means 'naked stemmed poppy'*.

DESCRIPTIVE LATIN SPECIES NAMES

acaulis	stemless	*lacteus*	milk-white
albus	white	*maculatus*	spotted
amoenus	pleasing	*meleagris*	speckled
argenteus	silvery	*nanus*	dwarf
atropurpureus	dark purple	*niger*	black
azureus	sky-blue	*nivalis*	snowy-white
baccatus	berry-bearing	*occidentalis*	western
caeruleus	dark blue	*parviflorus*	small-flowered
citriodorus	lemon-scented	*plumosus*	feathery
cordatus	heart-shaped	*reptans*	creeping
coronatus	crowned	*saggitifolius*	arrow-leaved
dentatus	toothed	*scandens*	climbing
farinosus	floury	*sinensis*	Chinese
flavus	yellow	*speciosus*	showy
floribundus	free-flowering	*spinosus*	thorny
fruticosus	shrubby	*tomentosus*	woolly
fulgens	shining	*tortuosus*	very twisted
glaber	smooth	*uliginosus*	of marshy places
gladiatus	sword-like	*venustus*	handsome
hybridus	hybrid	*vernalis*	of spring
japonicus	Japanese	*viridis*	green

PLACING YOUR PLANT

Plants in the wild have adapted to the soil and climate of the regions in which they grow. If you want to grow plants where they do not originally belong, you have to try and provide the conditions they are used to or they will die. Many plants from the tropics or the deserts will not survive out of doors in a temperate climate. Other plants may be half-hardy and able to withstand a certain degree of cold but will be killed by a hard frost.

CLIMATIC ADAPTATIONS

IN warm temperate regions such as the Mediterranean, plants have learned to grow where the soil is poor and there is a lack of moisture during the summer months. Often they have silvery leaves, the silver due to tiny hairs, which help to protect the plant from the sun.

❀ Plants in the tropics have a plentiful water supply and heat all year round and so grow non-stop – buds, flowers and fruit all out at the same time on the same plant. Succulents and cacti, on the other hand, are used to being in dry-as-dust deserts. They have adapted their stems as plump reservoirs for water and reduced their leaves to spines so that they lose very little moisture through the pores.

ABOVE: A low bench is used as a display area for a group of interesting small succulents in terracotta pots.

❀ Between the very warm and the cold, frozen regions, lie the temperate zones where the majority of plants are deciduous. Plants that have evolved in temperate zones have learned to cope with the wide variation of conditions in different seasons, having adapted to grow when the weather is warm and become dormant when it is cold. Deciduous trees drop their leaves and hibernate in winter, evergreens pause in their growth and perennial plants die down completely, sheltering their buds under the ground and not pushing up new shoots until the following spring.

LEFT: A sunny bench surrounded by succulents, including an imposing agave and pots of smaller succulent plants.

HARDINESS ZONES

How hardy a plant is depends on the lowest temperature it will have to endure. In the USA, where severe winters are common, plant hardiness zones (zones of consistent annual average minimum temperature) have been mapped out by the Arnold Arboretum of Harvard University.

❀ Zones are numbered and a plant might be described as 'Hardy to Zone 9'. This would mean it would survive an annual average minimum temperature of between 6° and 1°C (43° to 34°F). A similar map has been compiled for Europe.

ABOVE: *Frost can turn winter seed heads and stems into magically mysterious and attractive shapes with sugar icing coatings.*

Local climates

❀ Within each zone are areas with milder or more severe climates. Local conditions can vary considerably and altitude is an important factor. For every 100 m (330 ft) upwards, the temperature drops substantially. Unexpected frosts may kill the new shoots of plants that have survived a severe winter, while dormant and even hardy plants may be vulnerable to frost damage.

❀ Several things can make a difference to an individual garden. The climate in a city can be much warmer than the surrounding countryside, allowing more tender plants to be grown. Aspect is important, too, i.e. whether a garden is facing north or south, or whether it is at the top or bottom of a hill.

❀ South-facing slopes are much warmer than north-facing ones and will bring on growth early in spring. In a hollow, there is always a risk of frost. The stillness of the sheltered air contributes to the risk and what seems to be a sheltered corner of a garden can be far from sheltered in reality. If wind meets a solid wall, the compressed gusts have very high speeds and may damage plants.

LEFT: *Even without leaves, deciduous trees often have interesting forms. This Acer palmatum 'Oshio Beni' has leaves that turn spectacularly red before they drop.*

SUITING THE PLANT TO THE SOIL

GARDEN soil should be a fertile, well-drained loam, able to retain moisture. Soils have their own characteristics, which will suit some plants but not others. Some are mainly clay and rich in nutrients but slow to warm up in spring; others may be sandy and easily worked but water and nutrients will drain away very quickly; others may be too acidic for most plants.

❀ Soils can be improved enormously by adding organic matter but their basic type will remain the same. You will find it much easier to grow plants suited to the particular soil in your garden rather than trying to alter the soil fundamentally to suit particular plants you want to grow.

THE IDEAL SOIL

THE ideal soil is made up of 22 per cent water, 20 per cent sand, 20 per cent air, 15 per cent silt, 10 per cent clay, 8 per cent 'unavailable' water (that is, water trapped within the soil that the plant cannot use) and 5 per cent organic matter. Soil texture is how the soil feels when you handle it. This is due to the basic rock the soil is made of and cannot be altered. Soil structure is how the particles are held together in the soil. This influences whether the plant can get at the air, water and nutrients in the soil. It can be improved by adding organic matter, ensuring good drainage and digging in autumn to allow the breakdown of clods in heavy soils during winter. It is surprising how much difference adding organic matter can make to almost any soil.

Clay soil

Clay soils feel cold and heavy and can be moulded in the fingers. They are often very fertile but they are also heavy and may become waterlogged. They are slow to warm up in spring and may become very compacted when wet and covered with a cap or crust, which reduces the air available to roots and seeds. Plants from hot, dry areas are very unhappy in clay unless it has been much improved with sand, gravel and organic matter. Plants that grow well in clay include day lilies (Hemerocallis), roses, astilbes and peonies.

Sandy soil

Light, free-draining and easily worked, sandy soil warms up quickly in spring, giving plants a good start. Its disadvantages are that water drains through too easily and minerals can leach out quickly. Mediterranean plants and many herbs grow well in sandy soil.

Peaty soil

Very dark brown and often acidic, peaty soil is not very fertile and often poorly drained. Rhododendrons and heathers grow well in it.

Silty soil

This feels silky to the touch but not sticky and you can mould it in your fingers to some extent. It is moderately fertile and holds less water than clay soils but is easily compacted and can acquire a hard cap, which prevents both water and air from getting through to the plant's roots.

clay soil

sandy soil

peaty soil

silty soil

ABOVE: *Many woodland plants prefer a peaty or acid soil. Here, rhododendrons are growing with other acid-loving plants to make a pretty woodland scene.*

ABOVE: *Clay lovers include* Astilbe, Zantedeschia, Lychnis, *evening primroses* (Oenothera), *day lilies* (Hemerocallis) *and foxgloves* (Digitalis), *all of which are thriving in this garden.*

ACIDITY AND ALKALINITY

ACIDITY and alkalinity are important when considering what to grow. They are measured on a pH scale numbered 1–14. Acidic soils have a pH value below 7; neutral soils are pH 7 and alkaline pH value is above 7. Adding lime helps reduce acidity, while incorporating organic matter such as compost and manure will lower alkalinity to a certain extent.

❀ However, it is better to select plants that will thrive on the existing soil. Changing the pH radically is very difficult. Many plants prefer neutral to slightly acidic soils, others prefer acidic conditions and hate any alkalinity.

❀ Plants that like acidity are called calcifuges, those that like alkalinity are called calcicoles. Many plants, however, are happy with a neutral soil verging on the acidic or alkaline.

❀ Acid-lovers include heathers (*Calluna* and *Erica*), rhododendrons and camellias. A soil-testing kit will test your soil for acidity/alkalinity in different parts of your garden. It is well worth doing this to save your plants from succumbing to soils they are not suited for.

HELPFUL SYMBOLS

THE following symbols are widely used to indicate the sun and shade requirements of individual plants, their hardiness rating and how large they will grow.

Sun/shade requirements

Sun	☼
Sun or partial shade	◑
Shade	●

Frost tender

Half-hardy	❆	- Can withstand temperatures down to 0°C (32°F).
Frost-hardy	❆❆	- Can withstand temperatures down to -5°C (23°F).
Fully hardy	❆❆❆	- Can withstand temperatures down to -15°C (5°F).

Size

Typical height
Typical spread
Typical height and spread

10ft-3m

10ft-3m

LEFT: *The camellia is an evergreen shrub that produces spectacularly beautiful red, pink or white flowers.*

SOME PLANTS FOR PARTICULAR PLACES

THE following suggestions may help you to choose plants for some of the trickier places in your garden. No garden is exactly the same and plants themselves can be curiously reluctant to grow where you think they ought to, so a certain amount of experimenting with your own garden will be necessary.

PLANTS FOR ACIDIC SOILS

Many plants will grow on moderately acidic soil but few will thrive on very acidic soils, which are infertile. Many acid-loving plants are woodland in origin and many of the following plants will grow well in partial shade.

❀ If you do not have an acidic soil but would like to grow some of these plants, you can plant them in peat beds or containers filled with ericaceous compost.

Azalea
❀ See Rhododendron.

Bottlebrush (Callistemon)
❀ These shrubs have flowers that look just like bottlebrushes. They come from Australasia and need a mild climate and a sheltered site. *Callistemon salignus* has white flowers; *C. citrinus* 'Splendens' has brilliant red flowers and is probably the most hardy.

RIGHT: *The delicate sky blue bloom of the Himalayan blue poppy (Meconopsis betonicifolia) needs a cool climate in which to flourish.*

Scotch heather, ling (Calluna)
❀ This very attractive ground cover shrub is best grown in large masses, together with ericas. It also associates well with azaleas.

Camellia
❀ Extremely beautiful evergreen shrubs with shiny, leathery leaves and perfectly shaped red, pink or white flowers, camellias do well in large containers or can be fan-trained on sheltered walls. Camellias may grow to 3 m (10 ft). *Camellia. x williamsii* 'Donation' is one of the most popular with clear pink flowers, which do not go brown as they die.

Bell heather (Erica)
❀ This attractive ground cover plant is good grown in large masses near woodland and in association with calluna. Several species are available.

Dog's tooth violet (Erythronium)
❀ This is not really a violet at all but a bulb that produces charming little pagoda-shaped flowers in spring. Keep it moist and cool with plenty of well-rotted compost and it will spread into sizeable clumps.

RIGHT: *This beautiful ornamental rhododendron produces its mauve flowers during the months of spring.*

Gentiana sino-ornata

❀ Gentians need deep, acidic soil that never dries out and never becomes waterlogged. Given the right conditions, they will spread into grassy mats.

Lace-cap hydrangea
(Hydrangea macrophylla)

❀ These hydrangeas look well in natural settings such as light woodland, where they are sheltered from frost damage. They can become large and spreading. *Hydrangea macrophylla* 'Whitewave' and *H. m.* 'Bluewave' are recommended varieties. Blue flowers will turn pink if the soil is slightly alkaline.

Tiger lily (Lilium tigrinum)

❀ All lilies are grown from bulbs. Lilies like full sun, good drainage and lime-free soil. Plant several together for a strong effect in a mixed border.

ABOVE: *The bright pink spires of lupins look splendid in combination with a variegated cornus and deep blue columbines.*

Lupins (Lupinus)

❀ Lupins are hardy perennials with spectacular spikes of many coloured pea-type flowers in summer. They are short-term perennials but will often seed themselves and add height and excitement when grown in swathes in large borders from spring to early summer.

Magnolia

❀ This is a stately tree with spectacular fragrant flowers. Use magnolias as specimen trees or among other trees and shrubs. They like well-drained lime-free soils in sun or partial shade. *Magnolia grandiflora* is evergreen and suitable only for very mild climatic areas. *M. stellata* is a well-loved, exceptionally beautiful small tree or large shrub with star-like white flowers in early spring. Summer-flowering magnolias include *M. conspicua* (pure white, cup-shaped flowers) and *M. wilsonii* (hanging white flowers with crimson stamens).

Himalayan blue poppy
(Meconopsis betonicifolia)

❀ This beautiful blue poppy needs coolness and moisture. It may bloom just once after several years and then die. Where it has the right conditions, however, it may bloom for many years.

Primula

❀ Many primulas enjoy acidic soils. The common primrose (*Primula vulgaris*) is suitable for a woodland or wild flower garden. Most primulas need moisture.

Rhododendron

❀ This group, which includes large-flowered hybrids, dwarf hybrids, low-growing species and azaleas, is among the most beautiful of the spring-flowering shrubs. Low-growing species relate well to heathers, tall ones make imposing freestanding feature shrubs or may be planted in informal woodland walks.

Flame flower (Tropaeolum speciosum)

❀ A hardy, climbing form of nasturtium with the brightest scarlet flowers, it grows well on a north- or east-facing wall and contrasts well clambering up the dark green of a yew hedge.

PLANTS FOR HEAVY CLAY SOILS

There is a wide range of plants suitable for clay soils and you will have a much more successful garden if you stick to growing these. Plants suited to light sandy soils, for example pinks and silvery-leaved plants, will simply sicken and die in clay soil.

Michaelmas daisy (Aster)

❀ Hardy perennials with large daisy flowers in shades of pink and purple, these flower in late summer to autumn and are useful for damp soils.

Crocosmia

❀ These hardy perennials with strap-like leaves and brilliantly coloured red, orange or yellow flowers in summer need a sheltered site and good drainage.

Foxglove (Digitalis purpurea)

❀ The foxglove has tall spikes of trumpet-shaped purple or white flowers. It grows well in woodland and likes a moisture-retentive soil.

Helenium

❀ This is another hardy perennial with a daisy flower that will grow well in any garden soil, even if not well drained. The flowers appear in late summer and autumn in strong yellows and reds.

Day lily (Hemerocallis)

❀ The strap-like leaves of this hardy perennial form thick, elegantly arched clumps. The flowers vary from yellow to cream and brick red. They like moisture-retentive soil and will grow by the edges of pools.

ABOVE: *Although strictly speaking a wild flower, forget-me-not does well as a self-seeding ground-cover plant.*

Bergamot, bee balm, oswego tea (Monarda didyma)

❀ This has shock-headed flowers in pinks and purples, flowering in late summer to autumn. It likes moist, fertile soil.

Forget-me-not (Myosotis)

❀ A hardy biennial with sky-blue flowers that will seed itself, this likes moist, fertile, well-drained soil.

PLANTS FOR DRY SHADE

Very dry, very shady places in the garden are hard for most plants to cope with. A few, however, will thrive.

Anemone x hybrida

❀ This hardy autumn-flowering anemone grows to 1.2–1.5 m (4–5 ft) and each plant has many pink or white flowers and is useful in borders, *Anemone*. 'Honorine Jobert' is very effective and has single white flowers.

Cyclamen, sow bread

❀ Beautiful little tuberous relatives of indoor cyclamen, these are perfectly hardy and will grow well under trees. The flowers may be white or shades of pink and may be borne at almost any time of year, depending on the species. The leaves are heart shaped, often with silver markings. *Cyclamen coum* flowers in winter or early spring; *C. hederifolium* (syn. *C. neapolitanum*) flowers mid- to late autumn, before the leaves appear;

LEFT: *The day lily has leaves which grow in arched clumps and flowers in mid-summer.*

C. purpurascens flowers in mid- to late summer and prefers alkaline soil; *C. repandum* flowers in mid- to late spring. They may self-seed and turn up in unexpected places.

Barrenwort, bishop's hat (Epimedium)

This hardy perennial has wiry stems and delicate foliage with bronze tints in spring and colours well in autumn. The small cup-and-saucer flowers in white, pink, red, purple, beige or yellow are borne in spring to early summer in racemes. Its height and spread are around 20–30 cm (8–12 in). *Epimedium grandiflorum* 'Crimson Beauty' is deciduous; *E. pubigerum* is evergreen with creamy white flowers; *E. x warleyense* has yellow flowers.

Spurge (Euphorbia)

This genus includes annuals, biennials, evergreen and herbaceous plants. Some suit dry shady places. *Euphorbia amygdaloides* (wood spurge) has dark green leaves and greenish-yellow flowers; *E. myrsinites* is ever-green with succulent blue-green leaves and bright greenish-yellow flowers; *E. characias* subsp. *wulfenii* is a tall architectural plant with grey-green leaves and yellow-green flowers.

Fuchsia magellanica

This hardy fuchsia is an upright shrub, which produces small elegant pendant flowers of deep red and purple all summer. Once well settled in, it will put up with dry soil.

Dead-nettle (Lamium)

This low, ground-covering plant is grown mainly for its foliage but the flowers are worthwhile, too. It can be invasive if grown in moist soils but used in light woodland or among shrubs it is pretty and effective. *L. maculatum* is a low-growing perennial, with silver markings on the leaves. In summer it bears spikes of white or pink flowers.

PLANTS FOR DENSE SHADE

Some gardens, particularly those in towns and cities, have areas of dense shade, which get little sun and are shaded even more by overhanging trees and tall walls. Basement areas, courtyards and corners of larger gardens often pose problems in this way. Few plants will cope well under these conditions so you need to make the most of those that will.

Laurel (Aucuba japonica)

This large 1.5 m (5 ft) shrub has shiny leaves and bright red berries. The leaves of the dark green form shine like mirrors in the sun but the variegated form can bring a sunny feeling to a dark corner. It likes moisture-retentive soil but will grow in dry shade.

Privet (Ligustrum)

Deciduous or evergreen, *Ligustrum* is often used for hedging but can make pretty small trees. *L. ovalifolium* has golden and silver variegated forms and will tolerate deep shade; *L. lucidum* has some striking variegated varieties.

ABOVE: *Barrenwort comes in many colours, including white, pink and yellow, and flowers in the spring or early summer.*

ABOVE: *Once established, Fuschia magellanica can survive in dry soil, producing its pendant flowers in the summer.*

UNDERSTANDING PLANT CHARACTERISTICS

❦

The different ways in which plants have evolved is a fascinating subject in its own right. Understanding the origins and different characteristics of the various main groups of plants is helpful to all gardeners. Conifers are among the oldest plants; flowering plants appeared much later. Flowers themselves are amazingly diverse. Many have evolved to attract various creatures in very specific ways to ensure fertilisation. Others produce millions of tiny seeds that are dispersed by the wind. When you are buying and growing particular flowers, shrubs and trees for the garden, it is useful to have such background knowledge.

THE PLANT KINGDOM

ALL plants are represented in the plant kingdom, which is divided into two main groups and then sub-divided according to shared botanical characteristics, resulting in something rather like a family tree.

❀ Vascular plants have conductive tissue, which circulates water and nutrients. They come under two main divisions – non-flowering seed bearers (gymnosperms) and flowering seed-bearers (angiosperms). Non-vascular plants are those like mosses, liverworts, ferns and horsetails, which do not have conductive tissue and rely on a moist environment to survive. They are widespread in the wild but often not very interesting in appearance.

❀ Gymnosperms include the conifers, which bear seed on their cones. Many, such as yew and cedar, are very tolerant of heat, cold and drought and are therefore extremely useful in gardens.

❀ Angiosperms or flowering plants produce seed in an ovary. There are 300 families of flowering plants and 250,000 species. They may be monocotyledons or dicotyledons according to their seed leaves (cotyledons) and other differences in their anatomy and growth patterns.

❀ Monocots have a single seed leaf, leaves with veins that run along their length, slender non-woody stems and flower parts arranged in threes. They include grasses, bamboos and lilies. Dicots have two seed leaves, a network of veins on their leaves, thick, woody stems and flower parts arranged in multiples of 4, 5, 7 or more.

Family, genus, species

❀ The basic division of all higher plants is the family. All flowering plants are grouped into families based purely on the structure of their flowers. The plants in a particular family may all be clearly related, for example orchids (Orchidaceae), or one family may contain numerous and very diverse plants such as the Rosaceae family, which includes trees, shrubs and garden plants including roses, apples, strawberries, hawthorn and *Alchemilla*.

❀ Within the families, plants are categorised further into smaller groups, according to certain characteristics. Accordingly, they are given defining genus and species names, which are those used in the binomial system to identify plants in gardening encyclopedias and catalogues.

ABOVE: *A floribunda rose with large deep red flowers and a glorious scent, the epitome of what roses mean to gardeners.*

ABOVE: *Although they do not look like roses, the tiny little greeny-yellow flowers on the right of this picture belong to* Alchemilla mollis, *which is a member of the rose family, Rosaceae.*

ABOVE: *Conifers belong to the division of seed plants called gymnosperms, whose seeds are grown on the outside of the cone.*

THE LIFE CYCLE OF FLOWERING PLANTS

Flowering plants have evolved in many different ways to help them reproduce and survive in a range of habitats. Knowing how plants function and understanding their life cycles will make it much easier for you to grow them satisfactorily and work out an interesting planting plan in your own garden.

There are four steps in the life cycle of a flowering plant.

2. Growth
Seed leaves (cotyledons) appear first, then true leaves grow to build up food reserves for the young plants.

1. Germination
Once the seeds have fallen from a plant, they are stimulated into growth only when they have enough water, light and warmth. Seeds of some flowers such as alpines must experience a period of cold before they will germinate; others may require their seed coat to be nicked or 'sandpapered' to allow the seed to absorb water. In nature this happens when, for example, the seed travels through the digestive system of an animal or bird.

3. Maturity
The first leaves and stem rapidly develop into a mature shoot system. Their initial function is to gather energy from sunlight, essential for photosynthesis, which uses a complex series of chemical reactions to produce glucose from carbon dioxide. The initial growth of the leaves often slows down to allow the plant to put its energy into developing flowers. All the plant's energies are now focused into flowering and reproduction.

4. Seed formation
The flowers have been fertilised and develop into fruit containing seeds, which ripen and disperse.

Flowers

❀ Flowers have evolved innumerable forms to make pollination easy. Some are pollinated by insects, others by birds, wind or water. Insect-pollinated flowers are usually large, brightly coloured and heavily scented. Some are adapted to be pollinated by only one particular type of insect or bird. Wind-pollinated flowers are smaller and less conspicuous but there are millions on each plant.

❀ Most flowers contain both male and female reproductive organs. These may pollinate themselves or be pollinated by another plant of the same species. Other plants produce unisexual flowers. Monoecious plants have both male and female parts in separate flowers on the same plant.

❀ Dioecious plants are either all-male or all-female, so both male and female plants must be grown to produce fruit. A few species are polygamous with both bisexual and unisexual flowers.

❀ The parts of all flowers are borne in concentric circles (whorls) or spirals. The outer whorl or calyx protects the bud before the flower opens. It consists of sepals.

❀ The next whorl is the corolla, made up of the flower's petals. The next whorl is the male parts, the stamens, each consisting of a stalk (filament) and an anther containing pollen sacs.

❀ The inner ring is of female parts or 'carpels'. Each carpel has an ovary at its base, a stem (the style) and the stigma. For fertilisation to take place, a pollen grain must be deposited on the stigma.

Leaves

❀ The enormous diversity of leaves – their shapes, sizes, forms and the way they are arranged on different plants – enables the gardener to provide a huge variety of different effects in terms of texture and colour.

❀ Evergreen trees and shrubs are among the permanent features of a garden. Among them can be planted bulbs for spring and early summer interest, perennial plants for the summer and autumn border, alpines that brighten up the rock garden and climbers and roses that add magic to the scene.

❀ Understanding the contribution that these diverse plants can offer and the ways in which they may be intermingled to best effect is vital when designing a garden. The ground must always be prepared thoroughly before planting, to give the roots plenty of air, moisture and support.

ABOVE: *Buddleja is called the 'butterfly bush' because butterflies flock to feed on the nectar on warm summer days. Here, a red admiral enjoys the flower.*

BELOW: *Dahlias are among the most exotic-looking flowers, often looking as though they are made of paper. They owe their name to the 18th-century Swedish botanist, Anders Dahl.*

LEFT: *A fresh and charming spring border of* Crocus vernalis *(meaning 'of spring') and* Helleborus orientalis *(meaning 'from the East')*.

climbing hydrangea (*Hydrangea petiolaris*) displays this characteristic, as does ivy.

❀ Many low-growing plants like the periwinkle (*Vinca*) produce adventitious roots from nodes on the stems. This characteristic is used by gardeners to 'layer' or pin the stems down so that they root in the soil and produce new plants.

The whole picture

❀ A garden is made up of many different types of flowering and non-flowering plant, each of which contributes its special quality of height, permanence, texture, colour and form.

❀ Trees, shrubs, climbers, perennials, rock plants, annuals and biennials, bulbous plants and aquatics all have their place in a garden, as do the non-flowering plants such as grasses, bamboos and ferns. It is the way in which these types of plants are combined and contrasted that creates the most interesting sorts of garden.

❀ After the water and nutrients have entered the roots, they are drawn up through the plant by 'transpiration', which carries minerals to the leaves where oxygen and water evaporate through the stoma (pores) in the leaf surface. The movement of water allows the cells to remain swollen and upright. Plants soon wilt when they are short of water.

Modified shoots and roots

❀ Many plants have modified shoot and root systems. For example, tendrils of climbing plants are modified leaf stems, which have adapted for grasping supports – ivy is an example. In some plants a large part of the stem develops underground. These include bulbs, corms and tubers, which act as food stores.

❀ They produce baby bulbs called bulbils or offsets, which can be planted to produce new plants. Rhizomes are also stems but grow horizontally close to the soil surface, while 'adventitious' roots grow along the length of the rhizome. Bearded irises have slow-growing rhizomes and some bamboos have very fast and vigorous ones. Knowledge of such growth habits is important to avoid any plant becoming invasive.

❀ Adventitious roots are aerial roots rising from plant stems. They can cling to any surface and penetrate into tiny cracks and crevices, where they expand until they have securely anchored the plant. The

RIGHT: *The deep lilac flowers of* Vinca minor *(meaning 'small') can brighten up a woodland garden. It can be invasive when grown in a flowerbed.*

GROWING TREES AND SHRUBS

❦

Trees are woody perennial plants, usually with a single stem or trunk, and may grow to 90 m (300 ft) tall. Evergreen trees keep their leaves all year round while deciduous trees lose their leaves in winter. Shrubs are also woody perennial plants but produce several stems, which branch out from soil level. Most shrubs do not grow taller than 4.5–6 m (15–20 ft). Larger shrubs such as cotoneasters and lilacs (Syringa) can be grown as small trees. Subshrubs are plants that are woody only at the base, like Perovskia and Fuchsia, and which die back annually. They are often cultivated as herbaceous perennials. Trees and shrubs provide a good structural basis for a garden design and should be planted first before other plants.

TREES

BOTH conifers and deciduous trees grow in many different shapes and sizes. Conifers have distinctive shapes, regular branches and needle-shaped leaves. They can be useful both as specimen trees and as hedging.

❀ Deciduous trees have an extremely varied range of leaf shapes and sizes and many can be chosen for the interest afforded by their branch shapes or by their bark in winter when the leaves have fallen. Many of the birch family have peeling bark of interesting colours.

❀ Trees can introduce height and grandeur into the garden. They are also useful for introducing contrasts in size and form with other plants. A tall columnar tree can make a punctuation mark in the environment, whereas a spreading tree offers a more sheltering and protective view. Their leaves are often very decorative, and vary greatly in effect, depending on their size, shape, colour, surface texture and the way they are held on the twig. Poplar leaves are held so that they shake and rustle as they move in the wind, making a sound like the sea.

❀ Good specimen trees for large gardens include beech. All the beeches are beautiful, tall trees with smooth grey bark and fine foliage. The common beech tree is *Fagus sylvatica*, the weeping beech is *F. s. 'Pendula'* and *F. s. 'Roseomarginata'* is smaller than other beeches but still a big tree.

❀ Striking foliage colour can be important but try not to overdo it. Yellow can look marvellous, especially when placed where the leaves catch the low sun in the

LEFT: *Conifers of different varieties associate well together, as demonstrated by the tall shapes and varied colours of this mixed conifer border.*

LEFT: *The weeping pear (Pyrus salicifolia 'Pendula') is a small, highly decorative tree, which can be grown very successfully in a small garden. This one is underplanted with white tulips.*

Trees for the smaller garden

❁ For the smaller garden *Aesculus pavia*, one of the horse chestnut family, is smaller than most, with interesting flowers, and can be used as a large shrub. *Aamelanchier canadensis* is a small, pretty tree for any size of garden, eventually growing to 6.5 x 5 m (21 x 16 ft). It is covered in white blossom in spring and the foliage turns brilliant orange-red in autumn.

❁ Silver birches are delightful small trees, which can be planted individually or in close groups to form a coppice. The white-stemmed varieties are spectacular. *Betula papyrifera* (paper birch) has large leaves and peeling, paper-like bark. *Catalpa bignonioides* is the Indian bean tree and has attractive large leaves and panicles (heads of tiny stalked flowers) of white bell-shaped flowers with frilly edges and purple markings. It is exotic and makes a good shade tree.

morning or evening, but too much can be tiring to the eye. It is best to balance the foliage colours and not go for too many in a small area. Evergreens should be placed to create balance when the rest of the garden is dormant. Pines are best seen against the sky, where their interesting trunk shapes will stand out.

❁ Many of the maples are graceful and attractive. Snake bark varieties have good autumn foliage colour and very attractive trunks and branches.

BELOW: *Both dogwood and sumach, shown here in their autumn colours, can make shrubs and trees. Here they form a focal point on edge of a lawn.*

SHRUBS

Shrubs constitute an enormous range of plants suitable for gardens of any size and style. They are immensely varied in size, colour, shape and the interest they provide at different times of the year, and are therefore invaluable for giving shape and substance to the garden and for providing a framework.

❀ The smaller shrubs are good for bringing body, form and texture to summer flower borders. Larger ones can be used to create mystery or to screen off unsightly parts of the garden and many can be used as features in their own right. They are also useful hedging plants.

❀ Alternatively, use just one variety, such as box in a parterre, lavender to edge a rose bed or yew as a backcloth to a border. Use a mixture of varieties to create informal divisions or as a windbreak. Groups of compatible shrubs can be grown together to create a shrub walk or border, but bear in mind that a mass of unrelated shrubs can be most unsatisfactory, providing no unity or harmony at all.

❀ Choose a theme for your planting, perhaps a specific colour range or a choice of shrubs with similar shape or

habit. Acid-loving plants often relate well to one another and rhododendrons planted *en masse* can look spectacular. Two of the most useful contributions that shrubs can make to the garden are leaf colour and interesting berries in autumn.

Deciduous, evergreen or semi-evergreen

❀ A deciduous plant sheds its leaves every autumn, while an evergreen plant retains its leaves throughout the year. A shrub is described as semi-evergreen if it sheds some but not all of its leaves during the colder months. A plant's ability to retain its foliage varies according to the weather.

❀ During a mild winter, a normally deciduous shrub may keep some of its leaves, and in particularly harsh conditions an evergreen may shed more leaves than usual. Where the form of a shrub is an essential part of the framework of your garden, you should choose an evergreen unless you think the shrub's branches and twigs are interesting enough on their own to provide an imposing silhouette in winter.

RIGHT: Lavendula augustifolia, *the lavender shrub will look well edging a rose bed, but remember that a haphazard mixture of shrubs will lack harmony and look careless.*

Ornamental shrubs

❀ Shrubs that are important to the basic structure of the garden may also be highly ornamental with colourful, scented flowers, variegated foliage or attractive berries or stems in winter. But beware – it is easy to be seduced by individual plants and end up with too many varieties or simply too many shrubs, which will soon outgrow their welcome.

❀ Among things to consider are compatibility with the growing conditions, eventual height and spread and compatibility with other shrubs. Deciding where to place a shrub and, indeed, if it is really suitable for the garden at all, are important considerations.

Size and habit

❀ Shrubs differ enormously in size. There are mat-forming plants such as the creeping thymes, which will grow in a rock garden or between paving stones; there are small upright shrubs such as the lavenders, which can be used as part of a flower border or as low hedges, perhaps as a framework for a herb garden.

❀ There are also many silver shrubs, which contrast well in both habit and colour with pink, purple and red flowers. The curry plant (*Helichrysum italicum*) is good in this respect and easy to grow, as is *Artemesia* such as A. 'Powys Castle', with feathery leaves.

❀ Medium-sized shrubs can be used either as punctuation marks in a border or as features. The larger salvias make interesting medium-sized shrubs in

ABOVE: *An informal placing of an 'Easter Island' sculpture within a planting of a yellow azalea and the large leaves of a tree peony.*

milder areas. *Salvia microphylla* is an evergreen, which needs a sheltered spot and has deep crimson flowers at the tips of its branches right through summer into autumn. *Senecio laxifolius* is an easy-to-grow silver-leaved shrub with yellow daisy flowers. In sunny places it forms an upright bush 1 x 1 m (3 x 3 ft) and in shade it will scramble along the ground.

❀ The giants of the shrub world include smoke bush or burning bush (*Cotinus coggygria*), which can be used as a feature shrub or to divide up the garden. The cotoneasters are a versatile family, ranging from horizontal varieties, which look good stretching out in a sunny courtyard, to *Cotoneaster* 'Cornubia', which grows to 5 m (16 ft) tall and has the brightest of red berries in autumn.

LEFT: *A very pleasing combination of clipped, rounded shapes and contrasting spiky leaves in front of a tall, dark green clipped hedge.*

ABOVE: *Successful contrasts of foliage shape and colour can be seen in this shrub border, with the crinkled leaves of Swiss chard in the foreground.*

Features of interest

❀ The shapes, bark and stems of shrubs vary enormously, quite as much as their size. Some shrubs have a sprawling habit. They can be useful as ground cover but may look better trained up a wall. *Ceanothus prostratus* is one of these. It will form a mound of bright blue flowers in spring, but will take up less space if trained on a wall.

❀ The low-growing forms of willow (*Salix*) can be very pretty for rock gardens or for use by small pools. They have attractive foliage and catkins. A rounded form of shrub such as *Daphne collina*, an attractive dwarf, is ideal for a medium-sized rock garden, providing softness among the rocks. An arching form such as *Buddleja alternifolia* can provide a canopy over lower-growing plants at the back of a border.

Focal points

❀ Focal points or eye-catchers are important in the garden. Shrubs can do the job but they need to be of interest all year round. Many *Cornus* varieties make excellent feature plants, as do *Cotinus*, *Corylopsis* and hydrangeas.

❀ Phormiums have strong, strap-like leaves, giving a highly architectural, even tropical, effect. Yuccas, which grow to 2 m (7 ft), are useful for providing vertical interest and have elegant, creamy white flowers.

Links

❀ Shrubs are invaluable for providing links between one part of the garden and another, and between plants that otherwise do not relate to each other. They can mark an entrance to the house from the garden and, grown in groups or rows, they can flank a drive or a door. The shrubs chosen should be in sympathy with the style, scale and colour of the building.

❀ Evergreen shrubs are often chosen because they are continuously in leaf and are always good for a formal setting. Varied planting that includes deciduous shrubs, such as *Magnolia stellata* with its hundreds of white starry flowers, as well as evergreens will add interest in spring.

❀ Lilac (*Syringa*) is a good example of a plant to mingle with others because once its flowers are over it can look uninteresting and leggy. Spreading shrubs such as *Hydrangea quercifolia* can provide links between more upright plants.

Shrub borders

❀ Shrubs can be grown to great effect on their own in borders. Choose ones that will suit the soil and climate of your garden and provide a succession of colour and interest throughout the year if possible. Balance the shapes, heights and forms of the shrubs, and leave plenty of room for their ultimate spread.

❀ You can choose shrubs with interesting colour combinations or concentrate more on the textures. A border of mainly variegated shrubs with variations in the greens and yellows and the occasionally single colour to provide contrast should do well in a slightly shaded position.

❀ Evergreen and deciduous shrubs can be mixed together, provided you balance them well. Taller shrubs should be at the back, creeping ones at the front. Some shrubs will give months of interest while others tend to

mature and fade quickly. When planning the border, make sure the short-term shrubs are camouflaged by long-term ones. Fast-growing shrubs will probably need to be thinned out as the border matures.

❧ A larger shrubbery or shrub walk can be planted in grass. Here the shrubs should not be grouped closely as in a smaller border, but each should be given room to grow into its natural shape and still leave room for walking around it and standing back to admire it.

Shrubs in the mixed border

❧ Borders of herbaceous perennials only were popular at one time. Today it makes more sense to combine a framework of shrubs interplanted with a variety of herbaceous perennials to give all-year interest and a much more labour-saving border.

❧ Many shrubs act as ground cover, keeping down weeds and preventing moisture from evaporating. A mixed border can be planted next to a wall and can include wall-trained plants as a backdrop, as well as climbers.

❧ Other plants are positioned between the shrubs to present a balanced, colourful composition. It should be interesting from late winter to late autumn. In an island bed, shrubs can be planted with the tallest in the middle surrounded by other plants in clumps and drifts.

ABOVE: *A decorative wall forms the backdrop for a well-planted mixed border featuring roses, begonias, Achillea and Coreopsis.*

BELOW: *A low shrub border with great variety produced by the dark purple Berberis, variegated Euonymus, purple Salvia and pink-tipped Spiraea.*

TRAINING ROSES

❧

There are about 100 naturally occurring species roses and many natural hybrids growing in the wild. People have been growing roses in their gardens for over 2,000 years, however, and there are now thousands of cultivars, ranging from tiny ground cover roses to large shrubs and climbers, all of which have a part to play in modern garden design.

THE HISTORY OF ROSES

THE first garden roses probably occurred in the Middle East and spread via ancient Greece and Rome to the rest of Europe. These are the gallica, damask and alba roses. They are robust and highly scented but bloom only once a year. In the seventeenth century Dutch and French breeders crossed albas and damasks to produce large-headed roses with over 100 petals.

❀ In the 1780s merchant ships began to come home with roses from Chinese gardens, derived from two wild species – the 'giant' rose, a huge climber with big yellow flowers and *Rosa chinensis* found in the Ichang Gorge of the Yangtse river. Rose breeding between European and China roses has continued ever since and rose catalogues today include an enormous variety of rose types, both old and new.

ABOVE: *Roses and lavender always make a good combination, the lavender helping to conceal the bare 'legs' of many roses in the summer. This rose is called 'Cameo'.*

Rose groups

❀ Roses can be divided into several groups. Wild, or species, roses and their hybrids are large, arching shrubs flowering once only with single, five-petalled flowers in spring or midsummer. They have decorative hips in autumn and are useful for wild gardens.

❀ Old garden roses are best suited to informal gardens and include the gallica, damask and alba roses. Modern garden roses are best for formal rose gardens and include the patio and miniature roses.

❀ Climbing roses have long, strong shoots and large flowers borne singly or in small clusters. Some flower in summer only, but most will repeat-flower in autumn. Rambling roses are vigorous with long, flexible shoots, which bear small flowers in large clusters, mostly in early summer.

LEFT: *A seaside rose garden, heavily protected against the wind by a succession of clipped hedges and shrubs.*

TYPES OF GARDEN ROSE

The many thousands of species and cultivars available all fall within one of the categories below.

Old garden roses

Gallica: *Probably the oldest rose type. Usually forms small shrubs around 1.2 m (4 ft) high with strong, upright growth and many small bristly thorns. Flowers range from deep pink to purple and have a faint fragrance.*

Damask: *Also ancient but more elegant than the gallicas with open, arching branches, long elegant leaves and richly scented pink and purple flowers.*

Alba: *Closely related to the wild dog rose (Rosa canina). Large stately shrubs, once known as 'tree roses', with grey-green foliage and soft pink or white flowers.*

Centifolia (Provence): *Lax, open growth, big rounded leaves and globular flowers with a rich fragrance.*

China rose: *Much lighter in growth than European roses, with thin stems and sparse foliage giving them a twiggy look.*

Portland rose: *Short, upright habit; beautiful, strongly scented flowers with the invaluable ability to repeat-flower.*

Bourbon roses: *Similar to Portland rose but more lax and taller.*

Hybrid musk: *Vigorous, repeat-flowering shrub with abundant foliage and trusses of fragrant double flowers.*

Hybrid perpetual: *Vigorous, sometimes repeat-flowering; flowers borne singly or in threes in summer and autumn.*

Moss rose: *Lax shrub with furry, moss-like growth on stems and calyx. Flowers once only.*

Noisette rose: *Repeat-flowering with large clusters of flowers and a spicy scent.*

Sempervirens: *Semi-evergreen climber with numerous flowers in late summer.*

Tea rose: *Repeat-flowering shrubs and climbers with loose, usually double, fragrant flowers.*

BELOW: *An attractive mixed floribunda rose garden enclosed within a wall. The roses have been carefully chosen to grow to the same height and flower simultaneously.*

Modern garden roses

Large-flowered bush (hybrid tea): *Upright, repeat-flowering shrub with a single, large flower to a stem or in small clusters, summer to autumn.*

Cluster-flowered bush (floribunda): *Upright, repeat-flowering shrub with large sprays of flowers, summer to autumn.*

Dwarf cluster-flowered bush (patio rose): *Similar to cluster-flowered bush but with smaller, neater habit.*

Miniature rose: *Tiny counterpart of large- and cluster-flowered roses.*

Ground-cover rose: *Low-growing trailing or spreading rose.*

Modern shrub rose: *Varied group, ranging from low, mound-forming cultivars to spreading shrubs and giant, cluster-flowered bushes.*

Roses on their own

❧ The traditional way to grow roses is in a bed on their own. This is especially recommended for the large- and cluster-flowered bush roses, whose large and perfect flowers seem to ask for special attention.

❧ Avoid multi-coloured or undefined backgrounds. Most roses grown on their own look best against a smooth green setting – either a lawn or a clipped hedge as the background. They can also look attractive grown next to a paved, brick or gravel courtyard or path. The large- and cluster-flowered bushes become very bare and leggy, especially later in the year, and planted with only bare earth as the background can take on a somewhat moth-eaten look.

❧ The whole look of a bed devoted to roses can benefit from an edging of plants such as clipped box. Silver-grey plants seem particularly compatible with roses, and plants such as *Nepeta* and lavender also make very good low hedges that help to conceal the roses' bare 'legs', while providing a raised frame for the whole bed. It is important to choose plants that will last at least as long as the roses.

CHARACTERISTICS TO LOOK FOR

Roses offer a great variety of flower shapes and colours. Flowers may be single (4–7 petals), semi-double (8–14 petals), double (15–20 petals) or fully double (over 30 petals). As for shape, they may be flat, cupped, pointed, urn-shaped, rounded, rosette-shaped, quartered or pompon. About the only colour you cannot have in a rose is blue.

Hips

❧ Some roses will not set hips but the ones that do can provide clusters of really wonderful autumn colour. The rugosa roses with single or semi-double flowers have bright red decorative hips. Some of the species roses have yellow, red or purple hips.

Foliage

❧ Foliage is important where a rose is being used as a hedge or as a dividing feature in a garden. *Rugosa* roses have wrinkled, bright green foliage. *R. glauca* has feathery foliage of a dusky greenish-purple colour and deep red hips. Its arching habit makes it a most attractive plant as a specimen or as part of a shrub or large mixed border. The foliage of the large-flowered hybrids is often very attractive in spring when the young leaves are deep purple or bronze, although the leaves become sparser later in the year, but this can be concealed by other plants.

BELOW: Rosa 'New Dawn' is a popular silvery-pink climber, which flowers prolifically in summer. It can be grown up a wall or over a pergola or arch.

Roses in association with other plants

❀ In smaller gardens especially, it seems a pity to segregate roses or devote a part of the garden to one type of plant only. Roses are sociable and mingle well with smaller plants that do not compete for light or nutrients.

❀ Bedding plants are not usually very successful grown in association with roses, but many of the smaller geraniums, especially those with blue flowers such as G. 'Johnson's Blue', make very good bedfellows with roses, growing tall enough to conceal the angular lower rose stems in a mist of blue flowers. Clematis can be grown as companions for roses, too, adding colour during the summer when the roses are flowering less vigorously.

The formal rose garden

❀ In formal rose beds, as with any formal garden, it is best to restrict the colours to just a few in one bed. Too many different bright colours draw attention away from the beauty of the individual roses and confuse rather than please the eye. An all-white rose garden can be attractive.

❀ You can have a rose garden made up of different beds, each with its own colour combination: a bed of whites and pinks for example, another with shades of red, another with yellows and oranges. Yellows and whites can look good together, too.
A bed of mainly low-growing roses can be made

ABOVE: Shrub roses are among the most suitable for surrounding a seat. Their abundant flowers are prettily shaped and their strong scent wafts through the air.

more interesting by introducing a vertical element in the middle or at the four corners. Standard roses can be used in this way very effectively.

❀ Remember that not all roses will flower at exactly the same time, so mixing too many different varieties together may result in a patchy display. Cultivars also reach different heights, another thing to bear in mind at the early planning stage. Choose plants of the same height for a flat, open bed. A bed backed by a wall or hedge should have the taller roses at the back and the smaller ones in front.

RIGHT: 'Paul's Himalayan' musk, a deep pink with a glorious scent, and 'Blessings', a white floribunda, make a pleasing combination.

A more relaxed formality

✿ A formal rose garden can be created in a more relaxed way by dividing the plot into formal paths, by using water to enliven the space and covered seats to encourage the visitor to spend time there. Small rectangular pools with fountains can make the meeting places of paths delightful places to stop and rest.

✿ Standard roses or large- and cluster- flowered roses can be accompanied by climbers and ramblers growing over arches and arbours. Although such a garden has all the formality of the ancient Islamic gardens, the strict geometry is less rigid, with old roses and climbing roses creating height and a sense of freedom. Choose the most scented roses you can to add to the enchantment of this sort of garden.

Roses in containers

✿ Roses will grow quite well in containers, provided they are watered and given nutrients regularly – they require generous amounts or they will soon begin to suffer. They can brighten up a courtyard or patio and the tiny ones will even grow in window boxes.

✿ There are some excellent bushy plants in this category with prettily formed miniature flowers. Choose compact modern cultivars, which will form bushy mounds over the top of the pot.

✿ Miniature roses look charming in tubs or troughs. For pink, try R. 'Silver Tips', which is bushy with abundant, many-petalled flowers with a silver reverse, or R. 'Stars 'n' Stripes', a very pretty little rose with red and white striped flowers.

✿ For white you could use the ivory-coloured R. 'Easter Morning' and for something brighter, R. 'Little Flirt', a small, double orange-red flower with gold at the base and on the reverse of the petals. All these grow to about 30 cm (12 in).

✿ Patio roses are hardy, repeat well and are particularly useful for larger containers. They are larger and more robust than miniature roses but not as large as the cluster-flowered group. They have charming rosette-shaped flowers and a neat, bushy habit of growth. Ideal for sunny courtyards and patios, R. 'Bianco' has pure white pompon flowers in great profusion and bushy growth; R. 'Festival' has clusters of semi-double crimson-scarlet flowers with a silver reverse, R. 'Queen Mother' has semi-double soft pink flowers against glossy dark foliage and a slight scent.

BELOW: *Roses often look better in association with other plants than on their own, their angular stems softened by the form of many perennial plants. Here, Rosa 'English Miss' is grown with lavender and lavender-blue pansies.*

❁ Even quite vigorous climbers can be grown in large tubs or half-barrels and trained up a wall. Plant and train them as you would other roses but be sure to water and feed them regularly and replenish the topsoil, as it will be difficult to repot them. R. 'New Dawn' is one of the best and most vigorous modern climbers, with silvery-pink flowers in clusters, R. 'White Cockade' is a rather slow grower, which is advantageous in a pot. R. 'Danse de Feu' has repeating, semi-double brilliant orange-scarlet flowers and is suitable for a north-facing wall.

Roses as ground cover

❁ Most roses recommended as ground cover roses are not truly ground covering in the sense of plants that creep along the ground. They may be better described as dense, low-growing shrubs. They are usually very hardy and disease-free.

❁ Those that do spread along the ground form a dense carpet covered in flowers in summer. They are excellent for hiding the trunks of felled trees, manhole covers and other unsightly features you cannot actually remove. They can also scramble down a steep bank.

❁ There are several roses to choose from. Some cover the soil well but may grow too tall to look like a carpet. Others are too vigorous for a small garden, spreading rapidly and requiring constant control.

❁ The taller ones can be used to fill gaps in a mixed border where their healthy foliage and small flowers can blend in with many other plants. R. 'Max Graf' is prostrate with dense, glossy foliage and non-repeating single pink flowers with an apple scent. R. 'Raubritter' is a sprawling low mound with clusters of cupped pink flowers, which can be used to trail over a bank or low wall. R. 'Running Maid' has single pink flowers and a dense, low spreading growth that covers the ground well.

PLANTING CLIMBERS

Climbing plants are the dressing-up clothes of a garden. They provide great scope for the imagination and can bring colour to a garden in great profusion. They can be used to clothe unsightly buildings – from the standard garden shed to a concrete garage. Many are also sweetly scented and from their height on a support can waft fragrance through the whole garden. Some plants are not true climbers but can be trained up a wall, producing a curtain of flowers or berries. For example, the red berries of Pyracantha are a fantastic sight in autumn and the bright blue flowers of Ceanothus will cover a wall in spring or summer.

SOME POSSIBILITIES

SOME plants, like the beautiful single yellow rose 'Mermaid', are vigorous and will cover a whole wall or, like 'Kifsgate' with its profusion of tiny white flowers, will climb to the top of the tallest tree. These are not for small gardens. The stately wisterias, brilliant red Virginia creeper and *Hydrangea petiolaris*, with long-lasting flowers, will also cover a large expanse of wall. The large-flowered clematises will gently creep through the branches of supporting shrubs to produce wonderful large, colourful flowers in summer. They are then cut back in spring the following year.

Climbing methods

❀ Climbers have adapted in many different ways to raise themselves up towards the light. Some, such as the ivies (*Hedera*), are self-clinging and will attach themselves to their supports by aerial or 'adventitious' roots. Others, like Virginia creeper (*Parthenocissus quinquefolia*), adhere by tendrils. They cling to walls and tree trunks, needing no other support. Twining species all need permanent support.

❀ A few climbers attach themselves by curling leaf stalks. Others, like sweet peas (*Lathyrus odorata*) use tendrils. Passion flowers twine their axillary shoots around supports, while vines use terminal shoots.

❀ *Bougainvillea* species and jasmines produce long, arching stems, which need to be tied into their supports. Some species have hooked thorns to help them scramble through host plants. Blackberries are notoriously difficult to remove because of their ability to cling in this way.

ABOVE: *Virginia creeper* (Parthenocissus tricuspidata) *will cover a large wall and has leaves that turn a truly spectacular deep rich crimson colour in the autumn.*

Climbers on buildings

❀ Use plants to emphasise the good elements of a building. If it is built of pleasant materials and architecturally pleasing, you may want to keep to low climbers that will help anchor the house to the ground without concealing its shape or any architectural detailing. A boring-looking building, however, can be made more attractive by allowing climbers to cover the walls.

❀ *Actinidia kolomikta* has decorative variegated green and pink leaves with white tips and will cover red brick satisfactorily. Golden or yellow foliage plants such as *Humulus lupulus* 'Aureus' will complement red brick. A pale-coloured wall makes an effective background for deep red blooms such as *Rosa* 'Climbing Ena Harkness'.

ABOVE: *There are many beautiful and scented honeysuckles and this one, Lonicera 'Graham Thomas', is slightly unusual, with pale lemon-yellow flowers.*

Climbers for low walls and fences

❀ Low walls can be heightened by growing climbers up trellis. This will conceal unwanted views and create more privacy. If you are going to grow a vigorous climber, remember they can become very bulky and heavy so you will need a strong fence and the most robust form of trellis, otherwise the climber will pull it all down in a year or two.

❀ If you want to cover a fence quickly, use a quick-growing ivy. Some grow particularly fast and create an attractive 'curtain' of green. *Hedera canariensis* is a vigorous climber with large, glossy leaves. *H. c. algeriensis* has yellow-green leaves on smooth wine-red stalks. *Hedera* 'Dentata Variegata' has light-green leaves, mottled grey-green with broad, cream-white margins. Remember, however, that the quicker growing a climber is, the more likely it is to get out of hand and you will probably have a lot of cutting back to do eventually.

BELOW: *Hedera helix 'Goldheart' is an attractive variegated ivy with a very yellow centre to the leaf. It can be used to hide a garden shed, as it does here very successfully.*

Sun lovers

❀ Many climbers love the sun. Clematis love to have their flowers in the sun and their roots well shaded. If on a sunny wall, they can be shaded by a shrubby plant in front of them or by a large slab of stone laid above their roots.

❀ Many roses prefer full sun, although some will tolerate a little shade. In sheltered areas and very often in cities, where the temperature is several degrees warmer than in the surrounding countryside, you can often grow exotic climbers.

❀ The bright yellow *Fremontodendron californicum* really catches the eye. *Eccremocarpus scaber* has red tubular flowers with yellow shading and will scramble to a good height. The common passion flower (*Passiflora caerulea*), with its jellyfish-like flowers, looks spectacular in a sheltered spot. Other passion flowers are tender and need to be grown in a greenhouse.

Climbers for north walls

❀ There are several plants that will tolerate north-facing walls, including *Hydrangea petiolaris*, the pretty, white repeat-flowering rose 'Madame Alfred Carrière' and the deep black-red rose 'Guinée', which has a delicious perfume and dark green leaves on a well-branched stem.

❀ For shady and north-facing walls or walls exposed to cold winds, use vigorous, hardy climbers. Many ivies are good for this. If the wall is heavily shaded, use green-leaved varieties; you can use variegated or yellow leaves where there is no danger of frost damage. Some honeysuckles will do well in these conditions, too.

ABOVE: *This is an exciting combination of* Clematis tangutica *and* Clematis 'Perle d'Azur', *grown on either side of a sky-blue door.*

BELOW: *This absolutely enchanting rose 'Phyllis Bide', with chameleon-like flowers of pale to deep pink and masses of small blooms, looks particularly good against a brick wall.*

Climbers for pillars

❀ Freestanding supports such as pillars and even old tree trunks allow climbing plants to be viewed in the round and contribute a strong visual and stylistic element to the garden. The plants must therefore be carefully chosen and trained.

❀ Depending on the materials and design of the support, the climber may be formal and disciplined, or cottage-garden style and rambling. Metal obelisks look good in a formal rose or herb garden and their shape makes them easy to train climbers on to. They must be strong enough to bear what may be the surprisingly heavy weight of the climber chosen. Small obelisks are particularly good for summer-flowering clematis, sweet peas and honeysuckles.

❀ Pillars add a strong vertical element to a mixed herb border. A pillar can also be used as a focal point or at the end of an axis, at the corners of a border or at the top of steps where the garden level changes.

❀ A series of pillars alongside a path can be linked by rope swags with the climbers trained along them. Roses are probably the most popular climbers to use for this. A stout post with wire mesh fixed around it will provide good tying-in support for many climbers. If the supports you are using are particularly attractive, why not choose deciduous climbing plants such as the golden hop (*Humulus lupulus* 'Aureus'), together with the dusky summer-flowering *Clematis* 'Madame Julia Correvon'? Even when both plants are cut back, the support will still be a feature on its own.

Climbers for arbours

❀ An arbour covered with climbing plants provides privacy, a sense of relaxation and opportunities for growing spectacular climbing plants and letting them grow to their full potential. Arbours are used most in the summer, seldom in winter, so you can concentrate on summer-flowering climbers. Choose those that have fragrant flowers, as they will ensure that the arbour becomes a particularly enchanted and sweetly scented place, particularly in the early mornings and the evenings.

❀ *Rosa* 'Félicité Perpétue' has enormous heads of creamy-white double pompon flowers, whose petals are sometimes tipped with red. Its small, dark leaves are plum-red when young. It is vigorous and shoots freely from the base.

ABOVE: *Sweet peas like a rich, deep loam and plenty of water. They will then flower copiously up any support. This home-made bamboo wigwam is an excellent way of allowing the flowers support and plenty of sunlight.*

❀ If you prefer pink for your arbour, the old-fashioned, rich pink flowers of R. 'Bantry Bay' are highly decorative and a great favourite. Many honeysuckles have a glorious scent and very pretty flowers. *Lonicera* x *americana*, for example, has fragrant pink and cream flowers from summer to autumn. It is evergreen and needs a sheltered place in either sun or shade; L. 'Donald Waterer' has red and cream fragrant flowers in summer, followed by red berries.

foliage. All are twining, woody and deciduous. They climb vigorously and need plenty of room to look their best. A pergola gives them all this.

✿ Most wisterias are hardy but prefer a sunny, sheltered position. It is important to prune them correctly to get them to flower well. *Wisteria floribunda* has fragrant, violet-blue flowers; *W. f.* 'Alba' has white flowers tinged with lilac; *W. x formosa* 'Kokkuryu' is strongly fragrant with double purple flowers; *W. sinensis* is fast growing and vigorous with dense trails of slightly fragrant violet-blue flowers.

Pergolas

✿ Pergolas are often built over a patio near the house or in a prominent situation over a path that can be seen from the house. Because of this it is sensible to try and choose climbers that will retain some attraction in winter. Of course, if the structure itself is attractive enough, this is not always necessary.

✿ Make sure the cross beams on the pergola are high enough to allow the flowers to trail without touching the heads of people walking underneath.

✿ Wisteria varieties, although their flowering season is short, are among the most beautiful of climbers, and a pergola gives them the opportunity to hang their great trailing flowers elegantly and to show off their feathery

Growing climbers through supporting plants

✿ Many climbers will grow happily through other plants, although it is important to choose climbers that are not too vigorous for their hosts and that will not become so entangled in them that you cannot prune them effectively. It is important, too, to choose host plants that are not so vigorous that you will need to prune them while the climber is in flower.

BELOW: *This grapevine (Vitis vinifera) obviously makes the most of the sun reaching the small balcony and associates well with the pale pink and red pelargoniums peeping through the ironwork.*

LEFT: *Wisteria is perhaps the monarch of climbing plants with its enormous hanging heads of purple pea flowers. Here,* Wisteria sinensis *softens a red brick house and patio.*

✾ Other vigorous spring-flowering clematis such as C. *montana* can also be allowed to grow naturally; *C. m.* 'Mayleen' is an attractive variety with very dark leaves and single pink flowers smelling of vanilla. Another attractive *montana* type is C. *chrysocoma*, with large single white flowers tumbling in waves down its dark green leaves.

✾ In summer *Rosa* 'Kifsgate' (a famous one grows in the garden at Kifsgate in Gloucestershire) will reach right up into a very tall tree. *R.* 'Albertine' is another vigorous and much-loved rose that enjoys being allowed to grow to its full potential on a large pergola. *Vitis coignetiae* is one of the vine family with enormous, velvety leaves that will grow all along a pergola, offering shade. The Virginia creeper (*Parthenocissus quinquefolia*) really needs a large area to make the most of its hanging curtains of brightest red.

Climbers in small gardens

✾ For small gardens choose climbers that will not grow too tall. These can be grown in containers and will lend height to groups of other container plants. You can make a tripod out of bamboo canes, or alternatively you can buy small metal or cane obelisks to train the climbers up.

✾ Many clematis will grow well in pots. They can be used to brighten dull parts of a concrete yard area or along the walls of buildings. It is important to choose clematis with this in mind. C. *alpina* and C. *macropetala* can be grown in pots but their flowering period is limited to spring.

✾ Early, large-flowered clematis will flower in early summer. Good ones include C. 'Miss Bateman' (white with green anthers) and C. 'Pink Champagne'. Both are compact and ideal for training in pots. Slightly later-flowering clematis include C. 'Nelly Moser' (pink and white stripes) and C. 'The President' (deep purple and red).

✾ The grapevine (*Vitis vinifera*) is another wonderful plant to grow over a patio and the bunches of grapes will hang down invitingly.

✾ Climbers to use with shrubs include the large, summer-flowering clematises that are cut nearly down to ground level each year. *Clematis viticella* varieties can be grown through medium-sized shrubs. *C. v.* 'Polish Spirit' has rich purple flowers, which associate well with golden shrubs such as *Choisya ternata* 'Sundance' and silver-leaved shrubs such as *Senecio laxifolius*.

Climbers in large gardens

✾ In a large garden where pergolas can be long and wide and space is not restricted, you can choose the most vigorous and spectacular climbers. The early spring-flowering evergreen, *Clematis armandii*, will cover long lengths of wall or fence, looking like snowdrifts at a time when little else is in flower.

CLIPPING PLANTS

Any evergreen plants can be trained or clipped to create garden architecture such as hedges and arches. They can also be used to create living garden sculpture. Topiary, or the training and pruning of trees and shrubs in this way, has been popular since Roman times and many traditional gardens in Europe, particularly in France, Italy, Portugal and Spain, depend largely on clipped evergreen trees and shrubs for their planting. Colour is rarely used, except perhaps for the ubiquitous deep red rose used around front doors.

TIPS AND TECHNIQUES

TRAINING and clipping is suitable only on plants that have small leaves growing close together so that they will keep a clear shape. The technique offers scope for special effects, both in large gardens and the very tiniest of plots. In fact the modern garden relies more and more on such plants to create a strong skeleton to the garden and the architectural effects they can achieve can be used effectively to complement geometric modern buildings.

🌺 Most hedging and clipping is carried out in yew or box because these respond particularly well to the technique and grow into close shapes with good definition. You can use many other evergreen shrubs, however. For example, the Portuguese laurel (*Aucuba japonica*) can be clipped into an imposing hedge whose large and shiny dark green leaves catch the sunlight like mirrors. The shrubby honeysuckles such as *Lonicera nitida* also clip well; the variety 'Baggesen's Gold' is much more interesting than the ordinary green one.

BELOW: *This elaborate garden includes a box parterre, clipped yews and roses of one variety only, giving the impression of unity and variety at the same time.*

ABOVE: *The garden sculptures in this cottage garden provide a dramatic contrast to the rest of the plants, as well as forming a striking centrepiece at the front of the house.*

❀ As always, hedges should be of a height in keeping with the size of the garden, and trees should be shaped in a way that relates to their surroundings. It is nearly always a mistake to have many highly elaborate topiary sculptures because they will conflict with each other and diminish other aspects of the garden.

❀ Simple, rounded umbrella shapes can look good in association with each other and clipped ball shapes can look effective when repeated in pairs or multiples in a larger garden.

❀ The common yew (*Taxus baccata*) grows much faster than is often supposed if fed and watered generously. Box is slower growing but will still mature acceptably if cared for in the same way. The common yew is good for hedges, whereas Irish yew (*Taxus baccata* 'Fastigiata') has upwardly pointing branches and is therefore better if you want a narrow silhouette.

Maintenance

❀ If you are going to clip and train many shrubs in your garden, bear in mind that they require constant maintenance. Clipped evergreen shrubs should be fed with slow-release fertiliser in spring and watered during dry spells until the plants are well established – about two or three years. You will have to clip a formal hedge at least twice a year in order for it to maintain its shape.

❀ Hedges are mostly cut with shears or an electric trimmer. Use a straight edge or garden line as a guide. Informal hedges need regular pruning to remove untidy growth; cut back as far as you think is necessary. Flowering and fruiting hedges should be pruned only at the appropriate season, which will vary according to the species. Use secateurs to avoid damage to leaves, which would look unsightly.

❀ Old, neglected topiaries do not always need to be grubbed up to start again. They can sometimes be renovated. Hornbeam (*Carpinus*), honeysuckle (*Lonicera*) and privet (*Ligustrum*) will all respond well to pruning if they have become overgrown. Yew, in particular, can be pruned back hard and will sprout from what looks like dead wood. It is best to clip in stages over three years, cutting only one side of the plant at a time.

ABOVE: *The glowing red stems of Cornus alba are best planted in a group, where their massed branches can be seen in sunlight during the winter months.*

CLIPPED PATTERNS

PLANTS have been used since time immemorial to create patterns on the ground. Mazes were among the earliest patterns. The parterre became popular in France during the seventeenth century. They were often so complicated they became known as *parterres de broderie* or embroidered parterres. They were designed to be seen from first-floor windows or from raised terraces. In level gardens, a mount was often built with a little building on top from which to look down on the pattern.

❀ The knot is a complicated parterre pattern, which uses a continuous line of planting. This is usually made with box but other plants can be used such as marjoram, rue, lavender, rosemary, santolina or germander. You can use one plant interlaced with another, contrasting the silver foliage of santolina, for example, with the dark green of rosemary or box.

❀ A parterre does not interlace in a continuous line and is therefore easier to design and maintain. It is made up of separate patterns, often squares, and the middle is traditionally filled with coloured sands and gravels or flowers.

❀ Such designs can provide a unified design for spaces of almost any size. They are not too difficult to maintain and clip if the area is quite small. Coloured recycled glass beads are sometimes used instead of gravel. Bedding plants can also provide a brave show of colour. Perennial flowers such as small shrub roses mingled with foxgloves (*Digitalis*) or a mixture of herbs can be used inside the patterns.

HEDGES

WHEN choosing plants for hedging you need to choose the variety carefully for the particular place you have in mind. Yew can be burnt by the wind when young and will not tolerate boggy ground, while some conifers such as cypresses cannot regenerate from old wood so cannot be cut right back if they become too large. *Thuja* and *Lonicera* both grow fast and require much more clipping than yew.

❀ The best deciduous plants for formal clipped hedges are beech and hornbeam because they are easy to clip and they stay tight and compact. A hedge of beech (*Fagus sylvatica*) will hold on to its attractive brown leaves until new growth starts in spring. Good evergreens include *Aucuba japonica*, *Chamaecyparis lawsoniana* 'Pembury Blue' (an evergreen conifer with silver-blue foliage) and holly (*Ilex*). There is also a good hawthorn with polished dark green leaves (*Crataegus laevigata*).

❀ Informal ornamental hedges can be created with roses. *R. rugosa* 'Frau Dagmar Hastrup' has silvery pink flowers and big red hips and *R.* 'Mundi' makes a very pretty hedge with striped white and pink flowers. *Eleagnus pungens* 'Frederici' has dark green, glossy leaves with silvery borders; *Osmanthus delavayi* has evergreen, dark green rounded leaves.

Functional hedges

❀ If you are looking for security as well as ornament, try *Berberis* or *Pyracantha* varieties with long and unkind thorns, which are very difficult to break through. The flowering quince (*Chaenomeles*) has long, sharp thorns as well as pretty apple blossom-shaped flowers and it, too, can make an attractive and effective security hedge.

BELOW: *Pleaching takes a little effort but can create a formal division or avenue of great style. This pleached hornbeam avenue leads the eye to an arched exit at the far end.*

PLEACHING, POLLARDING AND COPPICING

PLEACHING is a method of planting trees in rows and training the side branches to meet in horizontal, parallel lines. Other growth is cut back or interwoven to form a vertical screen. Beech, lime, hornbeam and plane trees are all suitable for pleaching. This technique is particularly effective in a formal setting and often used to line paths or avenues in larger gardens.

❀ In smaller gardens it can make an elegant division between two adjoining areas. A pleached avenue automatically leads the eye to what lies at the end so it is important to make sure there is something worth looking at, such as a sculpture or a decorative seat.

❀ Pollarding, very popular in France, involves regularly lopping back the entire crown of a tree to short stumps, so producing many thin branches and a single mop head of foliage. It can be useful in small gardens where a natural crown would produce too much shade. Some shrubs such as willow (*Salix*) are pollarded to encourage colourful young shoots.

❀ Coppicing involves cutting a shrub such as dogwood (*Cornus*) down to ground level, again to encourage colourful young shoots. Eucalyptus trees can be coppiced to provide a constant supply of juvenile foliage and a more shrub-like effect.

LEFT: *These admirably sculpted yew chocolate pots at Great Dixter in the south of England guard the entry into another part of the garden and are echoed by the great battlemented yew hedge beyond.*

❀ Do not choose to have topiary in the garden unless you have time and patience, or a gardener, to care for it well. Every time you clip it, you are removing all the young, strong new shoots and leaves, which weakens the plant. Feeding, watering and weeding are therefore of the utmost importance. Use a slow-acting organic manure, which will improve the structure of the soil as well as provide nutrients.

Using topiary

❀ There are many types of evergreen shrub that can give shape and solidity to a design, whether formal or informal, or anchor the corner of a bed to a neighbouring path or the house itself to its surroundings. Most evergreens have a distinct habit. Some are naturally tall and slender, such as *Cupressus sempervirens* 'Green Pencil', which can add height without taking up too much precious space or light.

❀ Others can be clipped into various shapes. If you want to use topiary next to the house, you could echo some architectural feature of the building with your topiary shape. Topiary goes well with almost any

TOPIARY

TOPIARY is a way of making sculptures from living plants. By training and clipping you can make bold, often imposing structural shapes, including 'walls' and arches. You can also create birds and animals, trains, chess sets or simply cones, ball shapes and spirals, which can create formality or points of interest in even the smallest garden.

BELOW: *Pillars of box and juniper provide a variety of textures and add height to this attractively planted border of pink flowers.*

ABOVE: *The topiary evergreens here give a disciplined finish to this marvellous burgeoning border of roses, ferns and the exotic growth of the tree fern,* Dicksonia antarctica.

paving material and in gravel. If growing your topiary in containers, it always looks best in very simple ones. The main interest should be in the shape of the plant, not in the container.

❀ Single plants can make individual points of emphasis in the overall plan; pairs of plants can form or identify a gateway, or you can use rows of clipped plants to line a path or avenue.

❀ Plants clipped into similar or contrasting shapes can be grouped together to make a dramatic show against a plain background such as a stone or brick wall. One garden in the south of England has a complete chess game in clipped yew. The opposing pieces are ranged along either side of a green lawn and from there the eye is taken to a view of the distant countryside.

Simple topiary shapes

❀ Simple geometric shapes are the easiest to create. Box is particularly good for these because new shoots develop from the centre of the plant. Yew and shrubby *Lonicera* also respond well. To create a standard topiary shape – a round head on a bare stem – you can train a single leader up a cane then pinch out the top growth regularly until you have created a firm, rounded shape. This is usually quite easy to do by eye. The culinary bay tree (*Laurus nobilis*) turns into a neat little mop-headed shrub, which looks good in a tub.

❀ Trees that naturally grow into a conical shape, such as yew and *Cupressus macrocarpa*, can be shaped easily into geometric cones by making a wigwam of canes and placing it over the plant before cutting, to use as a guide.

❀ To make a spiral shape from an established cone, choose a plant at least 1 m (3 ft) high. Tie a length of string to the top of the plant, wind it in a wide spiral around the bush and secure it to the stem at the base. Following the spiral marked by the string, cut away the outer branches with secateurs. Try to keep the tiers even all the way round.

Topiary on hedges

❀ In some gardens you can treat the top of a hedge as topiary. It can be clipped into spheres, cubes, castellations or birds and animals. Simple scalloped shapes can be effective too. Always use string or wire to measure and mark out the pattern before you cut.

❀ Columns and buttresses can be created in large hedges with an interesting architectural effect. You must allow the sides of the hedge to grow out at regularly spaced points and take up to three years to trim it into shape. Round windows in a hedge can act as peepholes into the view beyond. They can be created by training pliable young branches around an iron frame on a rod firmly fixed into the ground.

CARING FOR BORDERS

A well-stocked, colourful border is one of the chief pleasures of a garden. Think about border colour only when the rest of the garden has been planned and given its basic spaces and framework. Perennials, annuals and biennials are the plants that bloom in spring and summer, then fade and die down during the winter months; these provide most of the colour for borders. There are innumerable varieties, and flowers in thousands of colour combinations. Some will last in the garden for years; others will flower and bloom in the same year and then die. Between them, they can provide colour from late spring until well into autumn.

PERENNIALS

PERENNIALS are non-woody plants, which live for at least two years and sometimes many more. Most of them are herbaceous, dying back in autumn to ground level. From roots thus safely protected from frost, they send up new growth in spring. There are varieties of most perennials suitable for almost any garden, and they can provide riotous colour or more subtle shades for a long season.

BELOW: Many border plants can be grown near the sea, provided they have protection from salt-laden winds. Here, poppies, pinks, santolina and other low-growing perennials are thriving behind an evergreen hedge.

❀ A few herbaceous plants are evergreen and provide valuable ground cover and colour during winter. These include the hellebores, including the Christmas rose (*Helleborus niger*). In some places this does, in fact, flower at Christmas, but in many areas and in heavy soils the flowers will not appear until spring.

Choosing perennials

❀ Perennials can range in height from the creeping bugle (*Ajuga reptans*) and dead-nettle (*Lamium*), which grow well at the edges of borders, especially if allowed to flow over on to brick or stone paths, to the regal delphiniums, which can reach 2 m (7 ft).

whereas *Iris sibirica*, which has more grass-like leaves, will begin to look untidy after flowering.

❀ Some perennials flower in later summer or autumn, bringing a welcome revival to the border after the difficult, dry summer period. The hardy chrysanthemums (*Dendranthema*) can bring a sprightly feeling to the autumn garden. *Dendranthema* Korean hybrids have pretty little flowers in shades of purple or rust and will flower from midsummer right up until the first frosts; *D. rubellum* hybrids such as 'Duchess of Edinburgh', a single bright red variety with a large yellow centre, are excellent.

❀ Low-growing perennials can be grown in containers but tall, statuesque plants will thrive better on their own, presiding at the back of a border over the lowlier inhabitants. Many of the taller plants need staking or they may lean untidily over the smaller plants in order to reach the sun. This will hide the smaller plants from view and also stunt their growth. Staking should be done early in the season when the plants have begun to sprout. Trying to tie them in later creates an untidy look and you will find their flowers facing the wrong way.

❀ Because there are so many beautiful perennials beckoning to you from garden centres and nurseries, it is tempting to 'buy and try'. But, as with all plants, check that the ones you choose are appropriate for your growing conditions – the soil, the aspect and the microclimate should all be favourable, otherwise they will probably die and will certainly become poorly.

❀ When choosing perennials remember that, in general, the foliage lasts much longer than the flowers. For example, peonies will give a really breathtaking display of flowers for perhaps three weeks in spring, but their foliage is so handsome that they still add 'body' and good looks to the border after the flowers have faded.

❀ The splendid early summer-flowering bearded irises have strong strap-like leaves and give definition to a border, especially among more rounded plants,

DESIGNING BORDERS

HERBACEOUS borders can be designed to emphasise the particular style you have chosen for your garden. In a formal garden, straight, geometric borders look appropriately well ordered and are best ranged in opposite pairs along a pathway, for symmetry. They should have a restricted colour scheme because in a formal garden the pattern of the garden as a whole is more important than colour. In an informal garden irregular, curved borders and freer, more adventurous planting is more in keeping.

✿ Always be generous with paths. If two borders are divided by a path, make sure the path is in proportion to the width of the beds and allows room for flowers to spill over on to it.

HERBACEOUS AND MIXED BORDERS

A TRUE herbaceous border is one that has only perennials in it – no shrubs, bulbs or other types of plant. This kind of border is very labour intensive and plants that are over before others are ready to flower leave unsightly gaps, so true herbaceous borders are seldom planted these days.

ABOVE: *This carefully designed border demonstrates the restricted colour scheme necessary in a formal garden. The border is made up of Lupinus texensis 'Texas Blue Bonnet' in brilliant pinks and purples.*

✿ A mixed border uses many herbaceous plants, but in association with shrubs, bedding plants, bulbs and perhaps even vegetables. In small gardens, where space is limited and precious, a mixed border is certainly the most satisfactory. During the growing season gaps are filled by shrubs with ornamental foliage and when the herbaceous plants die down in autumn and winter, evergreens and bulbs will still provide colour and interest.

✿ Formality asks for large, distinct groups of one type of plant. Indeed, more plants of the same variety generally look better, especially in small gardens, rather than one plant each of many varieties. Informal borders can be arranged in drifts rather than clumps so that groups of plants dovetail into one another.

✿ A completely unplanned medley of herbaceous plants will produce a traditional cottage garden effect of colour and variety, whereas a mixed border provides more structure and a sense of order. Every gardener is part plants person, part designer and the two will always be at odds, so it is usually necessary to come to some sort of compromise between too many plants and too austere a look.

Invaluable perennials for the border

❀ Plants characteristic of the traditional herbaceous border are the tall, white shasta daisies (*Chrysanthemum* x *superbum*), the pale mauve scabious with its pincushion flowers and the wonderfully fragrant, heavy-headed, sugared almond-coloured varieties of *Phlox paniculata*.

❀ All associate well with other flowers and have a good long season. Day lilies (*Hemerocallis*) and agapanthus have strap-like leaves, which contrast well with feathery or less well-defined plants.

Useful associations for the mixed border

❀ Yarrow (*Achillea*) has feathery leaves and flat heads of tiny daisy flowers. *Achillea filipendulina* 'Gold Plate' is a tall favourite with spectacular bright yellow flowers most suitable for large gardens. A. 'Moonshine' has gentler yellow flowers and a hummock of silvery-green leaves, retained throughout the winter. The genus associates well with many other herbaceous perennials including varieties of geranium such as G. 'Buxton's Blue', which will behave like a climber and peep out from among the achillea leaves. *Astilbe* x *arendsii* has ferny foliage with spires of tiny feathery flowers lasting throughout summer. A. 'Fanal' is a very dark red and contrasts well with the spiky leaves of day lilies (*Hemerocallis*).

❀ *Astrantia major* is an invaluable plant for shady borders. Its tall stems rise above coarsely dissected leaves, and the flowers are rosettes of tiny papery petals with a long flowering season. It associates extremely well with *Geranium psilostemon*, which grows to a similar height, has similar leaves and uses the astrantia for support. Its brilliant purple flowers with stylish black centres are startling among the ghostly mass of astrantia blooms.

❀ Lady's mantle (*Alchemilla mollis*) is a beautiful low-growing plant with downy green leaves and clouds of tiny green-yellow flowers throughout summer. This good-tempered little gem will harmonise with many other plants and grow in sun or shade. Try it as an edging plant all along a path or growing under rose bushes. It will seed itself freely and may know, better than you do, where it will look most at home.

BELOW: *Although this border is wonderfully bright, the colours have been limited to reds and yellows so that it is not too confusing to the eye. The nasturtiums at the front of the border are backed by the bright red stems of Swiss ruby chard.*

ANNUALS AND BIENNIALS

THESE are short-lived but valuable plants in the garden, often known as 'bedding plants' because they are used in beds for one season and then discarded.

❀ An annual is a plant whose entire life cycle, from germination to seed production and death, takes place within one year. Those that are able to withstand frost are known as hardy annuals. Those that are not frost hardy are known as half-hardy annuals. These have to be raised under glass and are planted out only after all risk of frost is over. Many of the most popular plants we use as annuals come originally from the tropics.

ABOVE: *A beautiful and confidently planted border, in which the colours have been carefully combined to provide a simple yet elegant feel; the garden bench offers a pleasant place to sit and admire the view.*

❀ Hardy annuals include forget-me-nots (*Myosotis sylvatica*), pot marigolds (*Calendula officinalis*), cornflowers (*Centaurea cyanus*), candytuft (*Iberis umbellata*), the very useful wallflowers (*Cheiranthus*), which provide cheerful colour and scent in spring, sweet peas (*Lathyrus odoratus*) and the majestic sunflower (*Helianthus annuus*).

❀ Half-hardy annuals include *Begonia semperflorens*, a perennial from Brazil grown as an annual, with clusters of flowers during the summer, petunias, lobelias, *Convolvulus tricolor* and *Cosmos bipinnatus* in a range of colours from blue-purple to crimson, single flowers and feathery foliage. *Dianthus chinensis* is a popular annual pink with some beautiful coloured forms, and *Dimorphotheca sinuata* has lots of daisy flowers with dark brown centres and a variety of petal colours, mainly in the orange and salmon pink range.

❀ A biennial plant takes two years to complete its life cycle. During the first season after sowing, it produces leaves. It then overwinters and the following year produces flowers. Examples of biennials useful in the garden are foxgloves (*Digitalis*) and hollyhocks (*Alcea*), which are in fact perennials but treated as biennials.

LEFT:*Hollyhocks, shown here growing attractively against a cottage wall, are actually perennials, but are treated as biennials.*

Characteristics of bedding plants

🌸 Most bedding plants have rather feathery, soft foliage and are neat and low growing rather than imposing. Some hardy annuals will seed themselves over the garden and can be allowed to remain, only being removed where they will smother other plants or where they are not wanted.

🌸 Forget-me-nots can resemble a blue mist over the whole flowerbed in spring, but should be removed if they start getting the better of some other plant.

How to use bedding plants

🌸 A complete border may be devoted to annuals and biennials and it may be a useful way to treat a new garden not yet planted, as they quickly produce a lively show of colour. In an established border they are invaluable for filling spaces left by early-flowering plants.

🌸 They make pretty 'edging' plants and add extra colour to containers on a patio. Plants with many small flowers, such as diascia, lobelia and verbena, form low mounds or carpets and grow well under tall flowering plants such as shrubby salvias or fuchsias.

🌸 Many provide a contrast of colour or foliage or a link between different perennials. Silver-leaved bedding plants such as *Senecio cineraria* look very pretty planted under roses or provide a link between blue and pink geraniums or the brighter colours of *Rudbeckias* and

ABOVE: *A striking border of warm yellow and reds is created using* Rudbeckia, *tobacco plants* (Nicotiana)*,* Tagetes *and* Dendranthemums.

the smaller asters. *Echeveria elegans* is another useful silver-leaved plant to use in this way.

🌸 Many bedding plants are true annuals and die down at the end of the season. Others are perennials but are treated as annuals because they produce the best displays in just one year, or else they are not frost hardy.

🌸 Pansies are hardy perennials but are treated as annuals or biennials. They are well loved as cottage garden flowers and can give a brave display of colour in winter and spring when the rest of the garden is looking a bit bleak. They are usually more effective if just one or two colours are used together rather than if all the colours are jumbled into one bed.

Bedding in containers

🌸 Half-hardy and hardy annuals are ideal as container plants. Many have a drooping habit just right for hanging baskets. Some pelargoniums are good for this.

🌸 Always plant generously, getting as many plants in as possible. The rootballs of the plants can touch, provided the container is deep enough to allow a little compost beneath them. The silver-grey foliage of *Helichrysum petiolare* acts as a good background and contrast to almost any container display, as do small evergreens such as ivies.

USING BULBOUS PLANTS

Bulbs, corms, tubers and rhizomes are perennial plants in which part of the plant has evolved into a below-ground storage unit where food created one year is used to nourish the plant in the next. They are valuable in the garden for many reasons. Spring bulbs appear early, before most perennials have properly started to grow again after the winter. They can also add colour to containers when other plants are not ready to face the danger of frost. In summer, bulbous plants such as alliums and lilies can provide stately interest, while autumn crocuses and tiny hardy cyclamen can cheer up the garden towards the end of the season.

WHAT IS A BULBOUS PLANT?

A TRUE bulb is formed from fleshy leaves or leaf bases, and often consists of concentric rings of scales attached to a basal plate. The outer scales form a dry, protective skin. True bulbs include the daffodils, reticulata irises and tulips. If provided with enough nutrients, they will often flower for many years.

❀ A corm is formed from the swollen base of a stem and is replaced by a new corm every year. They are common in crocuses and gladioli and usually have a protective skin formed from the previous year's leaf bases.

❀ A tuber is a swollen stem or root used for food storage. *Corydalis* and some terrestrial orchids such as *Dactylorrhiza* and cyclamen species are tubers.

❀ A rhizome is a swollen stem, usually lying horizontally almost above ground, and is found in the bearded irises and in some lilies. In general, all these bulbous storage larders are referred to as bulbs.

Spring bulbs

❀ There are bulbs for all seasons of the year but their glory is in spring when they epitomise the regrowth of a world that has seemed dead all winter. Among the first are the snowdrops (*Galanthus*) with snowy-white flowers and trim clumps of leaves.

❀ Daffodils, with their sunny yellows and oranges, can flower over a long period if the varieties are carefully chosen; the bold blue, pink or white heads and heavy scent of hyacinths are another spring delight, and the heavenly blue of swathes of scillas and *Anemone blanda* look good in flowerbeds or woodland settings.

RIGHT: *A striking annual border curving around a lawn uses reds and purples to give a warm low edging to a stone wall. Plants include busy Lizzies (Impatiens), petunias, Swiss chard and salvia.*

ABOVE: *This charming little blue Iris sibirica 'Swank' likes a damp position and will associate well with ferns and other moisture-loving plants. These sit under the shade of the large leaves of a Lysichiton.*

❀ Spring bulbs can be lifted and stored after flowering if they threaten to get in the way of other plants. Many bulbs will spread and increase naturally over the years in many parts of the garden. Crocuses, daffodils, snowdrops and spring-flowering anemones such as A. *blanda* usually increase rapidly.

❀ Bulbs are particularly useful under deciduous shrubs and trees, where they make use of the light available when the trees are bare and then die down when the trees begin to come into leaf. The bulbs then die down themselves and begin the process of storing and preserving nutrients for the following year.

Summer and autumn bulbs

❀ In summer bulbs can provide colour and texture in a mixed border without taking up too much space. An advantage of growing them in a border is that when the leaves die down other perennials will conceal them as they bulk out their leaves.

❀ Bulbs such as the allium family can provide interest with their often completely round heads of tiny flowers, while lilies and gladioli can add height and stateliness.

❀ In autumn there are the hardy cyclamen species with their heart-shaped, attractively marked leaves and exquisite, swept-back pink or white flowers.

❀ In late winter or early spring, the aconites appear, with cupped yellow flowers framed by a green ruff. They like woodland glades and can multiply well if they like their position but are often difficult to get started.

BELOW: *This delightful grouping of spring bulbs combines pale and darker yellow varieties of narcissi, tulips and fritillaries with a carpeting of bluebells.*

NATURALISING BULBS

Bulbs can be allowed to grow under specimen trees, in grass and in woodland. When left undisturbed, many will increase to form natural-looking drifts, lending interest to many parts of the garden.

Bulbs in grass

✤ Many spring bulbs look marvellous scattered in broad sweeps in a lawn. However, since the leaves should not be cut until at least six weeks after the flowers have died, it is best to plant them in a part of the lawn that can be left unmown for that period – perhaps under a small specimen tree.

ABOVE: *The very early flowering* Crocus tomasinianus *has naturalised here to create carpets of freshest violet in otherwise bare woodland. Shafts of sunlight through the tree branches light up the colour magically.*

✤ Species bulbs are more delicate in colour and form than most cultivars, and should be planted where they will not be dominated by other plants. Tiny little species crocuses such as *Crocus tomasinianus* always cause surprise by appearing overnight in early spring. Their pale lilac or white flowers show up well in short grass and soon increase to create a star-spangled patch of carpet.

✤ Some bulbs like moisture. The snake's head fritillary (*Fritillaria meleagris*) grows well in moist grass bordering a stream and, unlike some others of its family, will tolerate fairly heavy soils.

Woodland bulbs

✤ In light woodland, bulbs can be naturalised in informal groups. Many bulbs enjoy woodland conditions and blend well with other woodland plants such as ferns. Snowdrops, scillas, the wood anemone (*Anemone sylvestris*) and lily-of-the-valley (*Convallaria majalis*) can all spread and colonise beautifully.

LEFT: *Snowdrops are the most welcome of winter flowers. These* Galanthus elwesii *have larger leaves and they flower earlier than the common snowdrop.*

* The English bluebell (*Hyacinthoides non-scripta*), one of the most beautiful of woodland plants with blue carpet of flowers, is best planted on its own in woodland because it will invade and overcome other plants. The Spanish bluebell (*Hyacinthoides hispanica*) is less invasive in woodland, although not so elegant, but can be invasive in small gardens.

Bulbs under specimen trees

* Bulbs and deciduous trees or large deciduous shrubs can make good partners, if the trees have deep roots and a light canopy. Apple trees, magnolias, ornamental cherries and small weeping trees such as the weeping pear (*Pyrus salicifolia* 'Pendula') all look good with bulbs scattered under them in spring.
* Yellow shines out well from beneath a tree and the bright yellow 'Cloth of Gold' crocus is a good spring flower for underplanting. In general it is best to keep the yellows separate from the blue and purple shades of crocus. Autumn-flowering bulbs such as the sharp pink *Cyclamen coum* or soft pink autumn crocus (*Colchicum autumnale*) will flower when the tree is losing its leaves.

* If you have newly planted a small tree, use only dwarf cultivars under it for the first few years, such as species crocuses or species tulips. Rapidly increasing and large bulbs such as daffodils will reduce the available nutrients for the tree.

Bulbs in the alpine garden

* Many of the smaller bulbs like very well-drained soil and will thrive in a rock garden in sun or partial shade. Dwarf bulbs look attractive when planted in small gaps in the rock. They also look good in gravel or grit used as top dressing on a bed of alpines.
* The grit acts as a mulch and stops flowers from being deluged by mud in wet weather. *Fritillaria acmopetala*, *Narcissus bulbocodium* (the hooped-petticoat daffodil), *Muscari macrocarpus* (a tiny grape hyacinth) and *Crocus* 'Cream Beauty' are all delightful. The upright habit and spear-like leaves of bulbs contrast well with the low, mat-forming habit of many alpine plants.

Bulbs for a water garden

* Few bulbs flourish in damp, poorly drained soils but those that do can be well worth growing. Their strong shapes have a striking effect reflected in the water. The stately arum lily (*Zantedeschia aethiopica*) has large white flowers above arrow-shaped leaves and grows well in pond margins.
* Two plants that like moist but well-drained soil are the splendid purple *Iris kaempferi* and the arched sprays of *Dierama pendulum*. On a smaller scale, there is the delicate summer snowflake (*Leucojum aestivum*).

Bulbs in containers

* Bulbs can also be grown in ornamental pots, troughs and window boxes. Tufa troughs look good planted with dwarf bulbs and alpines. Grow the smaller fritillary species for their curious flowers. Larger bulbs, such as *Lilium regale*, can be grown in imposing containers outside a front door or on a patio where their strong fragrance can be enjoyed.

LEFT: *The elegant drooping head of the snake's head fritillary (Fritillaria meleagris) will brighten up any moisture-retaining position. These are among the few bulbs that do not seem to mind a heavy clay soil.*

TULIPS

THESE, too, are invaluable in the spring garden. The tall varieties can march in formal rows, their straight stalks standing stiffly to attention. They can just as well be used informally, intermingling with other flowers in a spring border.

❀ They have an astonishing range of flower forms – from the simple upright 'goblets' that look so well in formal situations, to the frilled and fringed petals of parrot tulips and the open, double blooms of peony-flowered tulips. Their colours are clear and bright and include the black-purple of *Tulipa* 'Queen of the Night', as well as vivid reds, clear pinks and the curious mixed colourations of the parrot tulips.

Botanic tulips

❀ These have developed from tiny species originally found around the Mediterranean. They are small with star-shaped flowers, often several to one stem. The hybrids developed from these dainty little bulbs are the *kaufmanniana* and *fosteriana* species, which flower in early spring, and the *greigii* species, which flower a few weeks later. They have large flowers and a variety of shapes and colours.

ABOVE: *Many spring bulbs will grow well in deciduous woodland, making the most of the light before the trees come into leaf. Here, Helleborus orientalis and pale-coloured Narcissus brighten up the bare ground.*

DAFFODILS

DAFFODILS are invaluable in spring, with their cheerful upright stems and sunny colours. They range from the tiny cyclamen-shaped species and hybrids such as *Narcissus triandrus* and *N.* 'Jumblie' with petals swept back away from the trumpet, to the great yellow giants such as 'King Alfred', ubiquitously planted in public parks but rather overpowering in a small garden.

❀ Daffodil flowers vary from those with long, short and hoop-shaped trumpets to swept-back or straight petals. Most have large single flowers but a very few are double. There are many small varieties, which can be planted in profusion in the small garden, varying in colour from white and very pale yellow to deep yellow and orange. The old favourite, the strongly scented 'Pheasant's Eye' (*N. poeticus* var. *recurvus*) has white petals and a tiny bright red trumpet.

❀ Chosen carefully, daffodils can flower over a long period in spring, starting very early in the gardening year with those like 'February Gold', a neat cheerful yellow, and *N. romieuxii*, a pretty, pale yellow hooped-petticoat type. Both are suitable for rock gardens and raised beds.

❀ The larger daffodils look best in large gardens or in formal beds. Smaller daffodils will grow in grass but it is important to wait for the leaves to die down before mowing, so choose a wilder part of the garden. They will grow well on grassy banks and look wonderful generously planted along a drive. In these situations they usually look best when one cultivar is planted *en masse*.

- The *kaufmanniana* tulips are only 15–20 cm (6–8 in) tall; 'The First' is white with carmine red, while 'Giuseppe Verdi' is carmine with yellow edging. The *fosteriana* tulips are taller, 35–40 cm (8–16 in); *T. f.* 'Red Emperor' is scarlet and *T. f.* 'Purissima' pure white.

- The *greigii* tulips are medium-sized, 20–30 cm (8–12 in) tall, and include the popular 'Red Riding Hood' and 'Cape Cod' (orange). All these tiny tulips make a brave display early in the year and have an innocent charm, unlike their more sophisticated soldier-like relatives.

- Larger-flowered hybrids used for general garden display look good with forget-me-nots or in clumps among herbaceous plants.

LILIES

THERE are short, tall and sweetly scented lilies, white ones and brightly coloured ones. Some look good in pots, others in the company of other plants or growing in the dappled shade of trees or shrubs.

- Tall lilies at the back of a border provide not only a vertical presence but also a sense of grandeur. Plant them in blocks of single colour because mixed colours or different cultivars within a block are confusing.

- Suitable lilies for the back of the border include *Lilium martagon* 'Album', a white Turk's-cap lily with masses

ABOVE: Lilium regale *is one of the stateliest of lilies and is very strongly scented. It will grow well in woodland or in any partly shaded border in the summer.*

of ivory-white flowers from early summer; 'Fire King', which has dense open clusters of purple-spotted bright orange-red blooms and *L. regale*, with trumpet-shaped clusters of very fragrant white flowers streaked with purple.

- Some lilies prefer dappled shade. These include *L. Henrii*, with tall arching stems and gently nodding spikes of small, black-spotted orange-red flowers from midsummer; *L. longiflorum*, with sweetly scented white trumpet-shaped blooms from midsummer; and *L. speciosum* var. *rubrum*, with its large, very fragrant spikes of deep carmine Turk's-cap flowers from late summer.

LEFT: *One colour will often be more telling than many colours together, as shown by this trough of* Tulipa *'Big Chief'. In this case a touch of blue is added by the low-growing forget-me-nots.*

CULTIVATING GRASSES AND BAMBOOS

Grasses have become popular in gardens over the last few years for very good reasons. They have elegant and architectural forms, long seasons of interest and need little attention. They can also cope with a certain amount of drought, an invaluable quality in the modern garden. They bring movement and a luminous quality into garden planting as they sway in the wind and their leaves catch the sunlight.

THE GRASS FAMILY

MEMBERS of the grass family (*Gramineae*), which includes bamboos, have rounded, hollow stems with regularly placed swellings or nodes from which the leaves appear. The flowers of grasses are small but are often held in large, showy panicles, spikes or plumes or stiff poker-like heads, well above the leaves.

❀ Although they lack bright colours, their golds, browns, greens and yellows catch the sun, producing beautiful subtle effects. Their arching stems, feathery flowers and subtle colouring can create marvellous displays, whether used as individual specimens or grouped together. Many have attractive flowers and seed heads that appear in midsummer and last well into winter.

The tall and the short

❀ Large grasses are admired for their statuesque quality and feather-duster plumage. Unfortunately, the overuse of the very tall and stately pampas grass (*Cortaderia selloana*) has given grass a bad name. It is undeniably beautiful in the right setting but at one time it seems to

BELOW: *The strap-like leaves of this purple phormium and the narrower leaves of the grasses go particularly well together, providing interesting movement and light for those sitting on the bench.*

ABOVE: *Although the leaves of the grasses* Imperata cylindrica 'Rubra' *and* Roscoea scillicifolia *have a similar strap-like quality, variety is provided in good measure by the colours, which light up when the sun shines on them.*

have been planted in almost every suburban garden as a matter of course, where it was out of proportion, out of keeping and badly maintained. It is indeed a regal plant but only for a very large garden or for planting in quantity by a lakeside or as a feature.

❀ C. *selloana* is the hardiest pampas grass but there are many more rewarding grasses to choose for the smaller garden. Choose *Miscanthus sinensis* 'Silberfeder' (silver feather), or M. *'Zebrinus'*, whose arching green leaves are intriguingly striped yellow. *Pinnisetum alopecuroides* has brown, caterpillar-shaped flower heads and can be grown in clumps under deciduous trees. Smaller grasses are more useful for their foliage effect, both in form and colour.

❀ Varieties of *Festuca*, *Milium*, *Elymus* and *Carex* are all excellent foliage plants and extremely useful in a border. They associate well with small perennials, dwarf conifers and shrubs, contributing a hedgehog roundness but feather softness that contrasts well with the upright shape of many perennials. Most are evergreen and so provide interest for the whole year.

RIGHT: *The tall, feathery stems of* Stipa gigantea *with the lower-growing* Miscanthus sinensis *'Silberfeder' and the fiery red of* Crocosmia *'Bressingham Blaze' make a really striking combination.*

CHOOSING GRASSES

IT is important to choose the right grasses for a particular effect. Clump-forming upright growers, such as varieties of *Calamagrostis*, will preside over lower-growing plants but lose all impact if crowded by plants of equal height. More open grasses, such as *Paricum virgatum* with loose flower and seed heads, can be used with taller perennials because of their almost transparent quality.

❀ Colour is important, too. If you grow the luminous green *Milium effusum* 'Aureum' in front of a bed next to the lawn, it will simply look like another bit of green grass. Choose the blue grass *Festuca glauca* instead, and it will contrast with the lawn grass very effectively.

Grasses by the sea

❀ Almost all grasses are invaluable grown in coastal or seaside gardens. Their ethereal quality seems to match that of the sea; they can cope well with wind and salt spray and are at home in a sandy and pebbly environment. The taller ones can be used for structure, the smaller ones for foliage, colour and for filling gaps.

ABOVE: *Grasses can look especially picturesque in a winter border after a heavy frost; they can lend a magical quality to an otherwise bland and colourless area.*

Grasses in the mixed border

❀ Many mixed borders will benefit from grasses grown among the shrubs and herbaceous perennials. *Stipa gigantea* is useful because its pale yellow stems and flowers make a significant shape but it is sparse enough for other plants to be seen through it. Its pale straw-like colour goes well with many of the later summer flowers such as *Echinaceae purpurea*, *Crocosmia* 'Lucifer' and *Aster amellus* 'King George'.

❀ Low-growing grasses look good at the front of mixed borders. Choose the tufted ones that build up slowly from a central crown. *Festuca glauca* 'Elijah blue' is evergreen and has vivid blue, needle-like leaves and blue-grey plumes of flowers in early summer. Vigorous, creeping grasses are not suitable for borders. *Phalaris arundinacea*, for example, will simply smother weaker plants growing nearby and will require endless weeding.

Grasses in winter borders

❀ When many flowers have died down for the winter, the grasses can come into their own, keeping a border alive when it has lost its summer and autumn colour. They can look spectacular when caught by a heavy frost so that their seed heads and leaves are outlined with a sugar icing coating.

❀ Taller grasses associate well with the sea hollies such as *Eryngium agavifolium*, whose seed heads continue to be attractive in winter, and also with *Sedum* 'Autumn Joy', whose flat plates of heads last well into winter, too, and contrast with the feathery heads of grass. In a large border the larger grasses look great with the seed heads of cardoons (*Cynara cardunculus*).

Grasses for paved areas and patios

❀ Some of the smaller grasses are suitable for growing between paving slabs. Purple moor grass (*Molinia caerulea*) has slender green upright leaves, which form into mounds with open panicles of purple flowers in summer. It will tolerate acidic, boggy soils, so can be used near pools.

❀ For a warm patio area try *Helictotrichon sempervirens* in a bed sheltered by a wall. Its slender blue leaves are upright and radiate stiffly so it looks suitably architectural next to a building.

Water's edge grasses

❀ *Glyceria aquatica* 'Variegata' has an attractive form, tolerates shade and spreads slowly. *Phragmites australis* is a tall species. It needs moist soil and will grow well by a pond or stream.

ABOVE: *The tall, feathery plumes of pampas grass* Cortaderia selloana *'Sunningdale Silver' give a spectacular display, which contrasts with the paddle-shaped leaves and bright red flowers of* Canna *'President'.*

Areas dedicated to grass

✿ If you have enough space, you might like to have a grass garden, creating your own area of American prairie. Varieties of *Cortaderia* and *Miscanthus* make a striking display. They are best grown in an open position where they will get the benefit of sun on their foliage and flowers and the wind will set them swaying.

SEDGES, RUSHES AND CAT'S TAILS

THESE plants are often confused with grasses but each belongs to a separate family. Although they will grow in sun or shade, they must have moist soil and are mostly useful for the bog garden.

✿ Sedges are grown for their attractive foliage. They thrive in bog conditions but are often tolerant of dryer sites. The flowers are grouped into spikelets, which may be richly coloured.

✿ The variegated species can offer good colour contrasts in a border. Members of the *Carex* family form dense mounds of evergreen hair-like leaves. *Carex* 'Bronze Form' has matt brown leaves, while those of *C. elata* 'Aurea' are bright yellow with narrow green edges.

✿ The rush family (*Juncaceae*) includes the rushes and the woodrushes, all of which have attractive leaves. Like sedges, they should be grown in a bog garden or a bed whose soil is reliably moist. The rushes prefer shade and make good ground cover plants. *Juncus effusus* 'Spiralis' has tiny brown flowers in loose clusters. Snowy woodrush (*Luzula nivea*) has light green leaves in loose tufts with clusters of white flowers in summer and will tolerate sun.

✿ Cat's tails are deciduous with invasive rhizomes. *Typha latifolia* is the common bulrush or reed mace, whose brown flower heads are poker shaped and topped with thin spikes. It is often seen growing in rivers or streams but it can be invasive. *T. minima* (dwarf reed mace) is less so and has dark brown flower spikes in summer.

BELOW: *Grasses and sedges are particularly striking when the frost catches them on a bright winter's morning. The grassy meadow by this wooden bridge has a silver frosty sheen, against which the dark pokers of the bulrushes stand out strikingly.*

BAMBOOS

BAMBOOS belong to the grass family (*Gramineae*). They are evergreen with woody hollow stems called culms and narrow, handsome foliage. Bamboos make excellent architectural plants; even when used as screens or hedges, they make a dramatic statement in any garden.

❀ They will grow in any dry, sheltered, shady spot and can create a lush tropical effect together with other evergreen shrubs. The tall vertical culms make interesting contrasts with the fronded foliage of ferns. Japanese anemones can be grown nearby, especially white ones such as *Anemone* x *hybrida* 'Honorine Joubert'.

❀ Most bamboos need plenty of space, since the larger ones will grow up to 4 m (13 ft) tall and many arch over 6 m (20 ft), but there are also some dwarf species.

❀ Some bamboos form clumps and make good specimen plants or focal points. Others have running rhizomes and need to be contained, unless grown in a wild garden or as ground cover. Canes can be green, brown, black, yellow, pink or purple, mottled or streaked. Do not expect bamboos to bloom, however. It may take 100 years for flowers to appear. On the whole, the flowers are untidy anyway and bamboos look better without them.

❀ Bamboos need a sheltered spot, protected from the wind, or they will lose excessive water. Although fully hardy, a bamboo in a container can suffer from drought in winter and it is wise to insulate the pot with fleece or plastic bubble wrap.

❀ Bamboos grow strongly in most soils once they have become established, and some spread very quickly. Many are tropical but plenty are hardy in temperate regions. They can be grown in beds in the garden or in tubs on roofs or in container gardens. A grove or specimen plant of bamboos can transform a prim garden into a much more mysterious and interesting area.

Bamboos in containers

❀ Bamboos can look superb when well grown in large containers. Terracotta and glazed Chinese pots are suitable but the plants can look just as stately grown in galvanised bins and buckets. The invasive, running types of bamboo are certainly best grown in pots, particularly in small gardens, otherwise they may spread and become a nuisance.

ABOVE: *Bamboos can be grown very effectively in pots and it is one way of making sure the invasive types do not spread. This small version sits well near a formal Japanese-style pond.*

❀ Bamboos are thirsty, hungry plants. Failure to water them sufficiently will cause the leaves to turn brown and even loss of nearly all the leaves. Once this has happened, they will be slow to recover. More vigorous and invasive species will fill up their containers in no time with rhizomes and roots and will then use up water and nutrients at an alarming rate.

❀ Such plants should be repotted every year but there are species that are more suitable for containers. These are slower growing and some may be kept in the same pot for five years or more. *Chimonobambusa marmorea* grows to 1.5 m (5 ft) and is a semi-dwarf Japanese variety with tightly bunched leaves. *C. marmorea* 'Variegata' has thin reddish stems and yellow striped leaves.

ABOVE: *This very Japanese scene includes a bamboo fence with the slim, black-stemmed bamboo* Phyllostachys nigra *growing against it, a stone lantern and two small hummocks of the low-growing blue grass* Festuca glauca *'Elijar Blue'.*

Bamboos in a Japanese garden

❀ Bamboos are more or less essential in a Japanese garden. Tall varieties such as *Fargesia murieliae*, which grows to 4 x 1.5 m (13 x 5 ft) and is particularly elegant as a specimen plant, can conceal the edge of a small garden, making it look much larger.

❀ A gravel area with a stone lantern on it will be given extra atmosphere by this arching plant. *F. m.* 'Simba' reaches only half the height or less and might suit a small garden better.

Interesting stems

❀ Some bamboos have striking stems, which are as much of a feature as their leaves. Plant these where the stems will really be noticed, rather than in some forgotten corner of the garden. They will look good in containers in a small area or as focal points and can be used as screens where they will please the eye while concealing what lies behind.

❀ Such bamboos include *Phyllostachys edulis*, whose distinctive culms are covered in a waxy white powder, which makes them look white. *P. nigra* has elegant, narrow ebony-black stems and is a very good variety for smaller gardens.

Ground cover bamboos

❀ A few bamboos can be used for ground cover. *Pleioblastus pygmaeus* (syn. *Arundinaria pygmaea*) is a dwarf bamboo with fern-like leaves with very slender culms. It looks attractive grown in a shallow container.

LEFT: *Bamboos have many uses in the garden and the canes, or culms, can provide as much interest as the foliage. This one is* Clusquea couleou, *which forms dense clumps of yellow-green to olive-green canes and will grow to 6 m (20 ft) tall.*

GROWING FERNS AND MOISTURE-LOVING PLANTS

Ferns are among the most delicate-looking of foliage plants. They grow in many different shapes and sizes and can add texture and atmosphere to many parts of the garden. They can enliven and cheer places the sun seldom reaches, act as foils to flowering plants and look very much at home grown in drifts as ground cover in woodland areas. They are particularly at home by streams and in damp, shady corners, and are therefore good for small courtyards. All in all, ferns offer an enormous variety of plants of invaluable use in a modern garden.

CHARACTERISTICS

FERNS may be evergreen or deciduous and they have leaf-like fronds, which usually begin to appear in spring. The young fronds, known as crosiers, are tightly curled and unfurl with great grace and beauty as they grow.

❧ The fronds of most ferns grow from rhizomes. These are coated in a furry, scaly covering, which may be black, brown or silvery white. Most rhizomes extend above and below ground, sometimes for a long distance. *Matteuccia struthiopteris* produces crowns of fronds at intervals along its rhizomes.

❧ Rather than producing flowers or seeds, ferns release tiny spores from capsules on the undersides of their fronds. You can often see these as brown markings on the backs of the fronds. These will germinate if given the right conditions.

❧ Some ferns, such as *Asplenium bulbiferum*, also reproduce by growing little plantlets or bulbils on their fronds. This particular fern needs a very sheltered position out of the sun and needs protecting in winter with a covering of straw or old fronds. It is probably better grown in a conservatory.

❧ Epiphytic ferns grow on trees, rocks or walls and draw their nutrients from rotting vegetation, which collects in the crevices.

RIGHT: *The feathery flower heads of the pink* Astilbe *'Erica' associate well with the tall and stately* Osmunda *and* Matteuccia *ferns, growing happily in a semi-woodland situation.*

❧ Almost all ferns require damp conditions if they are to thrive. A very few genera such as *Dryopteris* and *Osmunda* will tolerate dry conditions but only if well shaded. Many, such as *Allyrium* and *Osmunda*, die down at the first touch of frost so should not be grown in a winter interest garden. Some of the *Dryopteris* retain their fronds until well into winter. Leave the old fronds on the plant until early spring to protect the crown from frost but remove them as soon as the young fronds begin to unfurl.

LEFT: *This very natural-looking woodland planting scheme has tiny alpine-type plants growing from crevices in the wall and a mixture of wild flowers and ferns against the hedgerow.*

❀ There are lance-shaped fronds, such as those found in the shuttlecock or ostrich fern (*Matteuccia struthiopteris*), whose fronds turn brown in late summer and persist for over a year, creating a striking display. These are among the most graceful of ferns and they deserve a prominent position in a shady part of the garden, perhaps at the top of steps or as an eye-catcher in a paved corner.

❀ Simple strap-like fronds are found in the hart's tongue fern (*Asplenium scolopendrium*), a very hardy evergreen fern with a crown of mid-green fronds. The crosiers look intriguingly like small green cobras when the dead fronds have been removed.

❀ Antler-shaped fronds are seen only in the staghorn ferns such as *Platycerium bifurcatum*, whose basal fronds are shaped like kidneys and reach up to 60 cm (24 in) and turn brown when fully grown. They form a shield around the base of the antler-like fronds, which grow up to 80 cm (32 in) long and remain green. These are tropical plants and suited only to greenhouse, conservatory or indoor cultivation.

BELOW: *This congregation of shade-loving plants includes the small bleeding heart (Dicentra formosa), the Dryopteris fern, a large blue-green hosta and a purple Cotinus.*

Fern shapes

❀ Fern fronds comprise several basic shapes. There are triangular ferns, such as the five-fingered maidenhair fern (*Adiantum pedatum*), which has upright, lime-green fronds that die down in winter. They look attractive grown with other ferns in a shady border or woodland setting.

THE RIGHT CONDITIONS

FERNS are very tough and require the minimum of care and maintenance once established. Most ferns prefer neutral to alkaline conditions, and well-dug soil with added organic matter will suit most species.

❀ There are one or two that prefer acidic soil and which should be used in areas where other acidic soil lovers, such as rhododendrons and azaleas, grow. For example, the hard fern (*Blechnum spicant*), which has evergreen, leathery ladder-like fronds, is easier to grow in acidic soils, loves shady borders in woodland areas and associates well with acid-loving shrubs.

❀ The large ferns such as *Matteuccia* varieties will thrive in the damp conditions near ponds or streams. They associate well with large-leaved plants that love moisture, too, such as *Gunnera* and *Rodgersia* and reflect very prettily in still water.

Ferns in formal settings

❀ Ferns can be used successfully in formal settings. For example, they can be planted in clumps or rows behind a very low clipped hedge of golden box bordered by woodland.

❀ The dark trees will highlight the feathery outline of the ferns, while the ferns themselves soften the hard edge of the box. They also look good when they are used formally in a courtyard or paved area in the corner of a garden that gets little sun.

❀ If growing ferns in pots you must make sure they are kept moist at all times. They look good grown near formal water features, especially where a little water is allowed to escape into the surrounding soil.

ABOVE: *Most ferns and primulas prefer soil that will not dry out. Here, the large shuttlecock fern (*Matteuccia struthiopteris*) mingles with a cerise candelabra primula (*Primula bulleyana*) to make a delightful combination.*

BELOW: *An enormous, clipped shrubby Lonicera hedge, shaped like a pillow, is brightened and enlivened by the bright green feathery leaves of a large clump of Dryopteris.*

Ferns in rock crevices

❀ The lance-shaped fronds of the semi-evergreen *Ceterach officinarum* contrast well with the hard surfaces of the rock or brick that provides shelter and nutrients for them.

❀ If you build a double wall at the edge of a patio or front garden with a space in the middle for plants, these little ferns can be grown there, too, but remember that they should be in the shade.

Naturalising ferns in woodland

❀ Although woodland may sound a bit grand, in a small garden one good-sized silver birch or a small clump of deciduous trees planted close together can count as woodland. Where ferns are concerned, the woodland needs to be moist most of the time.

❀ Ferns planted in drifts in woodland look very pretty but they need not be grown on their own. They associate very well with lilies and also with groups of broad-leaved hostas and spring bulbs such as wood anemones and bluebells.

❀ The male fern (*Dryopteris filix-mas*), which keeps most of its fronds throughout winter, is a very accommodating plant and thrives in shade but will tolerate full sun. It will even grow at the foot of a privet hedge. Like most hardy ferns, it forms solid clumps and looks very pretty grown in drifts among trees and woodland shrubs.

❀ The common polypody (*Polypodium vulgare*) is drought tolerant and adaptable. It spreads easily and makes good ground cover. It will also grow on rocks and trees. It has dark green, lance-shaped, deeply lobed fronds and spreads via green rhizomes, which eventually form mats. It prefers an acidic soil, as does *Blechnum spicant*, a fern with a distinctive rich green colour.

Ferns as specimen plants

❀ Many ferns deserve a prominent position where they will be noticed and appreciated for some special quality. The Japanese painted fern *Athyrium niponicum* var. *pictum* is one of the prettiest, with metallic silver-grey fronds and purple midribs. It does not grow very tall, but put it in a moist, fertile soil and a sheltered position and it will thrive and look very pretty, particularly with small spring bulbs such as *Anemone blanda* and the charming little blue scillas and other small woodland plants.

❀ The royal fern (*Osmunda regalis*) is a large, stately fern growing to 1.5 m (5 ft) tall. It particularly likes waterside conditions in sun or shade. It makes a good container plant but must be regularly watered. It is best located near the house where it can be in a prominent position and its watering needs are less likely to be forgotten.

BELOW: *Foxgloves and ferns both grow in woodland conditions and associate well together under the canopy of deciduous trees.*

USEFUL PLANT ASSOCIATIONS

ELEPHANT'S ears (*Bergenia*), with large, shiny, rounded evergreen leaves, can be a little dull on their own when not in flower.

They look much more interesting planted next to ferns, especially the feathery ones, such as the beech fern (*Phegopteris connectilis*), whose lime-green fronds contrast with the dark green of the *Bergenia*. *Bergenia* 'Silberlicht' has loose white flowers and is a more elegant and interesting variety than the more usual pink-flowering ones.

LEFT: *This beautifully designed modern garden has a formal rectangular pond with a stone sculpture as a focal point. Water lilies float serenely on the calm surface of the water, and iries and other water-loving plants have been planted in the corners.*

❀ Even in the smallest plot you can have a trough with dwarf water lilies floating in it. In a larger garden a formal or informal pond can create a strong focus and set the garden's style. It may incorporate a fountain or waterfall to create movement, sound and liveliness and water lilies will complete the scene.

❀ Floating plants, marginal, deep water and bog plants all add to the interest of a garden but need to be catered for carefully. Ponds should be made with shelves at different heights so that pond baskets can be put at the heights best suited to the various plants.

Plants for formal ponds

❀ Plants with floating leaves and flowers, such as water lilies, are the obvious choice for formal pools. *Nymphaea* 'Froebelii' has deep red, starry flowers and

WATER PLANTS

Water in the garden – whether a formal pool, a small stream, a short cascade or a wildlife pond – will allow you to grow many plants that do not thrive in any other conditions.

BELOW: *This thoughtfully designed pond at the edge of a patio is planted with variegated hostas, which contrast with the large green-purple leaves of* Rodgersia, *the white and green strap-like leaves of* Phormium *and the slender leaves of a water iris.*

purple-green rounded leaves; N. 'Marliacea Chromatella' is a yellow-flowered variety with olive green-streaked leaves.

❀ Arum lilies do not float but stand upright and look marvellous at the edge of a pond where their arrow-shaped leaves and pure white flowers can be reflected in the water. *Zantedeschia aethiopica* is the hardiest and will withstand several degrees of frost.

Marginal plants

❀ Marginal plants are, in the main, very attractive plants grown at the edges of pools in shallow water about 7.5–15 cm (3–6 in) deep, but sometimes up to 30 cm (12 in) deep. Some species, such as water mint (*Mentha aquatica*) and *Veronica beccabunga*, also help to oxygenate the water.

❀ Ferns will grow well at the borders of informal pools and can form a good transition between a stream and the garden. Plants grown at pond margins also provide shelter for wildlife. *Iris laevigata* is tall and stately with fans of green, sword-like leaves and lavender-blue flowers.

❀ *Butomus umbellatus* has clusters of pale pink flowers in summer and early autumn and twisted bronze leaves. Purple loosestrife (*Lythrum salicaria*) has spires of reddish-purple flowers and lance-shaped leaves. The water forget-me-not (*Myosotis palustris*) has sky-blue flowers with yellow eyes all summer long.

❀ All these plants are valuable for breaking up the hard outline of a pond. In deeper marginal water you can grow the water flag (*Iris pseudacorus*), a tall, bright yellow variety of iris, but it may be too vigorous for smaller gardens.

Bog and moisture-loving plants

❀ Numerous colourful plants will grow happily in soil that is kept permanently wet. The water violet (*Hottonia palustris*) has pale lilac flowers and likes full sun; *Anemone rivularis* has blue or white flowers from spring into summer; and ragged robin (*Lychnis flos-cuculi*) is a very pretty sharp pink flower with ragged petals, which used to be common and now seems to be rare in the wild.

❀ If you have room you could grow something on a grand scale such as *Gunnera tinctoria*, which has enormous, rhubarb-like leaves up to 1.5 m (5 ft) wide. Spikes of greenish-red flowers are followed by red or purple fruits.

❀ *Rodgersia aesculifolia* is another tall, stately plant with leaves like the horse chestnut tree and plumes of tiny, fragrant white flowers. *Rheum palmatum* also has large, handsome foliage and unusual flower spikes on reddish-purple stems.

WATER GARDENS IN CONTAINERS

I N a small garden or a patio you can still have a pool without doing any construction work. Appropriate containers might be a sealed and lined half-barrel, a metal cauldron or a ceramic sink with the plughole stopped up. Although you will be able to grow only a few selected plants, the presence of even a little water can give great pleasure.

❀ Metal containers should be sealed with rubber paint or liner, otherwise the metal may be harmful to the plants and any fish you might want to keep. (If you do keep fish, they should be brought indoors over winter.) One suitable plant would be the tiny water lily, *Nymphaea pygmaea* 'Helvola', with pretty miniature yellow flowers. *N. tetragona* has white flowers no more than 5 cm (2 in) across and heart-shaped, dark green leaves.

LEFT: *The white skunk cabbage* (Lysichiton camtschatcensis) *is a marginal aquatic perennial, which flowers in early spring. Here, it is reflecting beautifully in the water.*

INTRODUCING EXOTICS

Exotic plants are usually thought of as those from tropical and subtropical climates that find it hard to survive in temperate conditions. However, in mild areas such plants may grow quite happily in a sheltered part of the garden and, even in colder areas, many survive outside if protected over winter. Some are so tender that they need the protection of a greenhouse or conservatory even in the summer. However, some exotic-looking plants are perfectly hardy and not actually tropical. Exotics include many handsome architectural plants grown as focal points for their height and interesting shapes and foliage. They also include plants with highly colourful and unusual flowers and evergreens with a jungly look.

CACTI AND SUCULENTS

CACTI and succulents come in an extraordinarily varied array of sizes, shapes, colours and textures. Many come from desert regions, where there is little rainfall and it gets very hot during the day and very cold at night.

❀ Some come from warm, humid rainforests. They have all adapted to their particular extreme conditions, turning their leaves, stems or roots into water storage tanks to help them withstand long periods of drought. Cacti differ from other succulents in having cushion-like growths on their stems from which spines, flowers and shoots develop.

❀ Succulents may have plump, smooth surfaces, a covering of silky hair or colourful spines. They may be symmetrical rosettes in shape or squat and globular or fluted like candlesticks. Many flower for only a short time and have large, brightly coloured flowers. Others flower for longer with many tiny blooms.

❀ In cool-temperate climates most cacti and succulents have to be grown in a conservatory or as houseplants, although there are some hardier species, which can make interesting garden displays. Nearly all need good drainage and will grow well in raised beds where the water can drain freely.

BELOW: *This secluded seating area has a wealth of container-grown succulents for colour and interest. Scented-leaved pelargoniums are fronted by the strong, spiky shapes of the Agave.*

ABOVE: *A row of succulents in terracotta pots sitting on a sunny wall by a patio will get the best of the daylight and warmth of the sun and will flourish accordingly.*

❀ Attractive collections of succulents can be grown outdoors in a relatively cool climate if you choose your varieties carefully. *Sedum* cultivars are often grown in mixed borders, although they usually look much more striking grown in a row or in swathes against a stone wall. There are some excellent deep purple varieties such as *S. spectabile* 'Abendrot'.

Succulents in containers

❀ Most succulents have shallow roots and are therefore ideal for growing in containers. Wide, shallow containers are best for low-growing and creeping species such as the hardy *Sempervivum montanum*, a variety of houseleek, which makes neat little rosettes and is ideal for a trough garden.

❀ *Lewisia* varieties have brilliant little blooms on delicate stalks and also grow well in a trough or gravel garden, given a sheltered spot. Troughs are good for creating mixed planting of different sizes and habits.

❀ Large pots or urns are better for large plants with strap-like leaves such as *Agave attenuata*. A raised bed with shallow soil and plenty of gravel is also a good place to grow mixed succulent plantings.

Succulents as focal points

❀ The agaves are spiky and statuesque. Grown in regions where the temperature seldom drops below freezing, *Agave parryi* has plump symmetrical rosettes of grey-green leaves and *Opuntia polyacantha* has brilliant yellow flowers. Each of these makes a splendid focal point on its own.

Trailing succulents

❀ Several succulents have a trailing habit and can be stunning planted in hanging baskets. *Ceropegia woodii* produces waterfalls of brightly coloured flowers and can be used in warm, sunny courtyards or in conservatories.

RIGHT: *Bananas are satisfyingly exotic with their enormous, shiny green leaves, which become tattered as they grow older. This young banana,* Musa acuminata, *requires a sheltered spot.*

ARCHITECTURAL EXOTICS

THERE are many splendid plants that can be grown for their architectural interest, to use as focal points and eye-catchers. Many are hardy; others can thrive in temperate climates, if they are given due care, attention and protection.

Tree ferns

❀ Tree ferns are true ferns, and come from tropical forests. They have enormous upright rhizomes, which look like tree trunks and which can grow up to 4 m (13 ft). They are so stately that just one could be the only plant needed in a city courtyard.

❀ The Tasmanian tree fern (*Dicksonia antarctica*) will certainly not survive several cold winters in succession but, given a shady position where it is protected from the wind by a tall evergreen hedge, it may well survive many years.

❀ Temperate climates are not really humid enough for tree ferns so in summer spray the trunk or rig up an automatic system to water it. In warmer areas, winter protection may not be necessary but it certainly will be in cold rural areas.

❀ Overwinter your fern by surrounding the trunk with convenient insulating material such as polystyrene plant trays tied around the trunk. Fill the crown with straw and fix a hat of polystyrene on top. Stack straw bales around the trunk and fronds as high up as possible.

❀ Tree ferns become hardier the taller they grow so buy the tallest one you can find. Young plants with no trunk are not suitable to overwinter outdoors except in very sheltered spots.

Yuccas

❀ Yuccas bring height and very exotic white blooms to the garden. Most are hardy enough for hot sunny sites in temperate climates. Use them as focal points in a border or on their own, or as effective eye-catchers on steps and terraces or in courtyards.

❀ If you want lots of lush growth, remove the yucca's spent flower spikes before they have fully faded as well as any dying or dead leaves. Some yuccas form a trunk and branch after flowering.

BELOW: *These purple phormiums, although they certainly look exotic, are reliably hardy in many temperate areas if grown in sheltered areas. In most places bananas should be taken indoors in winter.*

LEFT: *Despite its exotic, glamourous appearance, the yucca is surprisingly hardy and makes a spectacular statement, particularly as a feature in its own right.*

❀ *Trachycarpus* (fan palm) is a family of six species of evergreen palms from the temperate forests of subtropical Asia. They have a very attractive habit of growth with fan-shaped leaves and cup-shaped flowers. Fan palms are small enough to be grown in a courtyard but make splendid specimen trees in any garden. They like full sun or dappled shade and should be sheltered from cold, drying winds.

❀ The Chusan palm (*Trachycarpus fortunei*) is a single-stemmed palm with a head of fan-shaped, dark green leaves 45–75 cm (18–30 in) long, and small yellow flowers. Female plants have blue-black berries. It needs shelter, particularly from north and east winds.

❀ The dwarf fan palm (*Chamaerops humilis*) is a shrubby palm, which grows in Mediterranean regions. It has rosettes of long, graceful, finger-like leaves and tiny three-petalled flowers. It is a good specimen plant for a small garden. If there is danger of frost it is best grown in a pot and taken into a conservatory or indoors for winter.

❀ These include *Yucca floribunda*, *Y. gloriosa* (Spanish dagger), *Y. g.* 'Variegata' and *Y. recurvifolia*. Some form a clump of several plants without trunks. When one individual in the clump flowers, it dies and is replaced by a new plant from underneath. *Y. whipplei* may take many years to flower so grow it only for its leaves.

Phormium

❀ These evergreen perennials come from New Zealand. They form striking clumps of large, strap-like leaves, ranging in colour from yellow-green to deep purple. They create spectacular focal points in a border, next to a building or at the edge of a lawn.

❀ They give a truly jungly feeling, although many are perfectly hardy. *Phormium tenax* 'Dazzler' has arching bronze leaves with red, orange and pink stripes and looks strong in a mainly red border. *P.* 'Sundowner' has bronze-green leaves; *P.* 'Variegatum' is light green with cream and lime stripes and looks good against darker foliage plants or a clipped hedge.

Palms

❀ These stately trees always look wonderful swaying on the skyline in tropical countries. There are only two hardy palms and both can add an exotic feel to a garden. Grown in a border, they can give a truly splendid touch, or they may be grown as specimens on their own.

ABOVE: *These gardens at Tresco in the Scilly Isles have a remarkably mild climate, and many semi-tropical plants grow here that will not grow on the British mainland. Here, a tall palm gazes out over the other islands and an agave presides over smaller plants lower down the hill.*

ABOVE: *The strawberry tree (Arbutus unedo) is a spreading, sometimes shrubby tree with fascinating shredding, red-brown bark, white flowers and exotic round, warty red fruit.*

EXOTIC FLOWERS

PRIDE of Madeira (*Echium candicans*) is a wonderfully exotic, enormous woody perennial with cylindrical blue flowers 30 cm (12 in) long, on stems that reach 1.5–2.4 m (5–8 ft) and flower for a long time. It may survive for years against a sunny, sheltered wall. In colder regions grow it in a cool greenhouse.

❀ The large *Abutilon* family comprises deciduous shrubs and small trees from tropical and subtropical regions. They are not especially stately and they need staking, but their flowers are both showy and delicate.

❀ In frost-prone districts grow them in pots against a wall and bring them indoors for winter. *Abutilon* 'Ashford Red' is evergreen with red flowers from spring to autumn, while *A. megapotanicum* (trailing abutilon) has slender, arching shoots and bell-shaped flowers with astonishing yellow petals and purple stamens from red calyxes in summer and autumn. *A. pictum* 'Thomsonii' has interesting leaves mottled with yellow and salmon-pink flowers flushed with orange.

❀ *Fremontodendron* or flannel bush has spectacular showy yellow flowers, dark green leaves and hairy young shoots covered with scales. Grow it against a warm, sunny wall or at the back of a border, associated with something like ivy. The foliage and shoots may irritate the skin.

LARGE-LEAVED PLANTS

OFTEN best planted as individual specimen plants, some of these are good-natured enough to associate with smaller-leaved plants in a shady corner of the garden.

❀ *Fatsia japonica* is grown mainly for its huge, shiny, dark green leaves and sturdy habit. There is a bonus of creamy-white flowers and small round black fruit. It is ideal for a shaded courtyard, will perk up a dark corner of the garden and can be used in a shrub walk. *Fatshedera lizei* has a splendid jungly look for a shady position. It is a cross between an ivy and a fatsia and looks like it. It is evergreen and easy to grow.

LEFT: *The canna lily is usually grown for its brightly coloured, red and orange flowers but this, Canna striata, has exotic striped leaves. Grown with dark-stemmed red Dahlia 'Bishop of Llandaff' and fiery Crocosmia 'Lucifer', it helps to create a striking 'hot' display.*

❀ Actually evergreen perennials, banana trees are stately and full of character. The Japanese banana (*Musa basjoo*) is the only hardy one. It grows to 5 m (16 ft) tall and has leaves 3 m (10 ft) long. The yellowish-green fruit are not for eating.

❀ *Gunnera manicata* looks like a giant, hairy rhubarb plant, and makes a superb architectural plant at the edge of a pond or stream. Protect the crowns in winter by folding the leaves over the top and covering them with straw.

SOME EXOTIC TREES

THERE are many interesting trees suitable for small or medium-sized gardens and some splendidly exotic ones, which are not often enough tried.

❀ *Acacia dealbata* is the mimosa tree, which has the prettiest grey-green ferny leaves and is covered in a mass of bright yellow flowers in spring. It grows fast but is really only for mild climates or a conservatory.

❀ The foxglove tree (*Paulownia tomentosa*) is hardy, deciduous and a summer-long jungle plant. If you cut it down in spring it will grow 3 m (10 ft) tall and produce soft, velvety leaves 75 cm (30 in) across, in one season. It has fragrant pinkish-white flowers.

❀ The strawberry tree (*Arbutus*) is well worth growing. *Arbutus* x *andrachnoides* is a beautiful evergreen, which flowers in winter and has interesting, peeling red-brown bark. It is excellent for large shrub borders, in woodland garden or as a specimen, and can also be grown against a wall. It will grow to 7.5 m (25 ft).

❀ All the magnolias are exotic and there is one for every garden, large or small. M. *grandiflora* is evergreen with big glossy leaves and huge scented white flowers, to be used as a freestanding wonder, not as a wall shrub. M. *stellata* is covered in small, star-like white flowers in spring and is very good for a small garden.

❀ *Photinia serratifolia* is an aristocratic evergreen, which grows to 3.5 m (12 ft) with an exotic habit, bronze-coloured new leaves in late winter and interesting peeling grey and brown bark. It is good among other trees and shrubs in a grove, shrub border or walk.

❀ The loquat (*Eriobotrya japonica*) is a large-leaved small evergreen tree. It has pale green shuttlecocks of flowers from spring to autumn and large and wrinkled leathery leaves. It can withstand drought and if its pale orange fruit ever ripen, they are edible.

BELOW: *The brilliant oranges and vivid reds of dahlias look even more striking when complemented by the strong purple of annual or perennial verbenas.*

BELOW: *All the magnolias are spectacular and make good specimen trees. This is Magnolia x soulangeana, which will grow to 6 m (20 ft) and has large goblet-shaped flowers in mid- and late spring.*

KNOWING THE GROUND
RULES OF PLANTING

One of the most important things to understand when starting
to garden is that plants originating from different parts of the world
will thrive in the conditions they have adapted to and will suffer if you
try to grow them in conditions that do not suit them. It is much more
satisfying to grow plants that will enjoy the existing soil, climate and
aspect in your garden than to try and grow plants that would be more
at home elsewhere. If you garden on lime, for example, choose
lime-tolerant plants, and if you live in a frost pocket do not
choose tender plants from warm countries.

Plant associations

❀ Think carefully about plant associations. In fact, this is
made easier by understanding the origins of plants.
Those that come from similar regions of climate and
soil will nearly always associate well together, but
trying to grow rhododendrons, which are acid-lovers,
together with the daisy family will not only be
unsuccessful but will not look good either. Another
important thing is to try and choose plants that will
not outgrow their allotted space.

ABOVE: *Gravel is a very good mulch for a dry garden, keeping the moisture
in and preventing weeds from taking hold. Most of the daisy family will
respond well to dry gardens, as will rock roses, both helianthemum and cistus,
as well as alliums and verbascums.*

ABOVE: *Plants that like shady areas include hostas, like this* Hosta undulata
'Univittata', *euphorbias, lilies and the beautiful drooping white flowers of*
Dicentra spectabilis 'Alba'.

Plants for particular aspects

❀ A north-facing wall in total shade will be colder than other parts of the garden. Even plants that tolerate these conditions will grow more slowly than they would in other areas. In the main, plants grown for their foliage are better on north-facing walls than those grown for their flowers. There are a few flowering plants suitable for such walls. They include the evergreen climbing hydrangea (*Hydrangea petiolaris*), which will climb a large wall without help and produce lace-cap hydrangea flowers that turn a pretty tan colour as they fade and last into winter.

❀ Shade plants often have bigger leaves than other plants. They include hostas, foxgloves, bergenias, ferns and euphorbias.

❀ The climbing rose 'Guinée', with its deepest red flowers and rather sparse leaves will do well on a north wall, as will the almost thornless white rose 'Madame Alfred Carrière'. This rose has a first flush of flowers in early summer and keeps on flowering, although less profusely, for the rest of the season.

❀ East-facing walls are very difficult. After a frost the early morning sun may damage the buds of otherwise hardy rhododendrons, camellias and magnolias.

❀ Good climbing plants to grow include *Actinidia kolomikta*, which has large heart-shaped green leaves with cream and pink variegations. The colour will not show on young plants or old plants grown in too much shade. Virginia creeper is another good climber for an east-facing wall and the feathery yellowy-green flowers of *Alchemilla mollis* will liven up the area nearer to the ground.

❀ South-facing walls are hot and dry. Silver, scented Mediterranean-type plants and plants from Australia and New Zealand will thrive in this sort of area. There is a wide choice of suitable plants, including the asters and other daisies, many herbs and many plants with colourful flowers.

❀ West-facing walls are the kindest. They get the evening sunlight and suffer less from frost. Here you can grow delicate and exotic plants that need shelter. These often come from places like California and include the bright yellow, wall-trained fremontodendron, the Ceanothus family with their clouds of bright blue flowers and *Passiflora caerulea*, the hardiest of the passion flowers with its strange exotic blooms and oval orange fruits.

❀ *Carpenteria californica* is an evergreen shrub from California, which produces an astonishing display of large, yellow-centered white flowers in summer. It may become a little shabby-looking after a cold spell, but soon recovers its good looks.

ABOVE: *Wallflowers, verbena and parsley have all been planted in generous clumps to create this bright and cheerful summer border.*

Beds and borders

❀ By now you will be anxious to choose the herbaceous and colourful plants for your borders. This is the purely decorative part of planting and it is tremendously exciting.

❀ You can work out appropriate schemes, pinpointing which plants and how many are to go where. A dictionary or encyclopedia of plants is invaluable at this stage. A good plant book will describe each plant, tell you how large it will grow, where it comes from and how to cultivate it.

❀ It is best to write down the names of each plant on your plan. You can colour in the areas so you appreciate how the scheme will work. Place the large trees and shrubs first to give a good structural basis then work down to the smallest. Remember to allow for plant growth. Flowering times are important too. Mix early and late flowerers in the bed or border so that you get a balance through the summer and autumn. List the plants you have chosen separately and the number required of each. This makes it easier when plant shopping or ordering.

Bed or border?

❀ A flower border is a growing area backed by a fence, hedge or wall, whereas a flowerbed is usually something you can walk around and see from all sides. It is important to keep beds and borders in scale with the garden.

❀ In a large garden you can have long, deep borders and allot space to a specific type of plant in the form of a rose garden perhaps or a fernery, whereas in a small garden you may be restricted to narrow beds and mixed planting for year-round effect. Whichever you have, always try to break up the garden into workable units.

❀ Borders should always have a background. Hedges can make good backgrounds but they need maintenance and steal water and nutrients from herbaceous plants. Leave a narrow path or strip wide enough for a lawn mower between the border and the hedge to allow room for weeding and clipping. This should be wide enough to allow you to bend down. Allow, too, for the spread of hedge growth and the eventual width of the hedge.

ABOVE: *This large island bed has been given an informal shape and is planted with low-growing plants at the edges and tall plants in the middle to give it an interesting shape. The colour scheme relies very much on reds and purples.*

❀ Fences are also a possibility and again, you should leave a gap between border and fence so you can paint it. The gap can be trampled earth and just wide enough to use. If you are willing to do the maintenance in winter, the space can be quite narrow.

❀ All gardeners use trial and error when planning something as complicated as a bed or a border, but you can eliminate some of the error by researching the plants first. All beds and borders grow and change, so after three years you may want to thin out, move or replant.

ABOVE: *This neat gravel path is edged on either side by upstanding irises, which give it form and colour but also a 'marching' quality, taking you swiftly down to the foliage arch.*

Size of borders

❀ The deeper a border, the more plants you can grow in it. In a 1.2 m (4 ft) border you could grow one climber at the back plus two rows of ground cover plants or one of shrubs. Alternatively, you could grow a clipped, trained wall shrub and one row of ground cover plants.

❀ If you try to grow more, the plants will suffocate each other and you will be forever clipping, trimming and cutting back. In a 1 m (3 ft) border you could probably get away with climbing plants at the back and one row of small shrubs but you might decide to concentrate on tiny rock plants instead.

❀ You need nearly 2.7 m (9 ft) to get in three tiered rows of plants comfortably. In a 1.5 m (5 ft) border you could probably just get three rows in, thereby incorporating much colour. The tiers should not be planted in strict rows unless the garden is very formal. The plants should be planted in drifts, the taller ones mingling slightly with the shorter ones, so that you get a natural-looking mixture, producing a more varied, patchwork effect.

❀ The maximum satisfactory depth for a bed is 2.7 m (9 ft), unless you have decided on an island bed that you can walk all around. You can create a 3.5 m (12 ft) bed but you need much larger clumps so the size is more suited to a shrub and conifer border or certainly you will want to use some shrubs and conifers to break up the area.

ABOVE: *The cushioned quality of these rounded plants gives the whole of this large bed a quilted quality that is most attractive.*

Plant chart for borders and beds

❁ Designing a border or bed that will look good all
summer long and into autumn is complex. You need
to include plants of different heights, so that the area
will have a sculptural and harmonious shape.

❁ A chart that includes all the plants you want to grow
will enable you to tell at a glance whether you have
enough tall, medium-height and small plants and will
help you to place them on your planting plan. Make a
grid for each border or bed and as you choose the
plants for each, fill them in on the grid.

❁ You will soon see where there are gaps. This will help
you to graduate the height only. You will still have to
decide on a colour scheme, but it is an enormously
helpful exercise in getting to know more about plants
in general. You can include perennial plants, annuals
and shrubs in the chart, and bulbs, too, if you wish.

Ground cover planting

❁ It was once considered aesthetically pleasing to grow
each plant in a border individually, leaving an area of
bare soil around it so that each plant was treated as a
specimen. Nowadays it is considered more attractive to

ABOVE: *Effective ground cover can be given by using different heights of
plant and variety in the colour of flower.*

allow groups of plants to blend into one another,
creating a close blanket of green from which the
flowers will rise like Aphrodite from the sea.

❁ This creates a good-looking, colourful result and is also a
form of ground cover that helps keep down weeds and
reduces the amount of maintenance necessary in the
border. Ground cover is also useful under trees where there
is not enough light or moisture to support healthy grass. In
addition, ground cover plants can be used on steep banks
where mowing grass would be difficult or dangerous.

❁ The range of plants that can be grown as ground cover
is enormous. Even plants that do not spread of their

ABOVE: *Skilfully planted marigolds, petunias, hollyhocks and poppies in raised beds framed by a twig fence.*

own accord can be used as ground cover if planted densely. Ground cover plants have a practical purpose but they also have a unifying effect in a small garden, especially when one variety of plant is allowed to create a smooth sweep of foliage.

Useful ground cover plants

❀ The best ground cover plants are evergreen. St. John's wort (*Hypericum*) can be grown in a shady part of the garden where its bright yellow flowers will glow out of the darkness. Rose of Sharon (*Hypericum calycinum*) flowers from early summer to early autumn. It makes a good specimen plant in non-shady places, too, but if planted in a border it can be invasive.

❀ The periwinkles (*Vinca*) are excellent at covering the ground but can be invasive too, so plant them in woodland where they will have to struggle a little. *Vinca minor* grows to only just off the ground. It normally has pale lilac flowers but white and dusky red forms are attractive and slightly less invasive. *V. major* will reach 30 cm (12 in) and climb into nearby shrubs. It can be difficult to control when grown among other plants.

❀ Ivy (*Hedera*) does well in shade. Irish ivy (*Hedera helix* 'Hibernica') has large green leaves and will grow in dense shade. It is a good maintenance-free plant grown in a north-facing, little-used part of the garden.

❀ Dead-nettles (*Lamium*) make excellent ground cover plants under trees. *Lamium galeobdelon* 'Silver Carpet' has yellow flowers and evergreen leaves heavily spotted with silver. It is invasive but not difficult to pull up where it has outgrown its space.

❀ When planting under trees it is vital to prepare the soil well and to remove all weeds such as couch grass, nettles, and ground elder, otherwise their roots will entwine with your plant roots to disastrous effect.

❀ In a sunny, well-drained spot, the rock rose *Helianthemum nummularium* grows vigorously and makes excellent colourful ground cover. There are many named varieties in pretty shades of red, yellow and white. They should be cut back severely with shears when the flowers are over in summer or they will become leggy and lose value as ground cover. Do not prune in spring or you will remove the flower buds for the year.

ABOVE: *Bulbs can be used to provide a blanket of colouring in the spring months using such flowers as the crocus and the bluebell.*

Alpine and rock garden planting

❀ Some of the most enchanting plants available to the gardener are the tiny alpine and rock plants that originate high up on mountainsides. Gardens created for these little treasures should always be in a light, open, sunny situation to emulate their places of origin as nearly as possible.

❀ The rock garden should face south or west to provide the best and longest light. It should not be near trees, which will cast unwanted shade and damage the tiny plants with drips of water and falling leaves.

❀ It should be on a slope to ensure good drainage. In their natural habitat, alpines receive plenty of moisture from melting snow but the water drains through quickly and the soil does not become waterlogged. All alpines dislike bad drainage.

❀ The main features of a rock garden are terraces and flat areas, well-drained soil behind stone outcrops for growing small plants, and pockets and crevices for plants so that their roots are shaded.

ABOVE: *Tulipa Montana grows to about 15cm (6 in) and associates well with larger rock garden. It flowers in early to mid- spring and prefers sharply drained soil.*

Materials and arrangement

❀ Any rocks you use should not lie on the surface of the soil but should appear to emerge from it; as in natural rocky outcrops. Choose local stone if possible. It is less expensive to transport and will look more in keeping. Limestone, sandstone, granite or tufa can all provide a natural appearance by simulating natural rock formations.

❀ A scree is a flat or sloping area of rock fragments with a little soil, plus a few small pools to increase the humidity. In nature, a scree is virtually a river of loose stones found at the foot of a mountainside before the meadow begins.

❀ An increasingly popular way to grow rock garden plants is in a raised bed. This is easy, inexpensive and takes up less space than a purpose-built rockery. A height of 0.5–1 m (1½–3 ft) is recommended. The retaining walls can be of bricks, stone, reconstituted stone or railway sleepers. You can build a series of terraces to create extra interest and a place for trailing plants.

BELOW: Gentiana acaulis *makes a thick cushion of foliage and its beautiful blue trumpet flowers bloom in spring. It should be planted in a sunny position, turned slightly away from the sun in sandy soil that does not dry out.*

Choice of rock plants

❀ Rock plants coming from similar places of origin will associate well together and will thrive if you give them the conditions they are adapted for.

❀ Scree conditions are the most successful for growing plants from higher regions. A few flat stones here and there add interest. To show up against the pebbles, dark green is the best leaf colour, although many suitable plants have grey leaves, which also look attractive.

❀ Suitable plants include the tight green hummocks of *Armeria juniperifolia* 'Bevan's Variety', which are completely hidden by bright pink round flower heads in spring. *Asperula lactiflora caespitosa* and *A. suberosa* both make tuffets surmounted by pink tubular flowers with long flowering periods.

❀ *Veronica canescens* has bright blue flowers above silvery tufts and *Edraianthus pumilo* has lavender bellflowers. There are bellflowers (*Campanulas*) for all sorts of garden situations. Some good ones for scree are *C. allionii*, *C. bellidifolia*, *C. saxifraga*, *C. tridentata* and *C. aucheri*, all of which have stemless bells of violet-blue.

❀ There are many plants from Australia that thrive in scree conditions, and *Celmisia coriacea* from New Zealand has white daisy flowers with silvery leaves. *Lewisia tweedyi* needs winter protection from a pane of glass or half a clear plastic water bottle used as a small cloche.

Acid-loving alpines

❀ If you have acidic soil, this is a good opportunity to have a rock garden for a different range of plants. Many of these plants thrive in cool north-facing positions. If your soil is neutral or alkaline, you can build a raised bed 1 m (3 ft) or so above ground level and fill it with ericaceous compost to suit these plants.

❀ Many primulas will grow well in moist acidic soil, including *P. vialii* whose flowers are violet spikes with red tops. *Trillium sessile* associates well with *Anemone nemorosa* and the harebell poppy (*Meconopsis quintuplinervia*) has hanging heads of single pale lavender flowers on slender stems all summer. Gentians, so difficult to grow in ordinary soil, flourish on acidic soils. *Gentiana sino-ornato*, *G. pumila* and *G. verna* all have flowers of a lovely deep blue. Lastly, there are some tiny rhododendrons, such as *R. hanceanum* 'Nanum', which has pale yellow flowers and grows to 15 cm (6 in) tall.

ABOVE: *The pasque flower (Pulsatilla vulgaris), a native of the Carpathian mountains, needs a sunny, open place place in the rock garden and associates well with carpeting thymes and sedums.*

BELOW: *Some species of rhododendron will grow well in a rock garden, particularly one with acidic soil; this type of soil lends itself well to a mixture of plants.*

STRUCTURING YOUR GARDEN

❦

Imagine a garden of separate areas or 'rooms', each one with its own 'look', yet conforming to the overall style of the garden. Each should be hidden from the others so that every new one comes as a surprise. Link these areas with attractive 'gateways' or 'walks', however short. A narrow path between tall hedges will encourage you to walk quickly to the next point of interest; the lower the hedge and the wider the path, the more you are encouraged to wander slowly and enjoy the planting on the way. Creating sudden openings from one area to another is one way to deal with the transition. Some hedges are dense and close-knit, others more open and lace-like, giving glimpses through them.

ABOVE: A disciplined gravel path, marked by curved lines of brick, is flanked by a clipped hornbeam hedge, leading the eye to the open countryside and yellow cornfield beyond.

Backcloths

❀ Clipped shrubs can be used as a backcloth for a flower or shrub border. They can also create a backcloth for a pretty garden seat. A niche can be cut into a yew hedge to hold a sculpture or water feature.

❀ On the whole, dark green varieties of plant are more useful as backcloths than golden ones. Nearly all plants look good against dark green. Box has possibilities as a backcloth, but it takes longer to grow to a good height.

ABOVE: A generous wooden bench is surrounded by colour – from the tiny pink and white erigeron and scented thyme at ground level to the two 'Ballerina' rose bushes and silvery Artemisia 'Powys Castle' at the back.

ABOVE: *In this clever ground cover planting, everything has a positive shape and there are no gaps. The spreading plants are punctuated by the round heads of alliums and the tall spires of yellow verbascums.*

❀ Another good clipped backcloth plant is the Lawson cyprus (*Chamaecyparis lawsoniana*). This is not as dark a green as yew, but an attractive dark blue-green. Like yew, it needs clipping twice in the growing season, but unlike yew it will not rejuvenate from old wood, so if you let it get out of hand, it will not recover. In fact, if you are going to grow a backcloth hedge it must be kept clipped and tidy or it will ruin the effect of any planting or other features in front of it.

Shelter belts

❀ If you are lucky enough to have a garden right next to open countryside, it will probably have the disadvantage of strong winds sweeping in. On the principle that it is usually most satisfactory to keep the formal part of the garden near the house and to allow it to become more informal as it moves away from the house, an informal shelter belt can be made of mixed evergreen and deciduous shrubs.

❀ A hedge is better than a wall because it allows the wind through gently, whereas when the wind hits a wall, the force is severe and can be very damaging. If the wind really tears into the garden, it is advisable to have the double protection of taller trees and then a lower hedge.

❀ The Scots pine (*Pinus sylvatica*), larch (*Larix*), Lombardy poplar (*Populus nigra* 'Italica') and white willow (*Salix alba*) are all good shelter trees for the outer belt. In front of them you can grow dog roses (*Rosa canina*), common hawthorn (*Crataegus monogyna*), privet (*Ligustrum*) and other tough native shrubs, which look attractive and will offer food and protection for small wild animals and birds.

❀ There are several interesting variegated forms of privet; the roses and hawthorn are both pretty when in flower and have bright red hips or berries in autumn.

❀ If you live by the sea, you can use *Escallonia macrantha*, which has healthy-looking shiny green leaves, *Olearia* x *haastii* with its grey-green leaves and whitish daisy flowers, *Hippophae rhamnoides*, pyracantha or *Viburnum tinus*, all of which are attractive in an informal situation and can stand salt-laden winds.

ABOVE: *It is easy to divide up your garden with the careful use of plants, shrubs and hedges, creating attractive and verdant areas.*

Divisions

❀ Formal divisions in the garden can be made with evergreen plants such as yew, box, chamaecyparis or holly. These are all easy to shape and are useful for dividing the garden with growing 'walls'. They make strong architectural shapes and can be clipped into pillars or gateways, or given bobbles on top and arches within them. You can make a stunning display by growing the climbing nasturtium, *Tropaeolium speciosum*, with its small flowers of deepest red, up a dark green yew.

❀ For an informal, irregular garden, it may be more desirable to use hedging, which lets a little light through and through which you can just glimpse what lies beyond. Good plants for this sort of hedge are beech (*Fagus sylvatica*) and hornbeam (*Carpinus betulus*). Both are deciduous and make elegant hedges. They have larger leaves than the evergreens, are less closely packed and have an elegant habit of growth.

❀ If your garden suffers from severe winters, you may prefer to use evergreens for all hedges to give protection to other plants during winter. A technique known as tapestry or mosaic hedging combines a number of compatible plants within the same hedge to provide changing visual effects throughout the year.

❀ You can combine deciduous with evergreen species and provide a colourful and varied background. This kind of hedge is probably best only in larger gardens or very informal wild gardens.

Screening

❀ If you want to screen the utility parts of the garden such as the compost heap, the garden shed or an oil tank, you can use a complete blocking off device, such as a tall hedge, or you can use a low hedge or individual shrubs.

❀ You can draw the eye away from the work area with some interesting tree or other feature, or divide the path leading to it, having it curve away from the work area and leading perhaps to a small arbour.

❀ A garden shed can be made much more attractive with a coat of paint. Modern paint ranges include very good positive blues, greys and blue-grey colours, which should be used on anything else you paint, such as fences or doors, if you want to retain a feeling of unity.

❀ Evergreen planting next to the shed can also help disguise its workaday quality. If you want to disguise it during summer only, *Fuchsia magellanica* makes an

ABOVE: *A beech hedge makes a good, dense green garden divider in summer. Its leaves turn a copper brown and remain attached all winter so it is really attractive all year round.*

attractive tallish bush with lots of pendant flowers late into the autumn and will retain its leaves during winter. You can then cut it back in spring.

❀ The variegated form has pretty grey-green leaves with darker markings. If you want something taller, *Garrya elliptica* is an evergreen grey-green shrub with slender long catkins. It looks splendid grown next to *Viburnum bodnantense* 'Dawn', which has pretty pink flowers on bare stems in winter and grows its leaves when the flowers are over.

Noise barriers

❀ Hedges can help to screen out unwelcome sounds such as steady traffic. You will not eliminate noise altogether but can muffle it slightly, and the sight of the screen will help psychologically to make the noise less annoying.

❀ If you can do some earth moving and create a bank of earth, and then plant an evergreen shelter belt up the side of it, it should help, although it is difficult to keep out the sound of a nearby dual carriageway, no matter what you do. Other penetrating sounds,

such as children's playgrounds, workmen's drills and radios are almost impossible to block out.

Using Leyland cypress

❀ The Leyland cypress (*x Cupressoyparis leylandii*) grows very fast, which is why so many people plant it as a screen and perimeter hedge. Unfortunately, it often gets out of hand. If it is not clipped regularly it grows far too tall and if it has been left too long, it cannot be rejuvenated by cutting back hard, as yew can.

❀ However, it does respond well to regular clipping and can be shaped into hedges with interesting shapes. Although the golden form is frequently chosen, the dark green form is often more attractive, especially in association with other planting. If it does get too big and beyond control, the best thing is to cut it down and start again.

BELOW: *The disciplined clipping of this leylandii hedge into a low green 'wall' and gateway demonstrates that there is no need to let this fast-growing hedging tree get out of hand.*

Links

🏵 Links between one part of the garden and another can be leisurely, following a path that leads from one to another, or they can be sudden. One area surrounded by hedges or shrubs can let immediately through an opening on to the next.

🏵 A path hedged on both sides by tall evergreens such as yew hints at secrets beyond and will lead the visitor quickly from one area to another. A low hedge of box or the shrubby honeysuckle, *Lonicera nitida*, will slow the visitor down, encouraging examination of the flowers and shrubs behind the hedge. A curved path is immediately intriguing and asks to be investigated.

🏵 Links need not be made of hedges. A tiny piece of woodland or groups of shrubs on either side of a path can be division enough. Shrubs that make good linking plants are the evergreen *Viburnum tinus*, whose dark green leaves and pretty white flowers are produced in winter when little else is out.

🏵 *Choisya ternata* is another useful shrub, with a characteristic smell to its leaves – that you either love or hate – and white flowers in summer. The yellow *C. t.* 'Sundance' can look cheerful grown against a dark foliage shrub.

🏵 When grouping shrubs as an informal link you can include a small tree to give height and interest. Some of the hawthorns make pretty little trees. *Crataegus laevigata* 'Paul's Scarlet' has double red flowers in spring but may not produce berries; *C. persimilis* 'Prunifolia' has glossy dark green leaves, which turn orange and scarlet in autumn, and lots of dark red berries. They will grow to around 3 m (10 ft).

ABOVE: *From the brightly coloured planting of this bed you are invited through an imposing archway of sweet bay* (Laurus nobilis) *to whatever lies beyond.*

ABOVE: *A curved woodland path of slate chippings lined with rounded stones dug up from the garden itself, leads enticingly from the entrance gate to a more open area of the garden.*

Woodland links

🏵 Links can open out and become woodland walks. Paths through them should be fairly wide to give a feeling of leisure and encourage people to take time to enjoy the walk.

🏵 You can create a tiny bit of woodland in a very small transitional area using forms of birch. If you plant two or three together to keep their growth to a minimum, you will create a little grove in which none of the individual trees will grow too large. Interesting birches to try are *Betula pendula jacquemontii*, which has pure white stems that show up well in winter light with large areas of shaggy brown, peeling bark, an attractive autumn leaf colour and large catkins.

❀ The paper birch (*Betula papyrifera*) has large leaves and the bark peels off in large sheets to reveal white underneath. It prefers moist conditions. Some birches have orange or brown stems. *Betula albo-sinensis* has red to orange-red peeling bark. All of these look interesting in winter.

❀ The lacy foliage of birches allows a certain amount of light through so they can be underplanted with suitable small plants. Underplanting should be kept simple. Birches underplanted with tiny hardy cyclamen such as *Cyclamen hederifolium* and *C. coum* look enchanting in later summer and winter. The cyclamen grow well under trees, seeming to need little moisture. You can plant them right up to the tree trunks in generous drifts.

❀ Cyclamen need no associates since they look so attractive and dainty on their own. However, if you would like to add a little more greenery to the whole look, you can plant the area with ferns. They should be low-growing varieties because tall ones will dwarf the cyclamen, the true eye-catchers, on the ground. *Athyrium filix-femina* 'Frizelliae' is the tatting fern, found in Ireland about 100 years ago. It is a charming little fern, seldom growing more than 30 cm (12 in) tall.

❀ The Japanese painted fern (*Athyrium japonicum* 'Mettalicum') has soft grey leaves with purple midribs merging to grey-green at the margins. It likes a sheltered spot.

❀ *Blechnum penna-marina* is a tiny creeping species, which creates mats of dark green, roughly textured fronds. Another useful plant for light woodland is *Lathyrus vernus*, one of the sweet pea family. It is a low-growing shrub with matt evergreen leaves and bright blue-pink flowers in spring and summer, which turn almost turquoise as they age.

❀ If you create a narrow archway or perhaps a living gateway of evergreen shrubs at each end, this woodland can become a separate garden enclosure in its own right, as well as forming a transitional area.

BELOW: *A narrow stretch of woodland comprising silver birches, grown in a clump so that they will not grow too tall, leads the visitor to a separate enclosure.*

ABOVE: *This charming little summerhouse or gazebo with its tiled roof and red uprights marks the end of a grassy walk, which itself ends in a statue as a focal point.*

Meeting points

❀ Where two or more paths meet, especially along right-angle axes, you can mark the spot with seats or arbours at each corner. Or you can simply mark the spot with a vertical feature.

❀ You can create a circular or square paved space to give the meeting point some substance. At the centre you could place a sundial or a small circular pool or feature tree such as a weeping pear (*Pyrus salicifolia*). If you have chosen a 'built' feature such as a fountain or sundial, you can plant around it using low-growing plants, such as creeping thyme, that will smell delicious if trodden underfoot.

❀ Four tall junipers could also mark the space. The Rocky Mountain

juniper (*Juniperus scopulorum*) is a narrow, conical plant with foliage that varies from green to grey-blue in colour and consists of fleshy scales. It will grow to about 15 x 6 m (50 x 20 ft), so if your garden is not very big you may prefer to use *Juniperus* 'Blue Heaven', which makes neat, narrow pyramids seldom more than 5 m (16 ft) tall, with very blue foliage and many berries.

❀ The greenish-silvery leaf colour and tall, columnar habit of the junipers would contrast well with shrub roses in the borders along the paths, especially silvery-pink ones such as 'Madame Pierre Oger', 'Felicia' and 'La Reine Victoria'.

❀ The junipers would work well in an informal garden. In a very formal one you might prefer to choose box or yew, clipped into obelisks, corkscrews, domes or other geometric shapes. Along the paths you could grow rows of lavender or rosemary, interspersed with regular plantings of standard rose bushes.

❀ The white rose 'Iceberg' looks pretty planted like this, as does 'Ballerina', whose clusters of flowers are pale pink with a white eye. You could interrupt these plantings at intervals with plantings of box clipped into neat balls.

❀ Planting for an informal garden can include low-growing plants such as the blue geranium *Buxton wallichianum* 'Buxton's variety', which has deep blue petals with white centres.

❀ The fiercely puce *Geranium sanguineum* makes a good show. All the geraniums can be interplanted with silver plants such as *Artemisia* 'Powys Castle', as well as old-

ABOVE: *A round hole in a wall can be used to frame a beautiful view. This sort of viewing device is used very effectively in Chinese and Japanese gardens. Here, a brick edging has been used in a flint wall.*

fashioned roses such as the Portland rose, 'Rose de Rescht', which grows to about 1 m (3 ft) tall and has small rosettes of the brightest purple-red with a delicious scent.

ABOVE: *Four tall, narrow juniper trees mark the meeting point of several axial paths, lending height and interest to an attractive brick-paved area with a large planter placed in the centre.*

Framing a view

❀ If the garden opens on to countryside, make the most of the view. Any worthwhile view, whether it is a part of the garden created by you or green fields, rolling hills and ripe corn or a pine forest should be incorporated into your plan.

❀ Whatever the view, a path should lead enticingly to the best place to observe it and there should be a seat inviting visitors to do so. You can frame the view with planting to bring it to people's attention, and emphasise its interest by planting shrubs or a hedge along the edge of the garden and leaving an opening to emphasise the transition from garden to 'outside'.

❀ The opening may be wide and generous, with two tall trees such as Lombardy poplars on either side or, in a more formal setting, two obelisks of clipped yew.

❀ Another way of drawing attention to such a view is to create a wide path bordered by pleached limes or a hornbeam hedge leading the eye – and the visitor – directly towards the scene in the distance. A small gate always looks inviting, even if it does not actually lead anywhere.

❀ If the garden is bounded by an evergreen hedge, you can create a 'window' in the hedge by careful training and clipping so that people have a tantalising glimpse of what lies beyond.

❀ Circular 'windows' are not too difficult to achieve with a round template on a stem that you stick into the ground. This works particularly well in a formal rose or herb garden. Even a narrow slit in the hedge can provide a glimpse of the view. Here you could place two seats positioned at an angle so that both the distant view and the enclosed garden can be enjoyed.

Edging and bordering

❀ Edges and borders in a garden function like piping on cushions. They emphasise the shape and neaten the lines. Edging looks most striking when only one plant is used. This is essential for a formal garden and often true of an informal garden as well.

❀ Good bordering plants include the old standby known as elephant's ears (*Bergenia cordifolia*). Many people who have seen this planted in parks think it rather dull but, planted in long rows along a straight path, its large evergreen, dark glossy leaves look attractive and disciplined. *B. cordifolia* 'Purpurea' has bright purple leaves in winter and produces dark purple flowers in spring, while *B.* 'Silberlicht' has tall stems of loose white flowers and bright green leaves.

❀ Box hedges, when clipped low, make excellent edging plants. Their neat formality shows up the flowershapes and colours of plants grown behind them. *Ajuga reptans* is a low-growing plant, good for bordering a narrow path.

❀ The variety 'Atropurpurea' has very dark purplish-green leaves and dark blue flowers in spring. Even when not in flower its leaves are evergreen and attractive.

ABOVE: *Small plants planted near the front of the border are grown to cascade over the brick wall, which softens the line of planting.*

ABOVE: *The yellow peony flowers for only a short time but is worth growing for its wonderful flowers and its attractive leaves.*

In an informal situation, it can be allowed to creep back into a flowerbed and to creep forward to soften the lines of paving. It is not invasive and is easily controlled.

❀ Geraniums make good informal herbaceous edging plants. They will die back during winter, but some provide a very long season of flowers. Geranium 'Johnson's Blue' has deep blue flowers with pink centres, and flowers prolifically.

❀ Another good geranium is 'Wargrave Pink', which has silvery-pink flowers over a long period. Both these geraniums will line a path very prettily all summer long if you clip the spent flower heads regularly. *Geranium sanguineum* (bloody cranesbill) is a low-growing plant with bright purple flowers from late spring through to late summer and its leaves colour well in autumn; *G. s.* 'Album' has pure white flowers.

❀ A dark green hedge often looks as though it could do with something to edge its 'feet' but because evergreens are greedy for moisture and nutrients, it is difficult to find a plant that will survive. *Lamium maculatum* 'White Nancy', however, is a low-growing dead-nettle with very pretty white and green leaves and white flowers, which seems to grow almost anywhere and has even been known to clothe the feet of a north-facing yew hedge.

Concealing the garden perimeter

❀ In small town gardens particularly, you may want to conceal where the garden ends. A clipped hedge always looks neat but will define and emphasise a garden's narrow shape, whereas informal trees and shrubs will create a less clearly defined outline.

❀ Choose shrubs that give flower, foliage and fruit interest all year round, and the eye will concentrate on the shrubs rather than on what is behind them.

❀ Choose the shrubs carefully for variety of foliage and height. If you are planting a small square area as a garden room, your planting can make it appear oval. Plant the occasional small tree or tall shrub at the back. A smoke bush (*Cotinus coggygria*) can be grown as a small tree or, if you prune it back hard in spring, will throw out new shoots with larger leaves.

❀ The purple forms blend well with blue-green foliage so you can underplant it with *Hosta* x *sieboldiana*. Also at the back, you can plant a variegated weigela. These deciduous shrubs have pretty pink flowers in spring and leaves that contrast well with the dark cotinus.

❀ Next to the hosta, plant as much as you like of *Alchemilla mollis*, whose feathery yellow-green flower heads and pretty fan-shaped leaves go well with almost anything. Bergenia leaves are evergreen and their large size and shiny quality lend body, and will contrast well with the alchemilla. A peony will add colour in spring and its foliage will look attractive all summer.

❀ Allow enough space for the plants you choose, particularly for the larger shrubs. The smoke bush, for example, will grow to 1.8 x 1.8 m (6 x 6 ft) in five years and will look best if it can really expand into its allotted place.

BELOW: *Bergenias, or elephant's ears, make good plants for the front of a border with their positively shaped, rounded leaves, which turn good autumn colours of red. The crab apple 'Yellow Hornet' and the purple berberis make this a spectacular autumn border.*

USING COLOUR

❧

Colour is very much a matter of taste in the garden as anywhere else. Some people want their garden to be a riot of reds and bright colours; others prefer a more subtle approach of misty blues and pinks in association with silver leaves. Others again will find the variety of colours provided by foliage alone is all the colour they need.

✿ Colour is not a finite thing. It is affected by all sorts of things, including the other colours surrounding it, the quality of the light shining on it and the texture of the flower or leaf itself.

✿ Colours also appear different in different climates. In Mediterranean areas, the harsh overhead sun creates hard contrasts and shadows. Bright colours are necessary or they will not be noticed at all. The more intense the light, the more saturated the colour needs to be.

✿ In more northerly areas, the summer sun is lower in the sky and there is more moisture in the air. The resulting light is always slightly soft and blue, and pastel colours take on a particular glow not found in hotter areas.

Study of colour

✿ The science of colour was avidly studied by Victorian gardeners. When the French scientist,

LEFT: *The subtlest of greens, greys and yellows will pick up the light and transform a garden.*

BELOW: *It is best to restrict pink and red to a few shades in any one bedded area for simplicity and harmony of colour.*

ABOVE: *Use colour to surprise, like this simple thistle of the deepest purple.*

the Duke of Sutherland at Trentham Park, in Staffordshire, in the design of spectacular bedding schemes.

❀ Beaton and Fleming both introduced ribbon or 'promenade-style' borders at Shrubland Park and Trentham in the same year. Although the designs were nothing if not bright, the colours were restricted. Each border had three continuous lines of colour extending its whole length. Beaton described his like this: 'The first row on each side of the walk is blue, the second yellow and the third on one side is scarlet and on the other, white'.

❀ He used nemophila for the blue, calceolaria for the yellow and pelargoniums for the scarlet. Gardeners were also well aware that red seems to advance in broad daylight but blue advances in the evening light.

Chevreul (1786–1889), published a report on his study of colour for the Gobelins Tapestry Workshop in Paris, many British gardeners argued for the use of complementary colours, as recommended by him. Others argued that his colour theories took no account of green, which controlled the effect of complementary colours in a garden.

❀ Donald Beaton, head gardener at Shrubland Park, in Suffolk, in the 1840s considered that any variegated plant would function as a neutral colour and proudly described a bed he had planted with verbena and variegated pelargoniums, which a visitor had said looked like 'shot silk'. He used to compete with John Fleming, head gardener to

Colour complexities

❀ Whatever the complexities of colour in scientific terms, most gardeners will observe the effects of colours in their own gardens and decide for themselves which colours work in different parts of the garden at different times of day and in different seasons.

❀ Plant a purple-leaved plant in one place and it will catch the afternoon light so that its leaves become a magical stained glass window display; plant it elsewhere and it will never light up in the same way.

BELOW: *If you want to make a splash in your garden, mingle the perfectly formed flowers of the brightest red and white dahlias in a grand display of colour.*

USING THE
COLOUR SPECTRUM

The colour spectrum is a continuum of infinite gradations of colour between the six rainbow colours: red, orange, yellow, green, blue and violet. Colours have other qualities too. They may be very intense; they may be tinged with black (tones) or with white (tints). Examples based on the spectrum give a simplified idea but are a useful guide to the complex interaction of colours in a planting scheme.

THE COLOUR WHEEL

THE colour wheel shows the colours of the spectrum placed so that each colour is opposite the colour that it complements. Opposite colours and neighbouring colours both offer pleasing colour schemes. Less satisfactory results are usually produced by mixing the yellow-reds and blue-reds.

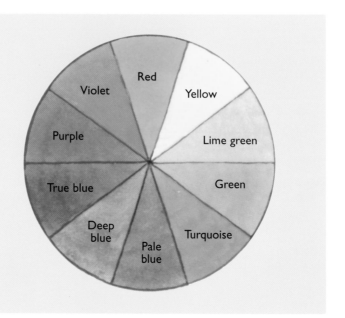

Colour in the garden

✿ Colours to choose for the garden are endless. There are dozens of different reds and different intensities of those reds, and the same is true of yellow, blue, green, in fact all the colours. Take red itself. There are blood reds, flame reds, poppy reds, rust, terracotta, wine, crimson, scarlet, beetroot, cerise and rose red, to name but a few.

✿ Green may vary from blue grass to turquoise, emerald, jade, pea green, grass green, olive green, coppery greens and true green, which is more or less epitomised by parsley.

✿ Yellow may vary from the greeny-yellow of many euphorbias to the sunny yellow of *Kerria japonica*. The term 'golden' is often used for yellow-leaved

plants, shrubs, conifers and other plants with yellow variegation, as well as for flowers.

✿ However, yellow is brighter than gold and many yellow tones have some blue in them, making them greeny-yellow rather than golden-yellow. 'Egg yolk' or 'buttercup' seems to describe many yellow plants better than 'gold'. The yellows include colours such as buff, sulphur, lemon, maize, saffron, primrose and canary.

✿ Blue is the most misunderstood colour of all and true blue is one of the rarest of flower colours. Most blues have some red in them, making them nearer to purple than blue. The shrubs, ceanothus and ceratostigma, are covered in very blue flowers in early or late summer; *Salvia uliginosa* and the Himalayan blue poppy

(*Meconopsis betonicifolia*) are among the true blues.

❀ The purples and violet-blues are easy to find. Many of the herbs such as the thymes, sages and oreganos have violet or purple flowers. Delphiniums, monkshoods, asters and campanulas are all rich in violets and purple-blues, too.

The colour wheel

❀ You can experiment very well yourself with different colours and colour schemes, but a basic knowledge of colour can be valuable, too. The colour wheel is a device for demonstrating the relationships between the colours of the spectrum by dividing them into equal segments.

❀ On a wheel like this, colours opposite each other are known as complementary. These colours nearly always go well together. For example pillar-box red is opposite dark green on the wheel and true blue is opposite orange. These colours usually look attractive together in a garden.

❀ Colours next to each other on the wheel usually look good together too, although less arresting. Some adjacent colours are more successful than others. For example, red and purple often associate well but yellow does not always look its best next to another yellow.

❀ The colour wheel is useful as a basic guide, but is nevertheless a fairly blunt instrument when choosing a colour scheme. Light will affect the colours, depending on the texture of the flower or leaf and depending how bright it is and how it is angled.

❀ Colours will affect each other as well. A particular red may look very bright against a pale colour, but become toned down if it is next to a deep colour. Orange and cerise may make a brash impression grown together, but if the cerise flower has a black centre, for example, it will alter the effect importantly.

ABOVE: *Yellows and reds give a bright, sunny, lively feeling to a border. Here, Gaillardia grandiflora with their yellow and red flowers are mixed with swathes of red lobelia in an informal scheme.*

ABOVE: *Blues and whites are cool and calming. Here, the tall spikes of a range of blue delphiniums combine with white to produce a striking 'cool' scheme, with the pink of the flowers in front adding a little warmth.*

COLOURS IN THE SPECTRUM

❀ Red, yellow and blue are described as primary colours. All other colours are produced by mixing these three. Side by side, they produce violent contrasts because they have nothing at all in common.

❀ Children love the primary colours, perhaps because they are so easily distinguishable from each other and so definite. The three colours separating the primary colours on the colour wheel are green, orange and violet. They, too, are in contrast but because they are secondary colours – made by mixing two primary colours – they harmonise rather than clash.

❀ Practice in mixing and matching colours greatly increases awareness of colour. You can use crayons, felt tips pens, watercolours or simply arrange colour samples from paint charts.

❀ In a practical gardening situation you can bisect the colour wheel, drawing a line between the green and red sides of the wheel. One side can relate to flowers and leaves with blue in their make-up, the other relates to flowers and leaves containing yellow.

❀ Many effective colour schemes have been made by the use of one or other of the two ranges, with only limited use of the other one in the scheme. There are some possibilities below for taking these colour associations a little further. Remember, in the garden they will be surrounded by other colours, particularly green.

OPPOSING COLOURS ON THE COLOUR WHEEL

THERE are some striking possibilities for the garden with these colour combinations.

Buttercup yellow and purple

❀ One example of this colour combination would be the tall perennial *Filipendula ulmaria* 'Aurea' with the creeping *Ajuga pyramidalis* grown in front.

True blue and orange

❀ Consider growing the funnel-shaped, deep blue flowers with white and yellow centres of *Convolvulus tricolor* with the hardy annual Californian poppy (*Eschscholtzia californica*).

Dark green and pillar box red

❀ This is exemplified by the deep red, semi-double flowers of *Camellia japonica* 'Adolphe Audusson', growing among its own dark green shiny leaves.

Adjacent colour combinations

❀ These two-colour schemes use colours that are next to each other on the colour wheel.

BELOW: *This exciting colour combination comprises opposing colours on the colour wheel – the deep orange and yellow plates of achillea contrasting strikingly with the purple spikes of* Salvia x sylvestris.

Red and purple

❀ *Rosa* 'Paul's Scarlet Climber' with its fairly small bright red double flowers will give a reliably generous display at midsummer, grown together with Clematis 'The President', whose deep purple flowers with their reddish-purple stamens will flower continuously from early summer to early autumn.

Pink and orange

❀ Many annual bedding plants have this mixture of colours. For example, *Dorotheanus bellidiformis* is a low-growing succulent annual with daisy flowers of crimson, orange, pink, red or white, sometimes with petal bases of a contrasting paler colour forming an inner zone around the darker central disc. They like a poor, dry soil and associate well with Californian poppies (*Eschscholtzia*) and pot marigolds (*Calendula officinalis*).

Orange and yellow

❀ The Welsh poppy (*Meconopsis cambrica*) is an annual poppy whose bright yellow, tissue-paper petals bloom from spring to mid-autumn. It looks even better interspersed with M. c. var. *aurantiaca* 'Flore Pleno', which has double orange flowers. If they like the position they will sow themselves and come up again, year after year.

ABOVE: *Orange and purple are at opposite ends of the colour spectrum and produce very positive and exciting planting schemes like this Zinnia 'Golden Sun' with the purple leaves of* Ricinis communis *'Carmencita'.*

Yellow and lime green

❀ The perennial *Euphorbia polychroma*, with its bright lime-green leaves and bracts, can be grown very effectively with the low-growing, front-of-border annual, the poached egg flower (*Limnanthes douglasii*), with its bowl-shaped yellow flowers with white centres.

Green and blue

❀ Baby blue eyes (*Nemophila menziesii*) is a trailing hardy annual with small bright blue flowers, which associates well with *Nemesia strumosa* 'Blue Gem'. Both have the brightest of blue flowers nestling among green foliage.

Blue and purple

❀ Woodland spring bulbs such as the lovely blue scillas and chionodoxas will associate beautifully with the small purple-blue *Anemone blanda*.

Three-colour combinations

❀ There are various triads of colours produced by turning an imaginary triangle in the colour wheel. Classic examples of successful three-colour combinations are sage green/plum/dried grass and citrus green/slate blue/rust red. These bear the same relationships to each other as red/yellow/blue but are easier to combine because they are secondary not primary colours.

❀ This is a simplified view of the colour spectrum and there are dozens of combinations to try. Many plants mentioned have other colours in them, such as white or red, and all will be surrounded by foliage of various colours. However, it should help the inexperienced gardener to look at colours with new eyes.

ABOVE: *kimmias are low-growing shrubs with attractive evergreen leaves and good clusters of bright red berries in autumn and winter. Here, they contrast highly effectively with the snow-white flowers of the common snowdrop (*Galanthus nivalis*).*

FOLIAGE COLOUR

IN general people think of leaves as being green, but look again. Leaves can be all the colours of the rainbow. In itself, green is paramount in the garden. It is the colour that induces calm and tranquillity. It has the ability to heighten pale colours and to tone down bright ones, and a pleasant garden can be created with no other colour but green. Gardens created entirely with foliage do have a particular quality of unity and peace but they need not be only green. Foliage comprises many other colours besides green, for example blues, silvery-greys, yellows, reds and cream and green variegations. Of course, these plants often have colourful flowers as well.

Blue-leaved plants

❀ The giants of the blue-leaved plants include *Crambe maritima* and *Thalictrum flavum* ssp. *glaucum*, both of which have blue-green leaves. Medium-sized blue plants include *Euphorbia characias* 'Blue Hills', a rounded compact dome with blue-green leaves, which grows to 1 m (3 ft).

❀ *Rosa glauca* is a species rose with glaucous purplish leaves and stems. Lower-growing plants include several

good blue grasses, including the evergreen *Helicotrichon sempervirens*, 38–46 cm (15–18 in) tall, and *Festuca glauca*, which makes little mounds of blue.

Silvery grey-leaved plants

❀ There is a really lovely selection of silvery-leaved plants available. They complement dark green leaves, as well as flower and foliage colours from deepest purple to pale pink and blue. They include the artemisias, for example *Artemisia* 'Powys Castle', which grows to 1 x 1.8 m (3 x 6 ft) and A. 'Lambrook Silver', 1 x 1.2 m (3 x 4 ft). *Brachyglottis Dunedin* Group 'Sunshine' (syn. *Senecio* 'Sunshine') grows to 1 x 1.8 m (3 x 6 ft); *Eleagnus* 'Quicksilver' has striking narrow silvery leaves and reaches 1 x 1 m (3 x 3 ft).

❀ Smaller silver plants include the curry plant (*Helichrysum italicum*) with narrow silver leaves, which grows to 30 cm (12 in). Lamb's ears (*Stachys byzantina*) forms dense mats of thick woolly grey leaves, 40 x 50 cm (16 x 20 in).

❀ *Convolvulus cneorum* is a charming, low-growing silver plant with white convolvulus flowers. *Artemisia schmidtiana* 'Nana' grows to 30 x 30 cm (12 x 12 in);

ABOVE: *The large, variegated yellow and green leaves of the Hosta fortuneii 'Aureo-Marginata' look extremely interesting against the deeply cut, feathery purple leaves of the Acer palmatum.*

LEFT: *Woodland always provides good opportunities for displaying autumn colour. Here, a gravel path leads through a variety of shrubs and woodland planting, with colours ranging from the orange of the Fothergillia gardenii to the green of the asplenium fern and the deep purple leaves of the heuchera.*

BELOW: *Sedum atropurpureum flowers well into autumn and has much deeper coloured flowers than the more common Sedum spectabile, as well as very dark purple stems.*

cotton lavender (*Santolina chamaecyparisus*) has finely dissected woolly leaves and grows to 60 x 60 cm (24 x 24 in). The woolly willow (*Salix lanata*) is a low, spreading bush for rock gardens, measuring 30 x 30 cm (12 x 12 in).

Red/bronze-leaved plants

❀ Red, bronze and purple leaves can be sensational if carefully placed. The red and bronze colours can complement other plants significantly. They look particularly good with greens and silvers, but may be less successful with variegated and yellow-leaved plants.

❀ *Cotinus coggygria* 'Royal Purple' is a splendid shrub with purple leaves, which turn bright red in autumn. *Berberis* 'Bagatelle' is a rounded shrub with bronze-purple foliage, often used as a hedge.

❀ Many roses have deep bronze young foliage in spring, which later turns green. *Cercis canadensis* 'Forest Pansy' is a deciduous tree or large shrub with bronze-reddish-purple foliage, which keeps its colour all season. It needs a sheltered, sunny spot and is slow growing but will eventually reach 12 m (40 ft).

❀ The palm-like *Cordyline australis* 'Pink Stripe' has leaves with purplish edges and a rich pink central stripe. It is not hardy so it should be grown outside only in mild areas or in tubs where it can be brought in for the winter.

❀ *Heuchera* 'Palace Purple' has coppery purple leaves and the leaves of H. 'Pewter Moon' are heavily marked with silver. *Berberis thunbergii* 'Atropurpurea', also known as 'Crimson Pygmy', is a deciduous berberis with rich purple new foliage. It is good as a colourful low hedge or a rock garden plant.

Yellow-leaved plants

❀ *Berberis thunbergii* 'Aurea' has spectacular yellow leaves and makes a rounded bush 1 x 1 m (3 x 3 ft). The Mexican orange blossom (*Choisya ternata* 'Sundance') is an evergreen shrub with very yellow young growth.

❀ *Cornus alba* 'Aurea' is a deciduous shrub, which grows to about 1.8 m (6 ft) tall. Golden privet (*Ligustrum ovalifolium* 'Aureum') has green leaves with broad bright yellow borders. *Hedera helix* 'Buttercup' is a good bright yellow ivy, which will grow to 2 m (7 ft).

PLANTING FOR COLOUR

For colourful beds and borders, a gardener will always be experimenting,
moving plants around and borrowing ideas from other gardens. It's a
wonderfully inexact science. One month the colours in a border will
harmonise beautifully, the next it has all changed and the harmony is lost.
One of the most exciting things about a garden is that it does not remain static
so you must always be rethinking. You may like deep, rich colours to dominate
the whole garden, or a patchwork of pastels or even one dominant single
colour such as white or red. Whatever your preference, a disciplined approach
is normally more satisfying in the long run.

Limiting the colours

❀ If you try and grow all the primary colours together,
too many reds, yellows and blues in close proximity
can have a very tiring and confusing effect. They may
be enjoyed in a large space such as a public park where
disciplined formal bedding can make some sense of
them, but they can be really hard on the eyes in a
small garden.

❀ Leave out just one of the primary colours and
concentrate on the reds and blues, say, or the yellows
and reds, or the blues and yellows in any single area of
your garden, and you can make it look as rich as an
oriental carpet. There is an enormous choice of plants
and colours even within this restricted palette.

❀ The successful garden designer, Gertrude Jekyll
(1843–1932), studied first as a painter and
subsequently treated the colours in her gardens as
though she were creating a painting. She would
graduate the colours in her long borders with great
skill, moving from yellows and whites through oranges
and reds to the blues and purples.

BELOW: *The pale yellow of these argyranthemums is a particularly attractive
colour, whether used on its own or mixed with other yellows such as lupins and
lilies as here.*

❀ The gardens she designed were large enough, so that these borders could be viewed from a distance and the visitor could get the full effect, as in a painting. In many of today's smaller gardens you could not do this, but you can still concentrate on particular colours in different areas of the garden.

❀ Red and purple are very dominant. White plants such as *Gypsophila paniculata* or Shasta daisies can help to tone them down a little.

❀ Pastel colours such as the violets, pinks or very pale yellows can be planted together. They may need the boost of something positive, perhaps a few black tulips in a spring scheme or some deep velvety-red pelargoniums in a summer patio scheme or the deep coloured leaves of a purple cotinus in a mixed border.

Single-colour schemes

❀ Of course, no scheme is truly made up of a single colour; all schemes are surrounded by the various greens, blues, silvers and bronzes of the foliage. Having single flower colour schemes can be effective but it is not wise to give the whole garden over to just one colour because of the difficulty in supplying it with enough of the colour for the whole season. In just one area or a border or a small front garden, however, you can certainly use a one-colour scheme quite successfully.

ABOVE: *Pastel colours are very much in the tradition of the 'old English garden'. Here, low-growing roses, catmint (Nepeta), Geranium 'Wargrave Pink' and stocks are grown in a grand profusion of pink and lilac.*

❀ White is the obvious colour choice and probably the most effective. You can get white varieties and cultivars of most plants so you can keep up the effect for a long time and the combination of white and different greens is a particularly charming combination. The structure of the border remains important or it will all begin to look like a bedraggled bridal bouquet.

ABOVE: *It is not often you find such a concentration of colour in a water garden, but here, candelabra primulas (Primula bulleyana) in the brightest reds, yellow and oranges are tempered only by a few zantedeschia lilies in the background.*

Suiting the mood of the garden

❀ Choose a colour combination that suits the mood of your garden space. Red can be heavy and overbearing because it has the quality of seeming to advance towards you, but it can have a stunning effect in a small courtyard or basement garden.

❀ Harmonious colour compositions, rather than strongly contrasting ones, will give unity and a bigger sense of space. If your garden is a cool airy terrace, fresh cream, pink, silver and yellow will complement the atmosphere.

Colour ideas for beds and borders

❀ A flower border is an immensely complex thing to design and an all-seasons border is the most complicated of all. For one thing, its shape and form are changing all the time as different plants reach maturity at different times of the year.

❀ The plants that are actually in flower change from week to week and, as the season progresses, plants may outgrow their spaces and begin to look untidy. It is a good idea in spring to rely heavily on bulbs because they tend to be smaller than plants that flower later and, as their leaves die down, new plants growing up nearby will conceal them.

ABOVE: *This pretty example of an informal cottage-style garden mixes the plate-like heads of achillea with cone-shaped echinacea and crosocmia.*

ABOVE: *The oriental poppy Papaver orientale 'Mrs Perry' is a beautifully shaped plant with superb salmon-pink flowers, which contrast well with the dainty pink spikes of Persicaria bistorta and with pale yellow irises.*

❀ It will help to make a plan of your colour scheme. Mark in any evergreens or firmly shaped deciduous shrubs first. Good structure with heights and masses will help integrate all the other plants.

❀ Now divide your bed or border into groups of plants, choosing some for each season. A large showy plant such as a peony can be grown singly but in general most plants give a better effect if planted in groups. Planting in threes or fives is usually best although in a very large border you could increase the numbers.

❀ If you want to include all the colours in your border, arrange them in harmonies or contrasts and make sure the transition from one group of colours to another is marked by a neutral colour such as green or white, or that the colours are interrupted by shapely foliage plants.

The yellow side of the spectrum

❀ There are several possibilities if you want spikes in your yellow-based colour scheme. *Verbascum nigrum* is a semi-evergreen plant with tall narrow spikes of brown-centred yellow flowers; red hot pokers (*Kniphofia*) are good for providing height.

❀ The hardiest of the plants in the yellow spectrum is *Kniphofia caulescens*, which has coral-red flowers turning yellowish-white; 'Bees' Sunset' has soft orange pokers and the smallest is 'Little Maid', which is a soft yellow. *Crocosmia* can create a splash of colour from late summer to early autumn. C. 'Lucifer' is deep red, C. 'Jackanapes' is yellow and orange.

❀ For clump-forming plants, try *Achillea* 'Coronation Gold', which has flat heads of tiny golden yellow flowers and silvery leaves for much of the summer and sometimes into autumn. *Helenium* 'Moerheim Beauty' is an upright plant for late summer, which has rich reddish-orange flower heads with a dark central boss.

❀ Chocolate cosmos (*Cosmos atrosanguineus*) is a tuberous perennial with single deep maroon crimson flower heads borne singly that make a good contrast with the yellows, and really do smell strongly of chocolate.

❀ For evergreen shrubs consider Halimium ocymoides, a dwarf shrub whose yellow flowers have black or brown spots at the base of the petals from early to midsummer. It reaches 0.6 x 1 m (2 x 3 ft).

❀ If you want to add something on the blue side, *Aster frikartii* 'Mönch' is a bushy perennial with daisy-like, soft lavender-blue flower heads. It goes well with the helenium and flowers continuously from midsummer to late autumn. *Phlox paniculata* makes large clumps of fine broad lilac-coloured flower heads on tall upright stems.

❀ For the front of the border you could use groups of *Alchemilla mollis*, with its long season of pretty foliage and feathery greeny-yellow flowers and *Eschscholtzia californica*, or pot marigolds (*Calendula officinalis*), whose bright orange flowers will counteract any blue in the alchemilla.

❀ Helianthemum provide a succession of colour from late spring through summer. *H.* 'Wisley Primrose' has pale grey-green leaves and yellow flowers; *H.* 'Rhodanthe Carneum' has carmine-pink flowers with orange centres and silvery foliage.

❀ In a small garden you may not have room for all these. Remember, if in doubt, it is usually more effective to have larger clumps of fewer cultivars.

A PLANTING DESIGN

Although this sketch is of a summer flowerbed, it has been planted with bulbs as well, so it will only be bare of flowers in the depth of winter. One half of the sketch shows the planting plan, the other gives an idea of the colours and heights of the plants when in flower. The colours are mainly pink and purple, with small touches of yellow and a little deep red here and there. The two shrub roses are pink and flower generously over a long period.

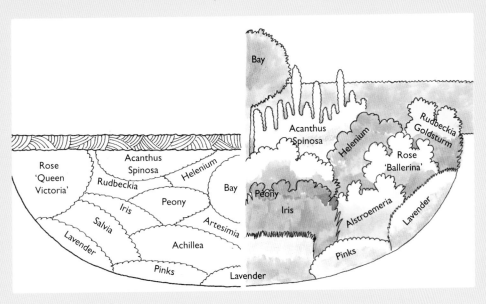

The blue side of the spectrum

❀ For tall spikes you could grow *Delphinium Belladonna* Group 'Cliveden Beauty', a compact variety of delphinium, which produces spikes of sky-blue flowers. It will continue to flower until autumn if the old spikes are removed.

❀ Delphiniums in the Black Knight Group are tall with deep violet-purple flowers with black eyes and those in the Blue Bird Group have clear blue flowers with white eyes.

❀ Upright blueish plants include *Campanula lactiflora* 'Prichard's Variety', which has branching heads of large nodding bell-shaped violet-blue flowers from early summer to late autumn. *Verbena bonariensis* has wiry stems with tufts of tiny purple-blue flowers in summer to autumn.

❀ For clump-forming plants look at *Eryngium* x *oliverianum*, which has large rounded heads of thistle-like blue to lavender-blue flowers. *Geranium psilostemon* is a fairly tall geranium with spectacular magenta flowers with black centres. *Salvia nemorosa* 'May Night' has deep violet-blue flowers, and *Erigeron* 'Serenity' has violet daisy-like flowers with large yellow centres.

ABOVE: *In this informal border, the pinks and reds of the colour spectrum have been chosen in the form of the large round heads of dusky red alliums, the tall spikes of* Verbascum phoenicium *and the oriental poppy* Papaver orientale *'Park Farm'*.

Plants for a red and silver autumn border backed by shrubs

❀ *Hydrangea villosa* is an interesting and attractive tall shrub for a deep bed. It has large lace-cap flowers of pale purple from midsummer to autumn. *Rosa moyesii* 'Geranium' is another tall shrub with bright crimson single flowers and flagon-shaped scarlet hips on arching stems.

❀ In front of these, plant *Sedum* 'Ruby Glow', an upright, fleshy plant with ruby-red flowers suffused with purple. *Artemisia* 'Powys Castle' is a rounded shrub with feathery silver foliage and *Acanthus spinosus* has large, deep green toothed leaves with long spines and spectacular spires of pale mauve and white flowers.

A rich border of reds and greens

❀ This colour scheme looks best against a dark green background such as clipped yew. These colours are directly opposite one another on the colour wheel so will

ABOVE: *This very pretty purple and blue mixture of low-growing spreading flowers such as verbena and geranium is set off beautifully by the silvery leaves of* Teucrium fruticans.

provide deliberate contrast and startling effect. Ruby chard is a spinach-like plant, grown for its bright red stems and crinkled green leaves with bright red veins.

❀ Penstemons are evergreen perennials with tubular foxglove-like flowers. They will flower all summer long. *Penstemon* 'Garnet' has deep carmine flowers; P. 'Cherry Ripe' is a warm red; and P. 'Chester Scarlet' has large dark red flowers with deeper red throats. Dhalia 'Bishop of Llandaff' has bright scarlet flowers with dark purple foliage.

COTTAGE GARDEN MIXTURES

THE charm of a cottage garden is its natural look, which appears to be made up of an unco-ordinated mixture of colours provided by annual and herbaceous plants, often self-seeded. In fact, modern 'cottage gardens' are carefully orchestrated and not as chaotic as is often supposed.

Plants for an early summer cottage garden

❀ This scheme is made up of purple, orange and bright pink. *Geranium magnificum* is a robust clump-forming geranium with deep blue flowers flushed red; *Eschscholtzia californica* is a hardy annual with silky smooth orange upturned flowers on feathery green foliage; *Tanacetum coccineum* 'Brenda' is a perennial with single daisy-like magenta-pink flowers with aromatic feathery leaves.

❀ Violas are well-loved cottage garden plants. Violas in the *Purpurea* Group have flowers of purple and violet and their leaves are often tinged with purple. They associate well with the spiky purple flowers of *Salvia* 'Ostfriesland' and with small silver-leaved plants such as the half-hardy *Senecio maritima* and *Tanacetum densum* subsp. *amani* with its silver-grey mop of feathered foliage.

❀ A midsummer mixture might include *Leucanthemum* x *superbum*, a hardy tall white daisy, more showy and more reliable than the simple marguerite. It associates well with bright red and yellow gazanias and all are easy to grow in a well-drained soil.

Using clematis

❀ Clematises are invaluable for providing colour in a garden throughout the year. In winter there are the bright yellow flowering species such as C. *tangutica* and the pale buff C. *balearica*. In spring the vigorous C. *armandii* and C. *montana* varieties can cover a whole wall or fence with white or pink flowers.

Summer-flowering clematis can be grown through many other plants, adding spectacular colour.

❀ The starry white flowers of C. *flammula* can be grown over dark green holly. Dusky red and purple clematis look good with silver-leaved plants. Try C. *viticella* 'Madame Julia Correvon' over *Brachyglottis compacta* – you can cut off the Brachyglottis' own yellow flowers.

ABOVE: *There is an enormous choice of colours among the clematis tribe. Here, Clematis 'Niobe' with its deep, velvety-red flowers is mingled with the paler pink of C. 'Comtesse de Bouchaud'.*

PLANNING
YEAR-ROUND COLOUR

It is impossible to cover the whole garden in bright colour all year round, but it is good to have some colourful, eye-catching plants somewhere in the garden at all times of the year. In a larger garden you can allocate particular spaces to specific times of year. Gertrude Jekyll, the famous garden writer and designer of the early 1900s, had part of her own garden dedicated to primulas in spring. For the rest of the year it was of little interest and visitors admired the summer border instead. In a small garden, where much of it can be seen at a glance, careful thought must be given to year-round interest and colour.

Succession of colour

❀ Colour is easy to provide in spring and summer when everything is burgeoning with blooms. In a large city the temperature tends to be several degrees warmer than in the surrounding countryside and you can make the most of this by growing flowers for longer in the season.

❀ Fuchsias flower well into late autumn; many roses will continue to flower into winter and a choice of different varieties of clematis can bring colour into the garden all year round.

❀ It is not difficult to arrange to have colour in autumn, too, with late-flowering herbaceous plants, red foliage and berries. Tender plants such as pelargoniums, busy Lizzies (*Impatiens*) and abutilons will carry on

flowering until the first frosts so, provided you bring them in before then, they can continue to brighten the patio until well into autumn.

❀ In winter, colourful stems and bark can add interest. Remember that both white and green can be counted as a colour. Your carefully planned framework of evergreen shrubs will give you a structural background.

ABOVE: *Among the most welcome of flowers in spring is the hellebore. This attractive form of* Helleborus orientalis *has dark pink petals, paler inside with very dark spots.*

ABOVE: *Heleniums are tall daisies, which flower over a long period and well into autumn. They are in the yellow to browny-red colour range and popular varieties include 'Septemberfuchs' and 'Moerheim Beauty'.*

❀ You just need to add colourful highlights to accentuate and brighten the picture. Stems and berries make a fantastic show of colour in winter. Some of the dogwoods (*Cornus*) have stunning coloured stems, ranging from crimson to orange or even black. They make a really good impact when two or three are planted together along a bank or as a hedge.

❀ Some of the snake and paper bark trees have marvellous colours, ranging from copper to white. Several birches, cherries and maples can also be used for the colour of their bark.

❀ Then there are the berries. Hollies, yew, cotoneasters, mountain ashes and many more shrubs retain their berries until well into winter, to attract birds as well as delight us. When choosing a shrub check how fast it will grow and how large. The spindle bush, for example, has fascinating pendent bright pink-red fruits open to display red capsules in autumn, but it is fast growing and needs a good 3.5 m (12 ft) spread to do it justice and you may not have room for such a giant.

❀ Skimmias, with their large, bright red berries will not grow to more than about 1 m (3 ft) and pyracantha, although potentially large can be grown up a wall and kept under control by clipping.

❀ Altogether, with disciplined planting, imagination and a choice of plants that will really work for their living by producing interesting flowers, foliage, stems and fruits, you should certainly be able to provide colour all year round.

❀ Of course, there are no sudden transitions between the seasons. Snowdrops, the epitome of spring flowers, will appear in winter and carry on to spring; many spring flowers contrive to flower well into summer and many berries start to form in autumn but will be retained on the plants well into winter, all helping to create a succession of colour.

BELOW: *The leaves of the vigorous decorative vine* Vitis cognetiaea *are a soft, furry green in summer, but become spectacularly coloured in autumn, creating a long season of colour.*

SPRING COLOUR BULBS

FROM the first delicate early snowdrops to the late-flowering sturdy tulips and daffodils, spring bulbs provide wonderful colour right through from winter to early summer. Many people worry about growing bulbs in a border because of the risk of disturbing them when planting herbaceous plants. However, if the bulbs are happy in their position, they will multiply rapidly, producing far more bulblets than you need, so do not worry if a few get dug up. You can replant some, give some to friends and discard the rest.

Snowdrops and aconites

 The common snowdrop (*Galanthus nivalis*) is actually a winter flower but will carry on flowering into spring and is among the most loved of flowering bulbs, naturalising readily in grass, woodland and shady flowerbeds. Snowdrops do best if planted while still in flower. The enchanting G. *caucasicus* has an eight-week flowering period and may start to bloom in late autumn or winter.

 Another favourite is the winter aconite (*Eranthis*). With its cup-shaped flowers and little green ruff, it makes a charming yellow clump under trees. Like snowdrops, winter aconites are best planted while flowering in early spring. They need a dry summer dormancy so are most at home under trees.

Crocuses

 Crocuses, with their wide-open flowers welcoming the sun, come in varieties of purple and lilac to yellows and white. Purples and yellows are usually best grown separately, although white will mix with either.

 The very early species are enchanting and delicate-looking planted under specimen trees on a lawn and will multiply freely. *Crocus chrysanthus* is an early-flowering species with over 20 varieties. C. 'Purpureus Grandiflorus' is an intense violet-purple colour, very free flowering and among the last to bloom.

ABOVE: *Anemone blanda are among the most enchanting of early spring bulbs. They come in a number of white and blue varieties and can carpet the ground with their bright little faces.*

Hardy cyclamen

 Elegant and tiny, the hardy cyclamen are essential bulbs for any garden. Like tiny versions of the better-known houseplants, they may be pink or white. They look very pretty naturalised in woodland or in pockets in the rock garden. C. *coum* flowers midwinter to late spring. Others such as C. *hederifolium* will flower in late summer and autumn. They thrive in sun or part shade and do not mind drought. They can also be grown in troughs or containers.

ABOVE: *These pale little narcissus appear on the woodland floor while the trees are still bare of leaves, bringing anticipation and colour to the garden.*

Erythroniums

❀ The European dog's tooth violet (*Erythronium dens-canis*) is not really a violet but has little pagoda-like flowers of pink, yellow or white on delicate stalks and attractive mottled leaves. It will grow on most soils in sun or shade.

❀ The American erythroniums prefer shade and are best planted among shrubs or trees. They include *E. japonicum* with purple flowers, *E.* 'Pagoda' with pale yellow flowers and *E. tuolumnense* with heads of up to 10 yellow flowers.

Daffodils

❀ You can provide a surprisingly long succession of colour with daffodils alone. For example, three months' worth of colour can be obtained by planting Narcissus 'February Gold', a cyclamineus type with swept-back petals, which is one of the earliest; 'Dutch Master', tall and vigorous with soft yellow, trumpet-shaped flowers with frilled cups; 'Tête-à-Tête', a dwarf daffodil with masses of multi-headed yellow flowers; 'Carlton', a large cupped, single yellow mid-season daffodil; 'Golden Ducat', a golden-yellow double daffodil; and 'Cheerfulness', with its clusters of sweetly scented creamy-white and yellow double flowers.

❀ It is not necessary to plant all of these in one place. Plant different types separately because confusion will detract from bold simple effects.

❀ 'Golden Ducat', 'Cheerfulness' and other large daffodils are useful grown in large pots in a quiet, sheltered corner of the garden, away from mice. In

ABOVE: Galanthus elwesii *is an attractive snowdrop with strap-like glaucous leaves and honey-scented flowers, which appears in late winter, brightening up the garden with its snow-like white.*

ABOVE: *These deep red tulips, accompanied by bright red wallflowers and yellow pansies, provide a very cheerful and colourful late spring bed.*

spring, you can place the pots in borders or inside larger pots to bring a splash of spring-time colour to a still-dormant area.

Tulips

❀ Tulips can also help to bring a succession of colour over a longish period. The kaufmanniana and greigii groups are early-flowering, short-stemmed tulips with handsomely marked leaves in a good range of flower colours.

❀ Single, later tulips include 'Queen of the Night', a deep blackish-maroon colour; 'Temple of Beauty', which is salmon rose, and the lily-shaped 'Union Jack', which is raspberry red on an ivory background.

❀ The later tulips stand up tall and straight like soldiers. It is tempting to plant them in serried ranks but they look better grouped naturally among other plants unless grown in a very formal garden.

SUMMER COLOUR HERBACEOUS FLOWERS AND SHRUBS

THERE is no problem in finding colourful plants for summer. The choice is enormous. In fact the real difficulty is in not overdoing things. The following popular plants can all add colour to the flower border. Primulas flower from spring right into midsummer. They form a rosette of leaves, from which grow flowering stems bearing from one to many five-petalled flowers, often with a white or yellow eye. There are species to suit every garden situation, from alpine gardens to bogs and borders. For a bog garden, the candelabra primulas are gorgeous.

For a sunny border

❀ *Convolvulus cneorum* is an evergreen low-growing convolvulus with silver leaves and white flowers carried intermittently for months. Rock roses (*Cistus*) bear papery flowers in white or pink, often with paintbrush marks of dark maroon in the centre. C. 'Silver Pink' is hardy with greyish-green leaves and likes a sunny position and poor soil.

❀ Lavender will flower all summer long with spikes of lilac, pink or white flowers above silvery leaves. It is one of the most useful low summer shrubs with the bonus of a lovely scent. Dwarf varieties are especially suitable for underplanting rose beds. Larger types can be planted as an informal low hedge.

❀ English lavender (*Lavandula augustifolia*) has pale lilac flowers on long stems. *L. a.* 'Hidcote' has deep blue, very thick spikes of flowers on grey-green foliage and compact growth. French lavender (*Lavandula stoechas*) has larger flower heads with petals sprouting out like a topknot.

❀ There are many varieties of sage (*Salvia*) worth growing for colour. Among the most colourful is *Salvia* x *superba*, a herbaceous perennial with masses of violet-blue flowers in midsummer with crimson-purple bracts that persist after the flowers have faded. *Salvia macrophylla* is a small shrubby sage with deep crimson flowers at the ends of the stems, appearing from early summer to the first frosts.

❀ Achilleas have tiny blooms forming flat-topped clusters of flower heads all summer and sometimes into autumn. A. 'Gold Plate' and A. 'Cloth of Gold' both have great platters of bright yellow flowers, which make an impact in a mixed border. A. 'Cerise Queen' has cerise or light cinnamon-coloured flowers.

❀ Sea holly (*Eryngium*) has bold, thistle-like flower heads in metallic blues and greens, adorned by spectacular

ABOVE: *Vibrant purples create a beautiful and dramatic summer border, contrasting well with the lush green of the lawns and surrounding plants. The smooth pebbles add to the tidy and well-kept feel.*

ABOVE: *The deep purple leaves of this beech hedge and archway contrast excitingly with the brightly coloured planting of red hot pokers (Kniphofia), lythrum and orange calendula.*

spiny bracts and flowers all summer. Many eryngiums are evergreen. *Eryngium* 'Blue Star' has deep blue flower heads and bracts; *E. bourgatii* has rounded flower heads, which change from steely blue and green to lilac blue; *E. variifolium* has small silver-blue flower heads and marbled leaves.

❀ Garden lupins are tall, stately flowers for early summer with astonishing colour combinations. The Band of Nobles Series has a range of yellows, pinks, reds, blues and violets.

❀ Rose campion (*Lychnis coronaria*) has handsome grey felted leaves and bold reddish-purple flowers throughout the summer months.

For a clay border

❀ Astilbes are tall, fluffy, plumed flowers in reds, pinks and white, springing from a skirt of fern-like green leaves. They like rich, moist soil and thrive on clay. There is a good range of hybrids, including A. 'Bridal Veil' (white) and A. 'Bressingham Beauty' (pink).

❀ Day lilies (*Hemerocallis*) are available in many colours – from cool yellow to pale creamy-pink or rich burgundy-red. Their strap-like leaves are useful as a contrast to more feathery or rounded plants.

❀ Bergamot (*Monarda dydima*) has a distinctive herby smell and ragged-looking dreadlock flowers in bright pinks, purples and reds. It will grow in part shade and likes a moist but well-drained soil.

❀ Border phlox (*Phlox paniculata*) have fine broad flower heads in blue, purple, pink or white from mid- to late summer. They are tall and upright, and like moisture and full sun or partial shade. They are intensely fragrant. *P. p.* 'Amethyst' has violet flowers, *P. p.* 'Bressingham Beauty' is pink and *P. p.* 'Red Sentinel' has deep red flowers with dark foliage.

❀ The daisy-like flowers of asters, rudbeckias, echinaecaes and heleniums provide colour on tall stems in late summer to autumn.

❀ Geraniums are essential in most gardens. They flower freely over a long period, especially if you remember to cut off the seed heads. There are many to choose from, including G. *psilostemon* 'Bressingham Flair', which has purple flowers and dark brown centres from early to late summer.

ABOVE: *The silvery-blue pointed leaves of* Artemisia ludoviciana, *with feathery grasses and the flat heads of* Achillea *'Fanal', make a really striking colour scheme in this summer border.*

AUTUMN COLOUR: FLOWERS, FOLIAGE AND BERRIES

FOLIAGE and berries are the obvious sources of colour in the autumn garden but there are still plenty of brightly coloured flowers to be appreciated at this time of year. If you intersperse them carefully among the earlier flowering plants, they will come into their own when the others are over. Many are tall, so put them at the back of the border and stake them early.

Herbaceous plants

❀ Many of the daisy family give a good show in autumn. Michaelmas daisies (*Aster*) offer a lovely selection of colours. *Aster amellus* 'King George' has large violet-blue flowers, while A. x *frikartii*, a clear violet-blue colour, is free flowering, vigorous and resistant to mildew.

❀ Heleniums specialise in yellows and orange-reds. H. 'Moerheim Beauty' has bronze flowers from midsummer. Rudbeckias have brightly coloured flowers with dark cone-shaped centres. *Rudbeckia fulgida* 'Goldsturm' is a wonderful yellow with a black centre, which glows brightly from green foliage at the back of the border.

ABOVE: *The stem of this black bryony (Tamus communis) has obligingly curved itself around the chestnut paling in this wild garden, giving emphasis to its bright red berries, which show up well in front of the ivy.*

Shrubs

❀ Ceratostigmas are low-growing shrubs with bright blue flowers, which bridge the transition between summer and autumn brilliantly. They are suitable for the front of a border, a rock garden or for containers. Their leaves turn red in autumn.

ABOVE: *Mahonia 'Charity' is an upright evergreen large prickly-leaved shrub, which really earns its keep in summer when it has spikes of bright yellow flowers, and again in autumn when its leaf colours and black berries provide winter interest.*

❀ Fuchsias are graceful and pendulous with flowers as elegant or as plump as you like. They start flowering in midsummer and will go on until late autumn. *Fuchsia magellanica* is graceful with narrow red flowers and purple calyxes. Its variegated form has pretty pale grey-green leaves with purple markings.

❀ Mop-headed hydrangeas are spectacularly colourful if you have the space. They do well in shrubberies or in large containers. The hortensia varieties have great round heads of red or blue flowers, which can be very spectacular in summer and autumn.

❀ As they die, they become 'dried flowers', retaining their colours effectively for a long time. *H.* 'Ami Pasquier' has many vivid crimson flowers (but light blue on acidic soil). It grows slowly, eventually reaching about 1 m (3 ft). *H.* 'Vibraye' is one of the earliest to flower and goes on into autumn. Many hydrangea heads will overwinter as a greenish-turquoise colour.

❀ Many roses will flower again in autumn. The hybrid musks are good value and *Rosa* 'Autumn Delight' and *R.* 'Ballerina', with its pale pink flowers with paler centres, are both excellent value.

❀ The smoke bush (*Cotinus coggygria*) is a large shrub whose inflorescences are just like smoke. The autumn foliage of the cultivar 'Flame' is brilliant reddish-orange. It should be planted in a place where the sun will shine through the leaves.

TREES

THE Japanese maples are outstanding for autumn colour and there is a good choice. *Acer palmatum* 'Dissectum' is a very small pretty tree at any time of year. It has an attractive shape, the leaves are individually enchanting and the autumn foliage is a lovely orange-yellow. *Amelanchier lamarckii* again has interest for much more of the year than just autumn with snowy-white flowers in spring and coppery young foliage, which turns a rich red in autumn.

For acidic soils

❀ *Photinia villosa* has dark green leaves with grey, downy undersides that turn vivid orange yellow. It is slow-growing but will eventually reach 3.5 m (12 ft). It goes well with rhododendrons and azaleas.

❀ For a larger garden, *Parottia persica* is a tree almost as broad as it is tall, with large leaves that turn vivid orange, yellow and red. Remove the lower branches to reveal the attractive grey, pink and yellow bark.

Berries

❀ Mountain ash trees (*Sorbus*) all have lots of good berries. The rowan (*Sorbus aucuparia*) is a well-known small tree, used freestanding or in a group. It has white flowers, dark green leaves with a grey sheen and clusters of spectacular red fruits. *S.* 'Sir Joseph Rock' has yellow berries and *S. vilmorinii* has interesting mauve berries.

❀ If you want to combine interesting fruits with security, try *Berberis aggregata*, which is very prickly and can be planted as a hedge or in a group. It has deep orange clusters of small fruits on wood that is two years old. *B. wilsoniae* is a very attractive berberis with pink and orange berries.

BELOW: Photinia villosa *is an attractive small tree with bronze leaves when young, turning orange and red in autumn. It has heads of small white flowers in spring, followed by red fruits.*

WINTER COLOUR

IN the winter garden, green is an invaluable colour in its own right and interesting evergreen shrubs make an important contribution. However, there are one or two shrubs that flower exquisitely in winter; there are some trees and shrubs with colourful and interesting stems and bark, and some berries last well into winter.

Stems and bark

❀ The red stems of the red-barked dogwood (*Cornus alba*) glow in the sun on a winter's day. The shrub is attractive all year round, with white flowers in spring, dark green leaves with red veins and silvery undersides and red autumn colour.

❀ Probably its best feature, however, is the colour of its bare stems in winter. Cut it back very hard in early spring to generate strong, well-coloured winter stems. Plant two or three together if space allows and make sure they are positioned so that they will catch the sunlight.

❀ The eucalyptuses, tall trees from Australia, are also good value all year round with an attractive growing habit, blue leaves and grey-green stems, often with peeling bark which reveals primrose-yellow underskin. Use them as ornamental trees or turn them into multi-stemmed shrubs by cutting down to the ground in spring.

❀ A hard frost may cause damage, but the snow gum (*Eucalyptus niphophila*) is a relatively hardy, slow-growing tree with an attractive trunk patched with green, grey and cream.

❀ Other trees worth growing for their bark are *Prunus maackii*, a decorative plum with very striking shiny

ABOVE: *Winter can be spectacular in the garden, but only if you do not tidy up too much and cut down all the old flower stems. It is the stems, seeds and old leaves that can come to life in winter frost and sunlight.*

mahogany-coloured bark, and several birches such as *Betula utilis*, which has pale, papery peeling bark and the very white bark varieties like *B. jacquemontii*. *B. albosinensis* var. *septentrionalis* is one of the finest orange-barked birches.

❀ For a larger garden, *Acer griseum* is a delightful slow-growing tree to grow on its own to get the full effect of its peeling brown bark, which shows a golden-brown underskin.

ABOVE: *Helleborus niger is the Christmas rose, and in some areas it will appear by Christmas Day. In others, and particularly in cold clay soils, it will flower in January or February.*

Winter flowers

❀ There are more flowering shrubs for winter than many people realise. The mahonias are large evergreen shrubs with small yellow flowers. They are often used rather unimaginatively in public parks but can be a great asset in a small garden. *Mahonia japonica* can be used in a shrub border and is useful in dark, dry places where its evergreen leaves and pale yellow, scented flowers can lighten the gloom.

❀ *Lonicera standishii* is a tall, shrubby honeysuckle with large, cream, highly scented flowers from midwinter and a bonus of red berries in early spring. Use it near the house or next to a path.

❀ *Viburnum* x *bodnantense* 'Dawn' is a tall, narrow shrub with very pretty, small pink and white flowers on bare stems in winter. The leaves follow on later. *Viburnum tinus* has dark green glossy leaves and heads of small flowers in pinkish-white throughout winter.

❀ *Daphne mezereum* is a very popular, attractive scented shrub, flowering from winter to early spring. It will grow to only about 80 cm (32 in) so plant it in a border, a large rock garden or at the edge of a shrub border.

❀ Winter jasmine (*Jasminium nudiflorum*) is not a climber but is good trained up a wall or pergola where its arching stems, carrying small dark green leaves and pretty yellow flowers, can be seen to advantage.

❀ The evergreen *Clematis cirrhosa* var. *balearica* has pretty, divided bronze or purple leaves and masses of creamy-yellow bell-like flowers with maroon spots inside which last all winter.

Winter berries

❀ Many berries last for a long time in winter and can be very cheering. *Skimmia japonica* 'Foremanii' has glossy evergreen leaves and long-lasting, large shiny red berries. They like acidic to neutral soil and dislike any alkalinity or waterlogging, and will tolerate shade.

❀ Choose them for woodland gardens or shrub borders. They also look good in large containers. The female form bears the berries when a male form is planted nearby.

❀ The cotoneasters have berries that last into winter. *C. franchetii* can be grown as a small tree. It has grey-green leaves on long, arching branches. Single white flowers in early summer are followed by dull red fruit, lasting well into winter.

BELOW: Hamamelis mollis *is a small tree with a pleasant shape and habit, whose rounded leaves drop in winter, which is when it produces its spidery, bright yellow or red flowers. Shown here are* Hamamelis x intermedia 'Sunburst' *and* Hamamelis x intermedia 'Diane'.

USING FORM AND TEXTURE

All materials in the garden have a shape, habit and texture.
It is useful to get to know a few plants with different shapes and
habits and see how they can be put together in interesting combinations.
Gardeners whose main interest is in the plants themselves will
want to buy every interesting plant they see, but from the design
point of view, simpler is better and fewer varieties will give
a more cohesive and unified result.

Knowing your plants

❦ It takes time to learn the qualities and characteristics of
different plants. Every garden you visit, whether it is a
stately home or a tiny urban back garden, will have used
plants in a way to interest you. The great skill is in
juxtaposing different forms and textures to create an
interesting complete picture, or rather a three-
dimensional sculpture.

❦ Textures are to do with the leaves and how they are held
on the plant. Feathery textures are soft but have little
structure. They will be most effective next to a plain
wall or planted next to large, leathery foliage plants.

ABOVE: *The contorted hazel (Corylus avellana 'Contorta') has a charming
weeping habit with bright yellow lamb's tails dangling down. This one has been
underplanted with snowdrops, adding to the excitement of spring.*

Clipped plants

❦ The textures of clipped plants should be dense, to give a
clear face or outline, which is why box, yew, hornbeam
and beech are so often used. They make tightly textured
backgrounds for flowers or for sculpting into shapes.
Shrubs used as divisions within the garden can be fairly
small leaved, giving a texture that will conceal what is
the other side but will not seem too forbidding.

ABOVE: *Contrast works well here with the deep green and gentle softness of the
lawn against the chard texture and cool greys of the brickwork step and the
spikyness of the variegated grass.*

ABOVE: *The enormous size of gunnera leaves gives them an open and coarse texture, made more interesting by their hairiness.*

❀ The shapes and structure of the plants used obviously affect the plan of the garden as a whole. In the flower border, feathery or strap-like plants can be offset by round or clipped ones.

❀ Plants with strap-like leaves will provide vertical interest among more undefined or rounded plant shapes. Large vertical plants such as yuccas can be used as focal points among shorter, bushier plants to get their full effect.

Differing shapes

❀ In fact there are few shapes that cannot be found in plants. Umbrella, dome and ball shapes, vertical columns and cones are all good shapes for the formal garden, where their geometrical qualities help to confirm the disciplined design, but they can also be used in the informal garden as 'punctuation marks' or to give height or solidity where needed.

❀ Habit is not so much the shape of the plant as the way in which it holds itself. Shrubs like buddleja have an arching habit, whereas junipers are upright, weeping willows droop and cedars of Lebanon spread.

❀ Roses, which have a rather straggly habit, often need something to cover their bare legs. Rounded shapes like lavender, and geraniums such as 'Johnson's Blue' or 'Buxton's Variety' make good petticoats for roses.

❀ Similarly in a shrub border or shrubbery, you can juxtapose the rounded form of *Hydrangea macrophylla*, especially the lace-cap varieties, with the lightness and elegance of *Cornus controversia* 'Variegata', keeping plenty of space between them so that each can be seen to full effect. When designing a garden, you are creating a kind of living sculpture and all of these textures, shapes and habits have their uses in creating a balanced and interesting whole.

TEXTURE

Every plant in the garden has its own individual surface pattern or texture. This textural effect is created by the size of the leaves, their shape and surface features – whether they are shiny, wrinkled, hairy and so on. Texture is also affected by the leaf edges, which may be curled or indented, and whether sunlight can pass through the leaves as it does in an open-textured tree such as birch, or is stopped by the numbers of leaves as it is in most plants. Texture is also affected by the thickness of the leaf, whether it is leathery, fleshy and so on.

Factors affecting leaf texture

❀ Plants draw water and nutrients up through their stems and then release the water vapour through all their aerial parts but mostly through the leaves, via pores known as stomata. This is known as transpiration.

❀ Plants have adapted in many ways to reduce water loss when necessary and these adaptations affect the texture of the leaves. Some grasses roll their leaves lengthways to protect the pores. The leaves of the blue grass *Festuca glauca* do this, giving them a rounded look with a very particular quality of their own. Plants with silver leaves are covered in tiny hairs to protect the stomata from hot sun and drying winds. These catch the light and give the leaves a silvery sheen.

❀ Other plants, such as cacti, have completely replaced their leaves with spines so as to conserve as much water as possible. Plants from humid tropical areas have enormous leaves so that they can transpire freely and the leaves are designed with drainage channels to allow

ABOVE: *Contrasts of texture here include the soft, almost velvety petals of the single French marigolds (Tagetes) and the stiff, shiny silvery leaves next to them.*

BELOW: *The wrinkled edges of the leaves of* Asplenium scolopendrium *give this fern a quality all of its own, particularly when edged by a winter hoar frost.*

excess water to run off quickly. All these things affect the texture of the plant and, incidentally, it is easy to see why particular plants will flourish in particular places in the garden and fail in others.

Leaf size

❀ Plants with tiny leaves have a fine texture and include the heathers. Large plants with small leaves such as yew, privet and box are good for clipping. Creeping small-leaved plants such as ajuga or periwinkles are good ground cover.

❀ Plants with medium leaves include trees such as beech and lime, and shrubs such as cotinus and laurel. Large leaves include climbers such as vines and Virginia creeper. Very large plants with enormous leaves, such as gunnera and Rheum palmatum have coarse textures. Some large leaves have a soft and floppy look, while others are very shiny and firm.

Leaf shape

❀ The shape of the leaf itself can also affect the texture. *Bergenia cordifolia* and *Cotinus coggygria* have rounded leaves, which provide a dense blanket of foliage; the grasses with their narrow leaves give a feeling of air and lightness as they are wafted around in the wind.

❀ Conical leaves, as in catalpas, hostas and polygonums, give a graceful look, and dissected leaves, for example *Acer palmatum* 'Dissectum', are also graceful and feathery. Lobed leaves such as those found in hawthorns and figs give a different texture again.

Surface features

❀ Surface features are equally important. They affect the way the plant reflects or absorbs the light. Hairs may give the leaf a velvety appearance, as in *Salvia officinalis*, or they may make it look silvery as in the curry plant. A furry surface such as that of *Stachys lanata* gives the plant a woolly appearance.

❀ Holly has a waxy coating, which makes it very shiny, and prickly leaves, which give it its characteristic look. The heavily veined leaves of viburnum absorb light and make the plant look very dense. *Magnolia grandiflora* has huge glossy leaves, while *Eleagnus pungens* has small matt ones.

ABOVE: *The ornamental cabbage has a leathery texture and a matt finish, which gives density to its attractive dusky pink and blue-green leaves.*

Large leaf textures

❀ If you want to create a dramatic effect in your garden, plants with large leaves are among the most spectacular. Large leaves often indicate that a plant comes from a tropical climate so many of them need to be planted in milder areas or in a sheltered part of the garden.

❀ The foxglove tree (*Paulownia tomentosa*) is deciduous. It originates in China and is an interesting rounded tree suitable for medium and large gardens as a specimen tree and for creating shade. It has 20 cm (8 in) hairy leaves on long stalks with a clammy coating for catching aphids, with the bonus of blue foxglove-shaped flowers in late spring. Its stems may become damaged in very cold winters but this allows the tree to branch more freely from buds below the damage.

❀ The Indian bean tree (*Catalpa bignonioides*) is a large round-topped tree with huge, ornamental, rich green leaves on long stalks, which form a large, shade-giving canopy and turn a good yellow in autumn. The spectacular white flowers only grow on 25-year-old trees. Catalpas make good eye-catching specimen trees and grow best in mild areas, away from strong winds but will tolerate urban pollution.

ABOVE: *The large leaves and rosette-like growth of hostas make them very attractive feature plants in garden woodland. This variegated Hosta 'Thomas Hogg' is deeply veined, which adds to its attraction.*

❀ Shrubs with large leaves include *Hydrangea aspera* ssp. *argentiana*, whose velvety, hairy leaves are up to 25 cm (10 in) long. It is a handsome, structural shrub with pretty dusky-pink lace-cap flowers and is good for woodland walks, as a freestanding shrub or a focal point among lower ground covering or as a large wall shrub.

❀ The caster oil plant (*Fatsia japonica*) with its huge palm-like leaves is one of the best shade-loving large shrubs and makes a good freestanding feature.

❀ There are several large-leaved climbers. The crimson glory vine (*Vitis cognetiae*) has heart-shaped leaves, which turn spectacularly yellow, orange, red, purple and crimson, especially if grown on poor soil.

❀ For moist soil there is nothing so spectacular as the giant gunneras. The leaves of *Gunnera manicata* sometimes grow to more than 1.8 m (6 ft) in diameter and the leaves of *G. chilensis* are only slightly smaller. They look majestic growing by the edge of a pond or stream.

❀ The cardoon (*Cynara cardunculus*) has silvery-grey leaves 50 cm (20 in) long and *Acanthus mollis* has dark green, deeply cut leaves 60 cm (24 in) long; both are of great architectural value in a border.

ABOVE: *The ruby-red Swiss chard has become popular for use in flower borders, not only for its spectacular stem colour but also for the interesting, deeply wrinkled texture of its leaves.*

Medium leaf textures

❀ There is an infinite variety of plants with medium and small leaves and these make up a large part of the background tapestry of a garden. Medium-leaved plants often create a rather amorphous texture unless they are clipped, and may require the occasional strongly architectural plant to provide structure. Very small leaves, on the other hand, can be so densely arranged on the plant that they create a very definite shape, almost as though clipped.

❀ Medium-leaved plants include many large trees such as beech, ash, lime and poplar. Medium leaves on a large tree will often provide a dense canopy for shade and the leaves move and rustle in the wind. The leaves of poplars in particular can sound like the sea breaking on the shore.

❀ Climbers with medium leaves include evergreen clematis, which can run along a fence or wall for some distance, creating a green blanket of overlapping leaves all shining in the light. Other evergreens with medium leaves include *Choisya ternata*, whose rounded leaves are attractively placed around the branches, and *Magnolia stellata* with its matt mid-green leaves growing on graceful branches.

❀ Roses are so much used in gardens; they deserve some special thought. Some roses have medium leaves, others have small ones. Their habit is often rather open. Only the species and old roses grow more densely and give better coverage, creating a more definite shape.

❀ The large-flowered and cluster-flowered bush roses are covered more sparsely with leaves and rely more on their flowers for interest. From the point of view of garden structure, therefore, roses are better grown together with other plants, unless you are growing a hedge of roses such as *Rosa rugosa* with their bright green, glossy, deeply veined and healthy foliage.

BELOW: *The Indian bean tree has an elegant shape and form, and a texture all of its own created by the large and handsome leaves. There is the added bonus of white flowers and, later, dangling bean pods.*

Small leaf textures

❦ The dividing line between medium and small leaves is not clearly defined. A plant's leaves may seem small when grown next to something like a gunnera, but much larger when grown beside a box bush. The choice here is fairly arbitrary and is intended as a rough guide only.

❦ The shrubby sages with their diamond-shaped, pale green leaves shining in the sun, the hebes with their evergreen compact foliage and the spindle berries (*Euonymus*) all make their own attractive individual contributions.

❦ The daphnes, although usually grown for their flowers, also have attractive small leaves. *Daphne* x *burkwoodii* 'Somerset Gold Edge' has extremely pretty yellow margined, round-edged leaves in rosettes around the stems. Myrtle is an attractive evergreen shrub with small pointed, dark green leaves. It is for mild areas and can be grown as a freestanding or wall shrub, or in a container.

ABOVE: *The narrow, arrow-shaped leaves of this spiky* Perovskia atripicifolia *give the whole plant an insubstantial feathery look, which shows up well against the rounded, denser purple cotinus behind it.*

Plants suitable for topiary

❦ Plants suitable for topiary all have small, closely spaced leaves. The most obvious are box and yew but the shrubby honeysuckle *Lonicera nitida* has tiny ovate mid-green leaves with silver undersides, which respond well to clipping; and the culinary bay tree (*Laurus nobilis*) with its thin aromatic leaves can be clipped into a mop-head standard. The evergreen *Ceanothus* 'Puget's Blue' has small shiny crinkled leaves, which make a good clipped hedge for mild areas. Clip directly after it has flowered in early summer.

ABOVE: *Here, a number of shrubby plants, all with small leaves, can nevertheless provide variety because some are matt, some shiny, some rounded and some pointed.*

ABOVE: The tiny leaves of the large shrub Abies balsamea *give it a fairly solid look; the creeping* Saxifraga moschata 'Densa' *makes a dense mat on the ground, and the narrow purple leaves of the nearby grass provide a more open look.*

❀ Conifers are useful with their dense tiny leaves. The western red cedar (*Thuja plicata*) is an evergreen conifer with flattened sprays of scale-like leaves. It will quickly grow into a tall tree but, if trimmed regularly, makes an easily controlled dense hedge.

❀ *Chamaecyparis lawsoniana* 'Pembury Blue' has flattened scale-like overlapping leaves and striking silver-blue dense foliage. It will grow to 4 x 1.2 m (13 x 4 ft) and can be clipped into a hedge or act as a backcloth for a flower border.

❀ Low-growing shrubs with small leaves make good hedges surrounding a herb or rose garden. Box is well known for this but does grow slowly. The lavenders make pretty hedges with their grey foliage and rosemary can also make a good clipped hedge. Less well known is wall germander (*Teucrium fruticans*), a low-growing evergreen sub-shrub for milder areas, with aromatic grey-green leaves covered in fine down.

Feathery textures

❀ Feathery plants do not contribute structurally but can add softness to a scheme that seems too rigid. Such plants include ferns with their regular shuttlecock shapes. Some of the artemisias create soft feathery silver mounds and the curry plant also has a feathery effect, especially grown next to a plant with flat, dark green leaves.

❀ The junipers have tiny leaves giving a feathery effect. *Juniperus scopulorum* with its conical shape contributes structure as well as softness.

❀ The tamarisk is a deciduous shrub with long graceful feathery plumes of dusty-pink flowers. It can be planted as an informal feathery hedge for summer interest and is often used in France to mark the spot where the septic tank is located. Broom (*Cytisus*) is another shrub whose flowers give a feathery effect.

❀ It can be useful in a shrub border, bringing lightness and freshness in spring. Alternatively, it can be used singly but it may begin to look a bit scrawny when the flowers are over so it is best in a place where it can be concealed by other plants.

❀ The white Portuguese broom (*Cytisus albus*) is particularly elegant but there are many, more colourful varieties to choose from. Astilbe is a useful hardy perennial with feathery flowers. The leaves are quite fern-like too.

❀ The flowers are mostly in shades of white, pink, lilac and red. The goat's beard family (*Aruncus*) is made up of tall hardy perennials with elegant feathery plumes of tiny cream flowers in midsummer. *Aruncus plumosus* has 20 cm (8 in) plumes of star-shaped creamy white flowers on tall stout stems. Both astilbes and aruncus thrive best in rich, moist soils.

❀ The cut-leaf forms of Japanese maples are among the most feathery of shrubs or small trees. Yet the positive shape of their trunks and branches makes a good combination of the shapely and the soft, and they make wonderful little specimen trees in a small lawn.

FORM AND HABIT

Having looked at plants as background material and at the way leaves provide different textures in the garden, we now need to look at the form or outline of the whole plant. This is the shape you would see in silhouette. You can see this best in summer with deciduous plants and all year round with evergreens and conifers. As well as its basic natural shape, a plant has its own individual habit. Habit is the way the branches are held on the plant. For example, a weeping habit is where branches hang down from the trunk, while plants with an upright habit have branches reaching upwards.

Structural elements

❀ Some plants are of architectural or structural interest in the garden because they have a strong individuality. They might have large-scale leaves, which is to do with texture; or perhaps there is a well-defined pattern to their growth, which makes them valuable in providing accents. These plants will show up against a simple background or planted somewhere where they will give emphasis to a group of less strongly defined shapes.

❀ Some plants hold their branches horizontally on upright stems and have flat flower heads. Such plants provide an excellent foil to vertical stems in the border and to tree trunks in woodland.

❀ Many are magnificent and will stand alone but they are also good as contrasts to amorphous, rounded plants with less-defined forms. They may give structure to a group of shrubs or a border of perennials, or they may be used to give definition to an avenue or path.

❀ In general, the shapes and forms described on the following pages are those that will add an architectural quality to the garden.

❀ Plant forms are partly inherent and partly created by the gardener. You cannot alter the basic way a plant will grow but you can train many plants to some extent so that they fit in with your scheme.

❀ Others can be cut back and 'moulded' to any shape you want. When choosing plants for any structural job in the garden, you must make sure you have left enough space for them to realise their full potential.

❀ You can choose large plants for a hedge and keep trimming it as you will, but if you want a plant because of its particular shape, it must have the space necessary. You do not want to have to move large, expensive plants just when they are coming into maturity and the true beauty of their shapes.

Contrasts

❀ The forms and habits of plants should be used to create interest and all designs need contrast. But if the contrast is too strong it can be distracting. An architectural plant should be placed where it will complement its neighbours, not where it will eclipse them with its magnificence.

❀ The tall, positive shapes of columnar conifers are so emphatically vertical they need to be carefully positioned, especially those with very dark colours. They can eclipse other plants in a border and lead the eye away from other carefully designed plantings.

❀ They can be useful in marking key spaces in the garden, for example a seating area or the meeting place of cross-axis paths. In formal gardens, round, square and conical shapes are in keeping with the geometric layout of the garden.

❀ Form and habit are perhaps most striking in the case of trees. The extreme forms should be used only where special emphasis is needed. These are the fastigiate (plants having erect branches) and plate-like or prostrate shapes. However, every tree and shrub has its own characteristic form, whether grown as an individual or as a group.

BELOW: *This delightful water garden shows many different plant forms and habits, some spreading, some stiffly upright, others prostrate and yet others arching.*

FORM AND HABIT

There are a number of forms and habits to be aware of when designing your garden. Remember that trees and shrubs with their leaves on provide a dense outline, whereas deciduous trees in winter have a more skeletal effect. The size and shape of leaves on a shrub will themselves affect the overall look of the plant.

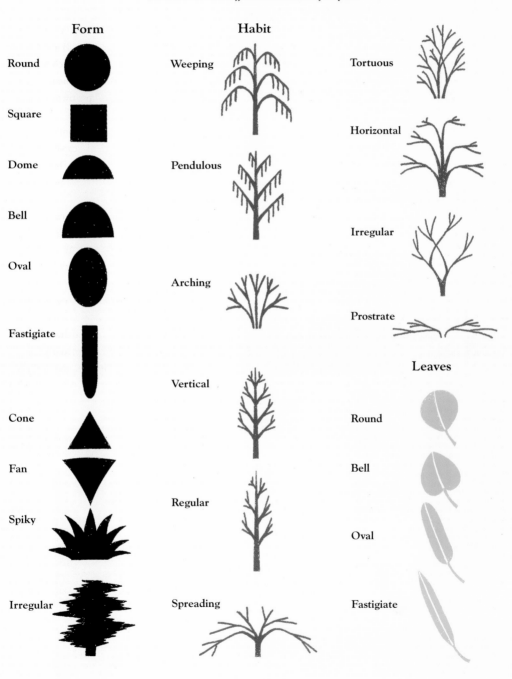

Form

Round

Square

Dome

Bell

Oval

Fastigiate

Cone

Fan

Spiky

Irregular

Habit

Weeping

Pendulous

Arching

Vertical

Regular

Spreading

Tortuous

Horizontal

Irregular

Prostrate

Leaves

Round

Bell

Oval

Fastigiate

FORM

THE shape or form of a plant is its outline pattern seen in silhouette. The plant world has many forms but most can be categorised into a few basic shapes. Each has its own individual value in the garden. Plants with strong forms are valuable in giving strength to a design or as complements to buildings.

❀ All borders need a solid background. When this has been provided, whether as hedge, fence or wall, plants of some solidity can be planted at intervals along it to give a buttressing effect to integrate background and border. For a formal border you could use clipped yew or box. For an informal border you could use plants with solid mass such as choisya, eleagnus or hebes.

❀ Many plants with smallish leaves can be clipped into particular shapes, and these are useful when you want to make a particular statement or create a structural quality in a certain area. Arches, gateways, buttresses and columns can all be created with clipped evergreen shrubs.

❀ When it comes to herbaceous perennials, you may find that the species form is more graceful than modern 'improved' hybrids. Many dwarf cultivars, theoretically ideal for the small garden, have often lost much of their original elegance.

Round shapes

❀ Round shapes are always very formal but will add impact to any garden. Round-headed trees include the black walnut (*Juglans nigra*), a useful quick-growing tree for giving shade to medium or large gardens and avenues.

❀ *Malus floribunda* is a pendulous crab apple with red buds opening to a staggering profusion of pink flowers. It is best grown as a specimen tree. Most of the sorbuses are round-headed and have attractive fruits.

❀ Round shrubs include *Choisya ternata*, a neat shrub that grows quite large but normally needs no pruning unless it outgrows its space when it can be cut back hard and will regenerate. Low-growing hebes such as *Hebe albicans* make neat, round evergreen shrubs for borders, low hedging or containers. Sweet bay, box, standard roses, yew and *Lonicera nitida* can all be successfully clipped into balls, either on long stems or at ground level.

Dome or hummock shapes

❀ These can be like mushrooms or buns or slightly flatter. A dome is a good shape to plant near a building as it softens other shapes. Domed trees are umbrella-like and make good shade trees. They include *Crataegus prunifolia*, a good autumn-colour form of hawthorn and *Catalpa bignonioides*.

❀ Smaller shrubs include *Erica carnea* and *Salvia officinalis*. Saxifrages, heathers and arbutus make bun-shaped mounds and the flowers of rudbeckias and echinaceas are dome shaped, too.

Bell shapes

❀ These are similar to domes but taller. They can add height in a mixed border and make good background plants and screens. Bell-shaped trees include apples, horse chestnuts and many of the larger trees.

❀ Shrubs include olearia and some evergreen rhododendrons. Bells, domes and round shapes tend to complement each other and can be used well together.

LEFT: *This pretty little clipped tree has been given a bun shape on a slender stalk, which marks it out from its surroundings and gives it a character of its own.*

Oval and fastigiate shapes

❁ Oval shapes are formal bodyguards, adding strength to the garden. They can be used as gateways or in single file along one side of a large lawn. Only a few plants are this shape naturally. One is the fastigiate yew (*Taxus baccata* 'Fastigiata'), but the common yew (*Taxus baccata*) and other shrubs can be clipped into the shape.

❁ Fastigiate plants are tall and thin with erect branches. They can be eyesores if they are not placed correctly, but used as focal points in groups or in a line – not singly – they can be very dramatic. Trees include Italian cypresses, often used to repeat a columnar look, the fastigiate beech (*Fagus sylvatica* 'Fastigiata'), the fastigiate oak (*Quercus robur* 'Fastigiata') and the fastigiate hornbeam (*Carpinus betulus* 'Fastigiata').

Square and rectangular shapes

❁ The square, so often found in human architecture and design, is not found in nature at all. It is particularly suitable for formal situations. Trees in French streets and squares are often pleached into regular blocks, which let light in and integrate well with the geometry of the architecture. The shape is used in pleached hedges, usually of lime, hornbeam, box or yew.

RIGHT: *The spiky leaves of this cordyline, all sprouting from the same point on the stem, create a ball-like form with an interesting open texture.*

BELOW: *The cut-leaved maple,* Acer japonicum *'Green Cascade', has a feathery texture that needs to be seen on its own or with a very plain background for full effect.*

HABIT

MANY plants within the same family have different habits. This is the way the stems and branches are held on the plant. They may be upright or weeping, pendulous, arching or spreading. This not only contributes to the overall shape and form of the plant, but also contributes a quality or mood of its own. This is particularly important in trees but many shrubs have interesting habits, too. Some trees ask to be given a place of honour as single specimens. The Scots pine and the cedar of Lebanon are well known for their stately habit of branching and the beauty of their trunks; weeping trees, too, have particularly attractive forms. Other trees such as hornbeam, ash and alder are best planted in groups or groves.

Vertical habit

❀ Upright plants give a strong line in winter. They include *Salix alba* and *Cornus alba*, whose bare stems in winter can provide superb colour.

❀ Similarly, there are several herbaceous perennials that carry the same characteristics into the flower border in summer, including the sea hollies (*Eryngium*), *Thalictrum glaucum*, *Echinops ritro*, *Acanthus speciosus* and *Acanthus mollis*, delphiniums and verbascums. All have a certain rigidity, which gives backbone to plants with less distinctive growth habits.

Spreading habit

❀ Plants with a spreading habit reach out rather than up, often growing wider than they are tall, creating a horizontal effect. It is important to recognise how much space they will need to grow to their full width.

❀ Trees with a spreading habit include *Parrotia persica*, a wide deciduous tree with large leaves that turn a spectacular mixture of reds, oranges and yellows in autumn. The medlar (*Mespilus germanica*) makes a wide-spreading ornamental tree with good autumn colour and is interesting as a specimen plant on a lawn.

Prostrate habit

❀ Prostrate plants reach out rather than up, rather like spreading plants, but they cling close to the ground. They can be useful in rock gardens, or narrow borders where there is no room for tiered rows of plants. Plants such as Juniperus horizontalis make good ground cover.

ABOVE: *All the leaves of these grass-like plants, including the phormium and the palm, have arching habits and together, give a loose, informal look to the garden.*

❀ Several of the cotoneasters have a prostrate habit, including *Cotoneaster cochleatus*, a slow-growing evergreen, and *C. dammeri*, another slow-growing evergreen, which can be used for carpeting banks and bare ground beneath taller trees and shrubs as it has ground-hugging stems that root where they touch the soil.

BELOW: *The alliums and the tall silvery onopordum have upright habits, standing stiffly as if to attention.*

Tortuous habit

❀ These plants, with their strangely contorted stems and branches, are exciting but difficult to place satisfactorily. They really need to be seen against the sky or reflected in water and are best grown on their own as specimen plants.

❀ *Robinia pseudoacacia* 'Tortuosa' is a slow-growing large tree, reaching 15 m (50 ft) with twisted shoots and pea-type leaves. *Arbutus andrachnoides* is a tortuous form of the strawberry tree; *Corylus avellana* 'Contorta' is the corkscrew hazel. It is slow growing but can eventually reach 3 m (10 ft).

Weeping and pendulous habit

❀ This is an appealing habit in which branches 'weep' from the trunk. Weeping plants are usually used as specimen plants on their own and make good focal points. Many weeping trees are smaller than their upright equivalents.

❀ Large trees include the weeping beech (*Fagus sylvatica* 'Pendula'); the weeping willow (*Salix babylonica*), a particularly fine specimen tree to plant beside a large pond; *Prunus pendula*, a weeping ornamental cherry; and the weeping ash (*Fraxinus excelsior* 'Pendula'). Small weepers include the weeping pear (*Pyrus salicifolia* 'Pendula') and the Kilmarnock willow (*Salix caprea* 'Kilmarnock').

Arching habit

❀ Arching plants have branches that grow upright from the ground and then arch over. They are very graceful but may take up more room than expected. Many grasses have an arching habit, as do many old roses.

Strap-like and spiky habits

❀ Strap-like leaves can provide strong contrasts to feathery and other not so well-defined shapes of plant. The fan-like leaves of bearded irises and sisyrinchiums contrast well with plants of horizontal and spreading habit.

❀ Spiky shapes are difficult to use well. They work well with rocks or used on their own, for example at the end of an axis, and if you want to give a tropical look to the garden. They suit urban situations and respond to being planted in relationship to modern buildings, in courtyards and by steps. Spiky plants include *Yucca filamentosa* and *Phormium tenax*.

BELOW: *The silvery-leaved weeping pear (*Pyrus salicifolia*) always seems so sprightly and cheerful for a weeping tree. It can take pride of place in any small garden or stand at the end of a vista in a larger garden.*

GLOSSARY OF GARDENING TERMS

Acidic soil
Soil containing no free lime, and with a pH of lower than 6.5.

Aeration
Opening up the soil structure and changing its texture by introducing increased air space.

Aerial root
A root growing from a plant's stem which absorbs moisture from the atmosphere; not generally rooted into the soil. Some aerial roots, such as those found on ivy stems, may help support the plant.

Alkaline soil
Chalk or limey soil with a pH of higher than 7.3.

Alpine plants
Plants growing naturally in, and adapted to, mountainous conditions. This group of plants is widely used in rock gardens.

Annual plants
Plants which germinate, grow, flower, set seed and die within a single growing season.

Aphids
Sap-sucking insects which cause severe damage to fruits, decorative plants and vegetables by attacking the fruits, stems and leaves. Aphids can also cause plant damage by transmitting viral disease. There are many different species, including the greenfly and the blackfly.

Backfilling
Replacing compost or soil around a plant's roots after planting.

Basal
Buds or shoots which develop from the base of a plant.

Bed
A defined area of cultivated earth.

Bedding plants
Plants, generally annuals, but sometimes perennials or biennials, which are raised in large quantities and used for a temporary display in a bed.

Biennial plants
Plants that complete their life cycle over two growing seasons; germinating and forming leaves in the first year, flowering, setting seed and dying in the next.

Black spot
Unsightly fungal disease causing black spots on affected leaves.

Blight
A common name for a range of diseases, often fungal, particularly those causing serious, sudden leaf damage.

Bloom
A waxy or powdery coating.

Bog garden
An area with permanently wet soil, usually around a natural or artificial water garden or stream. This type of garden is particularly suitable for growing plants such as rushes and water irises.

Botrytis
Also known as grey mould, this fungal disease is unsightly and affects both living and dead plant tissue.

Broadcast sowing
Sowing seeds by scattering them directly onto the soil surface.

Bud
A swelling containing developing petals or leaves.

Bulb fibre
Well-drained planting medium for growing bulbs.

Calyx
The outer green ring of a flower comprising numerous sepals which enclose and protect the petals whilst in bud form.

Chipping
Nicking the outer coating of a hard seed, such as sweet pea, to hasten germination.

Clay soil
A heavy, sticky soil made of minute mineral particles.

Climbing plants
Plants that travel upwards towards the light.

Cloche
Predominantly clear structure of glass or plastic, used to protect plants from inhospitable weather conditions.

Compost
Either sterilised soil for planting, or organic material formed from decomposed animal/vegetable matter used to improve garden soil.

Contact action
The action of a herbicide, fungicide or pesticide which kills on contact.

Coppicing
Severe pruning method in which trees are cut almost

down to ground level to promote growth of new shoots from the base.

Cordon training
Restricting a fruit tree's growth by pruning back to a main, spur-bearing stem, which may be at an oblique angle or upright, and can be single or multiple.

Corm
Swollen, short, underground, bulb-like plant stem, comprising solid tissue, not scales. It shrivels at the end of each season and a new corm grows at the sides or top of the old, withered one.

Crocks
Pieces of broken pot placed inside the bottom of a planted container to improve drainage.

Crown
The point on a herbaceous plant where the stem joins the roots and at which new shoots appear.

Cultivar
A cultivated variety of a plant rather than a naturally occurring type.

Cutting
A piece of leaf, root or stem taken from a plant that is prepared in one of a variety of ways in order to produce a new plant.

Damping-off
A fungal disease which infects the stems of seedlings at ground level causing them to collapse and die.

Dead-heading
Removing dead flower heads from plants to give a tidy appearance, and make a better display of blooms by conserving the plant's energy that otherwise would go into producing seed.

Deciduous
Plants which shed their leaves in winter.

Die-back
Tips or shoots dying, generally because of disease or damage.

Disbudding
Removing unwanted buds in order to direct all of a plant's energy into a few buds. Used to produce exhibition-quality blooms. Fruit trees are shaped by removing buds on young

shoots, a process also known as disbudding.

Dormant season
The time when active growth ceases, generally in winter.

Double digging
A more intensive digging technique than single digging, in which two spits' depth, rather than one, is dug or forked over.

Drill
A shallow, generally straight furrow in which seeds are sown.

Dwarf
A plant with a restricted height and root spread, such as dwarf apple trees. Dwarf plants are especially useful for small gardens and dwarf fruit trees may even be grown in containers.

Ericaceous plants
Plants which hate limey conditions; requiring a soil with a maximum pH of 6.5. Rhododendrons and azaleas need ericaceous soil.

Espalier training
Training a tree, often a pear or an apple, into horizontal tiers leading regularly off from a vertical trunk.

Exotic
Plants introduced into one country from another.

Fan training
Training a tree, generally a fruit tree, into a fan shape against a wall.

Foliar feeding
Spraying liquid plant food directly onto the leaves, rather than the soil around a plant.

Formative pruning
Pruning from the early stages of a plant's development to produce a particular shape and branch configuration.

Frost pocket
Area susceptible to trapped cold air in winter; such as the ground at the bottom of a hill. Plants grown here will be at greater risk of frost damage.

Fungicide
A substance used to control fungal diseases.

Fungus
A primitive form of plant life responsible for a range of common infectious plant diseases

such as rusts and mildews.

Genus
A number of plant species which share similar characteristics.

Grafting
Joining a bud or stem of one plant onto another.

Ground cover
Planting specifically designed to cover the earth, in order to reduce weeding and, if used on sloping areas, to help consolidate the soil.

Half-hardy
Plants which cannot withstand frost.

Hardening-off
Gradually acclimatising plants grown under glass to outdoor conditions.

Hardy
Plants which can tolerate average winter frosts.

Heeling-in
Temporarily placing plant roots in soil and lightly firming with heel pressure until permanent planting can take place.

Herbaceous
Plants producing soft, non-woody growth which usually dies back in winter.

Hybrid
Plant bred by crossing two genetically different plants.

Inorganic
Not originating from a substance which has previously lived i.e. one which is of plant or animal derivation.

Insecticide
Substance that is used to destroy insect pests.

Intercrop
A fast-cropping plant grown between the rows of another, more slowly developing plant to best utilise space, especially in the vegetable garden.

Lateral shoot
A shoot branching off from a main or leader shoot.

Layering climbers
Propagating climbing plants by growing on sections of rooted stem.

Lifting
Digging up plants for storage or planting elsewhere.

Lopping
Severe cutting back of the large, upper branches of a tree.

Mildew
Fungal disease which is unsightly and attacks the vitality of a plant.

Mulch
A top-dressing, usually of organic material such as compost; applied to conserve soil moisture and add nutrients to the soil. Inorganic mulches such as gravel are sometimes used to retain moisture within the soil and suppress weed growth.

Naturalise
To establish plants in the garden for a naturalistic appearance; for example, planting snowdrops in drifts within grass.

New wood
Stem growth produced during the current season.

Nitrogen
The most essential element in plant nutrition, promoting dark green foliage and above-ground growth. Nitrogen is used up quickly and needs to be replaced frequently.

Old wood
Stem growth produced prior to the current season.

Organic
Substance derived from a source which has once been alive, i.e. a plant or animal. Also a term used to describe a method of gardening that does not use inorganic substances and which respects ecological issues.

Ornamental plants
Plants which are grown purely or predominantly for their decorative attributes.

Oxygenating plants
Aquatic plants which release oxygen through their leaves. These plants are essential to the survival of fish in a pool.

Parasitic plants
Plants which grow on and take their nourishment from another living plant, such as mistletoe growing on apple trees.

Parterre
A formal geometric arrangement of beds, usually edged with low-growing clipped hedges such as dwarf box.

Peat
Dead, partially decomposed vegetable matter often derived from heathland or bogs, used as a soil conditioner, planting medium or mulch, due to its moisture-retaining properties.

Perennial
Plants which live and flower for at least two years. The term is generally used in reference to flowering perennials which die down each winter and produce new growth each spring.

Pergola
A series of arches, straight or curved, which form a covered area.

Perpetual
Flowering plants such as perpetual carnations which bloom intermittently throughout the year.

pH
A numerical scale used to measure alkalinity or acidity, meaning parts Hydrogen.

Pillar training
Training a plant to grow in a limited space by restricting and encouraging its growth into a pattern of a central trunk approximately 2 m (6.5 ft) high which produces a succession of lateral shoots.

Pinching out
Removing the tips of growing shoots to encourage the formation of sideshoots and limit extension growth.

Pollarding
Pruning method in which tree branches are repeatedly cut back to the trunk to encourage new shoots to develop from this point.

Pollination
The transfer of male pollen onto the female flower pistil to produce fertilisation.

Potbound
A plant is potbound when its pot is full of roots. This is often indicated by a plant draining too quickly or showing checked growth.

Potting on
Transferring a plant from one pot to another, usually because the plant has become potbound.

Pricking out
Transferring seedlings from the container in which they were sown to larger pots or trays.

Propagation
Multiplying plants either vegetatively, i.e. by layering, grafting, budding, dividing and cuttings, or seminally, i.e. from seed.

Pruning
Selectively cutting away parts of a plant in order to improve its overall health and performance and/or alter its shape.

Rhizome
A thickened, modified stem with leaf buds and roots; a bulbous plant which grows horizontally underground or may be visible just above the ground. Rooted sections of rhizome are easy to propagate.

Rock plant
Compact plants suited to rock gardens and growing on walls.

Rootball
The compacted mass of soil and roots at the base of an established, container-grown plant.

Rootstock
Host plant onto which a desirable cultivated variety is budded.

Runner
A horizontally extending shoot, e.g. the rooting stems which develop from strawberry plants.

Seedbed
An area of carefully prepared, level soil set aside for seed-sowing.

Seedling
A young plant with a solitary, unbranched, soft stem.

Semi-evergreen
Plants which retain their foliage in mild winters but which may lose some or all their leaves in particularly harsh winters.

Shrub
A plant with woody branches and stems, with no central trunk.

Spot treatment
Applying substances such as weedkillers or fungicides to individual plants, or to a specific part of a plant.

Staking
Supporting plants using canes, sticks or other materials to help them maintain an upright habit.

Standard
A trained shrub or tree with a single, bare stem clear of branches from ground level up to a height of approximately 2 m (6 1/2 ft). Half standard trees have a clear stem up to a height of approximately 1.5 m (5 ft).

Stem
The bud-, leaf- and shoot-carrying part of a plant which is above the root system.

Sterile
Unable to breed. The term is widely used to describe plants which produce fertile pollen but no seed. Some plants, such

as some fruit trees, are called sterile, but the term is slightly misleading, as they can set fruit with a pollinating partner.

Stopping
Pinching out or removing growing tips to encourage the development of side shoots and control flowering. A practice often employed to produce better-quality, late-flowering chrysanthemums.

Sub-tropical
Plants of tropical origin which may be grown outside in summer, but which cannot tolerate any hint of frost.

Succulents
Plants with fleshy, water-retaining stems or leaves well adapted to life in arid environments.

Suckers
Unwanted shoots growing from below the ground at the base of a plant, such as the suckers which develop on the original rootstock of hybrid roses. Remove suckers at their point of development to prevent the plant reverting to its pre-graft origin.

Tap roots
Long, sturdy, anchoring roots such as those formed on carrots, which grow straight down from the base of a plant.

Tendrils
The fine, curling, modified leaves or stems which emerge from the stems of climbing plants and entwine themselves around available supports.

Thinning out
Reducing the number of seedlings in a seedbed or container so that the remaining plants have sufficient room to grow well with minimal risk or disease and maximum access to light, good airflow, water and nutrients.

Tilling
Cultivating the soil by raking, hoeing, forking or digging either by hand or powered tools such as rotary cultivators or mechanical ploughs.

Top-dressing
Applying compost, soil or fertiliser to a lawn or the soil around a plant.

Topiary
The art of training and clipping shrubs and trees into ornamental and decorative shapes.

Training
Encouraging and restricting plants to a particular growth

pattern by tying them into a framework and by selective pruning.

Treading
Walking methodically over freshly tilled soil in order to firm it so that it is ready for planting or sowing. Treading encourages good contact of plant roots with the soil for efficient take-up of nutrients and water.

Tuber
A swollen, bulbous, underground stem which acts as a food-storage organ and produces a scattering of buds over its surface. Begonias, anemones and cyclamens are all tubers.

Tuberous root
A swollen, bulbous underground root which acts as a food storage organ and bears buds at the top of the root. Ranunculus and dahlias are tuberous root plants.

Tufa
Porous type of hard limest one popular as the basis of a rock garden because of its ability to absorb and retain moisture.

Underplanting
Low-growing plants around and beneath taller trees or shrubs.

Variegated
Flowers or leaves of two or more colours. The term is widely used to describe leaves with cream, yellow or white markings.

Vermiculite
A natural substance which is heated until it expands, producing air-filled granules. These lightweight, absorbent granules are often used as part of a planting mixture to encourage good drainage. Tubers lifted from the ground seasonally are also often stored in vermiculite.

Virus diseases
Plant viruses are tiny particles present in plant sap spread throughout all the tissues of a plant. Sap-sucking insects, primarily aphids, suck sap from affected plants and transfer the disease to other plants.

Weeping
A shrub or tree with branches which have a drooping, pendulous habit.
esent attacking the water-conductive tissues of the plant stems leading to collapse.

INDEX

ACKNOWLEGEMENTS

AUTHOR'S ACKNOWLEDGEMENTS

Many people have been generous with their advice and help in writing this book. I would particularly like to thank Graham Cousins, whose garden has been an inspiration, Ruth Chivers for providing many of the photographs, Ken Baker, Michael Clark, Josephine Cutts, Graham Hopewell, John and Dorothy Knight and my editor Katie Cowan, for constant encouragement under pressure.

PUBLISHER'S ACKNOWLEGEMENTS

The publishers would like to thank the following for their kindness in allowing us to photograph their gardens: Anne Birnhack, Ken Baker, Michael Clark, Derek Guy, Graham Hopewell, John and Dorothy Knight and Gae Oaten.

Thanks also to the following companies have been more than generous in loaning equipment, props and plants for photography: Chairworks, Clifton Nurseries, Draper's Tools Ltd, Idencroft Herbs and Queenswood Garden Centre. Extra special thanks to Jardinerie in Swindon, Wiltshire for allowing us to shoot within the garden centre.

PICTURE CREDITS